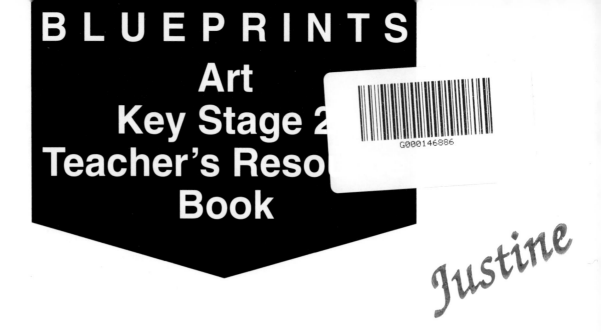

BLUEPRINTS

Art
Key Stage 2
Teacher's Resource
Book

Justine

Ron Adams

Stanley Thornes (Publishers) Ltd

Do you receive *BLUEPRINTS NEWS*?

Blueprints is an expanding series of practical teacher's ideas books and photocopiable resources for use in primary schools. Books are available for separate infant and junior age ranges for every core and foundation subject, as well as for an ever widening range of other primary teaching needs. These include **Blueprints Primary English** books and **Blueprints Resource Banks**. **Blueprints** are carefully structured around the demands of the National Curriculum in England and Wales, but are used successfully by schools and teachers in Scotland, Northern Ireland and elsewhere.

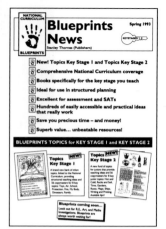

Blueprints provide:
- *Total curriculum coverage*
- *Hundreds of practical ideas*
- *Books specifically for the age range you teach*
- *Flexible resources for the whole school or for individual teachers*
- *Excellent photocopiable sheets – ideal for assessment and children's work profiles*
- *Supreme value.*

Books may be bought by credit card over the telephone and information obtained on **(01242) 577944**. Alternatively, photocopy and return this **FREEPOST** form to receive **Blueprints News**, our regular update on all new and existing titles. You may also like to add the name of a friend who would be interested in being on the mailing list.

Please add my name to the **BLUEPRINTS NEWS** mailing list.

Mr/Mrs/Miss/Ms _____

Home address _____

_____ Postcode _____

School address _____

_____ Postcode _____

Please also send **BLUEPRINTS NEWS** to:

Mr/Mrs/Miss/Ms _____

Address _____

_____ Postcode _____

To: Marketing Services Dept., Stanley Thornes Ltd, FREEPOST (GR 782), Cheltenham, GL50 1BR

First published in 1993 by:
Stanley Thornes (Publishers) Ltd
Ellenborough House
Wellington Street
CHELTENHAM GL50 1YD

Reprinted 1994, 1995

A catalogue record for this book is available from the British Library

0–7487–1646–7

Typeset by Tech-Set, Gateshead, Tyne & Wear
Printed and bound in Great Britain at The Bath Press, Avon

CONTENTS

What is *Blueprints: Art*?

Blueprints: Art is a practical teacher's resource that provides structured materials for developing art in line with the requirements of the National Curriculum. It is, however, organised in such a way that it can be used just as profitably by teachers and schools not following National Curriculum courses. It is intended to be used flexibly, either as an ideas bank for individual teachers or as a workable core resource for a whole school scheme of work in art.

Blueprints: Art consists of material for Key Stages 1 and 2. For each stage there is a Teacher's Resource Book and a book of Pupils' Copymasters. This Teacher's Resource Book provides hundreds of practical ideas and activities for 7- to 11-year-olds and can be used on its own, as a freestanding resource, without the accompanying Copymaster book. The book of Pupils' Copymasters provides 105 photocopiable worksheets linked to the many activities in this book. The worksheets are not colouring sheets. They reinforce and extend activities already done and provide opportunities to develop art skills in a structured and specific way.

Blueprints: Art will provide you with coverage of all the requirements of National Curriculum Art. It is written around the requirements of the Programmes of Study and provides complete coverage of the Statements of Attainment at Key Stage 2. You will find a full explanation of National Curriculum Art and how it is covered in the following pages. The key feature of *Blueprints: Art* is that it is a skill based, progressive resource not a collection of isolated one-off activities, and this is reflected in its structure, as well as the contents.

The general features of *Blueprints: Art* are in line with both the requirements of the National Curriculum and the realities of the primary school classroom, as follows:

- It provides a balanced programme of art, craft and design which allows children to meet the full range of art activities, in both two and three dimensions and in a variety of scales.

- It provides activities which integrate the two art Attainment Targets, as recommended in the Non-Statutory Guidance on art.

- It stresses the newly emphasised role of art history in children's artistic development.

- It allows you to work flexibly from either topics or skills or directly from the National Curriculum programmes of study if you so choose.

- It assumes a realistic amount of time in class and takes account of the need to fit art into an over-crowded primary curriculum.

This book consists of two parts. The first part uses eight common junior topics to provide a bank of structured, skill based art activities. The second part provides a section of basic skills and knowledge, in line with the requirements for AT1 and AT2. You will find the skills and knowledge also referred to quite widely during the topics, and the sections are closely cross-referenced. The content of the topics is in fact structured around these areas of study to provide the balanced programme of art, craft and design activities that the National Curriculum demands. The areas of study are:

 Art history

 Ceramics

 Design

 Drawing

 Modelling

 Painting

 Print-making

 Textiles.

Art history relates to AT2: Knowledge and understanding, the other areas to AT1: Investigating and making. The logos for these areas are used widely throughout the book.

Art through topics

Constraints on time and the nature of the primary day mean that topics will provide the most frequent opportunities for art. With this in mind eight topics have been chosen as a context for developing art skills. These are:

- Ancient Egypt
- Ancient Greece and Rome
- The sea
- Colour and light
- Food and farming
- Advertising
- Lines and shapes
- Seasons and weather.

You will find that cross-curricular links are made but each topic is focused quite specifically on art, and the activities are related throughout to art in the National Curriculum. You can see the coverage in outline on the chart on pages xi–xiii. The topic webs are structured in such a way that all the main areas for study mentioned earlier are specifically covered in each topic and highlighted through the use of logos mentioned earlier. The topics include a huge range of activities that provide coverage of all these specified areas of National Curriculum art. You will also find that a topics index has been included on page xvii to enable you to use many of the ideas in the eight topics to resource a wide range of other topics.

Although they may be used in any order you like, the order of the topics is loosely developmental. Whilst most topics provide considerable coverage of AT1 and AT2 the earlier topics make fewer demands on knowledge and understanding. They include many investigating and making activities (AT1), many of which are simple rather than ones which link together a number of processes and skills. They are therefore more suitable for younger classes. Later topics include activities that combine more complex processes and planning. You can see the coverage of the topics in the chart on page xiv.

Skills and knowledge in art

The second substantial section of the book is structured around the specific requirements of the two ATs. Art history provides activities that relate to AT2, the other seven skill areas relate to AT1. One of the fundamental aims of the National Curriculum is to develop the notion that art involves the progressive development of particular skills, that there is a vocabulary of visual literacy and skills which needs to be taught and developed systematically. Whilst the National Curriculum sees that 'there is more to learning in art than acquiring technical skills', it does also emphasise a systematic development of these skills through practical activities as set out in AT1.

The idea of developing art skills systematically will be an unfamiliar one to many teachers. There is a common tendency to regard art with children as being primarily about inspiration and imagination, and that these qualities must not be interfered with by the structured teaching of skills. The progressive development of skills is, however, one of the key features of the National Curriculum. In this respect art is not unlike music: music teachers know how essential it is to use a variety of exercises to build up skills. Similarly, language teachers know that leading children towards verbal literacy includes a number of well established methods and approaches. Common to all literacy skills is the foundation of the alphabet, followed by exercises to build listening, reading and writing skills: children are not expected to come across the alphabet by accident. The same applies to the field of visual literacy. Artistic skills can and must be taught. Teaching skills, individually, in groups or as class activities should enhance children's adventurous and daring spirits, while a balance of activities will give scope for individuality, flair and a sense of craftsmanship. The Copymasters are quite specifically provided to help with this structured skill development.

The skills section aims to provide a developmental alphabet of knowledge and skills in each area through a course of progressive activities. You will find that the development of these areas of study is threaded through the topics, but this section provides you with a coherent development for the eight areas mentioned previously:

 Art history

 Ceramics

 Design

 Drawing

 Modelling

 Painting

 Print-making

 Textiles.

The skills are very firmly linked to practical activities. Art history relates to AT2 (Knowledge and understanding). The remaining skill areas comprise AT1 (Investigating and making). These are based on an analysis and breakdown of the activities set out in the examples in the programmes of study. Of the practical activities, drawing is dominant because it is a basic skill which underpins art. The National Curriculum recommends that ratio of work in AT1 to AT2 should be approximately 2:1.

The skills activities can be used either as a reference source or to build a course that relies on class teaching rather than topic work. There are no hard and fast rules about the levels of the activities. A few skill activities have been brought forward from *Blueprints: Art* for Key Stage 1. It is important that you do not set the exercises in isolation. Ensure that you provide a relevant and well resourced context for all work. You may also find the skills section invaluable for enhancing your own skills.

Assessment in art

There is no statutory end of Key Stage assessment in art, but the non-statutory guidance does make suggestions about teacher based assessment which are interesting, if rather complicated. It is important that you do find a simple and straightforward way to develop a critical awareness of your pupils' performance in art so that you are able to help them develop further and provide a progressive programme. It will also be necessary to provide parents and future schools with information.

With this in mind *Blueprints: Art* provides a simple record keeping sheet at Key Stage 2 (Copymaster 105) which is straightforward, comprehensive and easy to use and also provides a checklist of criteria to use when assessing children's work. Alongside this it will be helpful to keep a portfolio of annotated and dated samples of your children's work. The skill based copymasters can comprise a useful part of this portfolio. When taking photographs take care to include a rule alongside the work and to use a tripod and light it properly. Fuzzy photographs of vague objects in the distance are worse than useless as records and as exemplars in the visual arts.

How to use this book

Blueprints: Art can be used flexibly to meet your needs. It allows you to work from either Topics or Skills or directly from the National Curriculum. You do not need to have the Copymasters to use this Teacher's Resource Book, but the Copymasters are dependent on it.

If you have only this *Teacher's Resource Book:*

If you want to work from topics integrated into the rest of your curriculum planning, you can use any of the eight core topics to do so. You will find that the cross-curricular links are clearly stated and that the map of art activities is outlined in the web at the front of the topic. If you are planning to integrate art into topics other than the eight specifically covered, go to the Topic Index on page xvii which will allow you to access ideas across the book.

If you want to treat art as a separate subject and start from skills, go to the relevant skill section and start from there. You will find each provides a bank of skill based activities which can provide a module of progressive learning. You can also use the skills index on page xviii to help you do this. Remember that it is important to provide interesting contexts in which to develop skills. Although art history (AT2) doesn't provide many specific activities, it may be seen as a vital first step. The way it is arranged relates the knowledge specifically to practical areas.

If you want to start by looking at the National Curriculum programmes of study, go to the charts on pages xiv–xv where you will find an outline of how the activities provide coverage. Again it is important that any subject-based approach to art is securely grounded in contexts which have real meaning for juniors. In general we recommend that you work mainly from a topic approach, that you integrate art into your overall curriculum planning and use the record sheet to record pupil progress. You will probably want to dip into the skills section at certain points to focus learning as you

work within a topic, as well as to provide yourself with a basic alphabet of necessary art skills.

I recommend that you allow an hour a week for specific art activities whether they are related to a topic or not. You will find that making a practical link between AT2 and practical activities is both logical and enriching.

If you have the pupils' *Copymasters* as well:
At first sight it may appear odd to provide copymasters for a subject such as art. The copymasters in *Blueprints: Art* are all designed to do specific and purposeful tasks, either by providing opportunities for developing quite specific focused skills, or by providing a bank of visual resources that can be used to stimulate activity in a wide range of situations. The sheets can also form part of a child's art portfolio. Many sheets are locked quite specifically into particular activities in this book and you will find them referred to in the text where notes on their use are provided. You will find the appropriate sheets

referred to in this book with this symbol:

Acknowledgements
Many thanks to Veronica Parker, Headmistress and her staff at St Stephen's Primary School, Bath; Fiona Godfrey, MA, of Birmingham University.

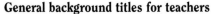

BIBLIOGRAPHY

General background titles for teachers

Berger, J., *Ways of Seeing*, Penguin, ISBN 0 14 013515 4. (Very theoretical.)

Carlson, *Guide to Landscape Painting*, Dover, ISBN 0 4862 2927 0

Carr, W., and Leonard, M., *Looking at Paintings*, British Museum Press, ISBN 0 7141 1725 0 (Very good.)

Children's Books of the Year, Children's Book Foundation, from Book House, 45 East Hill, London, SW18 2QZ. Tel. 081 870 9055

Kellog, R., *Analysing Children's Art*, Mayfield Publishing, ISBN 0 87484196 8

Leach, B., *Potter's Book*, Faber, ISBN 0 571 10973 4

Picture this Century – an introduction to 20th century art, Hodder & Stoughton, ISBN 0 340 54867 3. (Very good.)

Read, H., *The Meaning of Art*, Faber, ISBN 0 571 09658 1. (Very theoretical.)

The Craftsman's Directory, Angle Press from The Rural Crafts Association, Brook Road, Wormley, Godalming, Surrey, GU8 5UA

Art books linked to National Curriculum requirements and as a visual stimulus

Barnicoat, *Posters, A Concise History*, Thames and Hudson, ISBN 0 500 20118 8

Burn, *Greek and Roman Art*, British Museum Press, ISBN 0 7141 1297 6

Carpenter, *Hiroshige*, Kodansha International, ISBN 4 77001658 1

Duchen and Cook, *Understanding Modern Art*, Usborne, 1991, ISBN 0 7460 0475 3

James, T. G. H., *Egyptian Painting*, British Museum Press, ISBN 0 7141 2038 3

Lister, *Paintings of Samuel Palmer*, Cambridge University Press, ISBN 0 521 31855 6

McHugh, C., *Animals*, Wayland, 1992. This title is part of the *Discovering Art* series

Master of Art Series, Thames & Hudson. Titles include: *Van Gogh, Cezanne, Constable, Klee, Leger, Monet, Picasso,* and *Turner*

Micklethwaite, L., *An Alphabet in Art*, Collins, 1992. ISBN 0 00 664184 9

Prats and Okuyama, *Art Playbook Series*, Abrams. Titles include: *Magritte – the Double Secret*, ISBN 0 8109 3601 1, *Picasso the Minotaur, Delauney the Eiffel Tower, Kandinsky Sky Blue*

Richardson, W. and R., *The World of Art Series*, MacMillan, 1989. Titles include: *Animals, Cities, Water, Families, The Natural World, Entertainers*

Vallance, *Art of William Morris*, Dover, ISBN 0 4862 5647 2

Wilkin, *Braque* from the *Abbeville Modern Masters* series, Abbeville, ISBN 0 89659947 7

Woolf, *Picture This*, Hodder & Stoughton, ISBN 0 340 55991 8

Wrede, S., *Modern Poster*, Museum of Modern Art, ISBN 0 87070 571 7

SUPPLIERS AND USEFUL ADDRESSES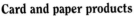

Card and paper products

Celloglas Mirri Products (Mirriboard), Unit 12C, Exeter Way, Theale Commercial Estate, Theale, Reading, Berkshire, RG7 4AW. Tel: 0734 303656

Daler–Rowney Ltd, Southern Industrial Area, PO Box 10, Bracknell, Berkshire, RG12 4ST. Tel: 0344 424621

Frisk Ltd, 4 Franthorne Way, Randlesdown Road, London, SE6 3BT. Tel: 081 698 3481

Oram and Robinson Ltd, Cadmore Lane, Cheshunt, Waltham Cross, Hertfordshire, EN8 9SG. Tel: 0992 27376

Paperchase Products Ltd, 213 Tottenham Court Road, London, W1. Tel: 071 580 8496

Slater Harrison & Co Ltd, Lowerhouse Mills, West Bollington, Macclesfield, SK10 5HW. Tel 0625 73155

Wiggins Teape Ltd, (Paper Point) 63 Poland Street, London, W1. Tel: 071 439 4414

Clay

Clayglaze Ltd, Kings Yard Pottery, Talbot Road, Rickmansworth, Herts. Tel: 0923 87107

Wengers Ltd, Etruria, Stoke-on-Trent, ST4 7BQ. Tel: 0782 25560

General art supplies

Berol Ltd, Oldmeadow Road, King's Lynn, Norfolk, PE30 4JR. Tel: 0553 61221C

Caran D'Ache, Jakar Int. Ltd, Hillside House, 2–6 Friern Park, London, N12 9BX. Tel: 081 445 6377

Faber–Castell (UK) Ltd, Crompton Road, Stevenage, Herts., SG1 2EF. Tel: 0438 316511

Reeves Ltd, Whitefriars Avenue, Whealdstone, Harrow, Middlesex, HA3 5RH. Tel: 081 427 4343

Staedtler 9UK0 Ltd, Pontyclun, Mid-Glamorgan, Wales, CF7 8YJ. Tel: 0443 237421

Winsor & Newton, Whitefriars Avenue, Whealdstone, Harrow, Middlesex, HA3 5RH. Tel: 081 427 4343

Textile Techniques, 47 Storths Rd, Birkby, Huddersfield, HD2 2XW

General educational suppliers

E J Arnold & Son Ltd, Parkside Lane, Dewbury Road, Leeds LS15 5TD

James Galt & Co. Ltd, Brookfield Road, Cheadle, Cheshire SK8 2PN

Hestair Hope Ltd, St. Philip's Drive, Royton, Oldham, OL2 6AG

Nottingham Educational Supplies, 17 Ludlow Hill Road, West Bridgford, Nottingham NG2 6HD

Materials for print-making

Daler-Rowney, Westminster Road, Wareham, Dorset BH20 4SW. Tel: 09295 6621

Hunter Penrose Ltd, 7 Spa Road, London, SE16. Tel: 071 407 5051

T. N. Lawrence & Son Ltd, Bleeding Hart Yard, Greville Street, Hatton Garden, London, EC1N 8SL. Tel: 071 242 3534

Process Supplies Ltd, 19 Mount Pleasant, London, WC1. Tel: 071 837 2179

Sericol Ltd, 26 Parsons Green Lane, London, SW6. Tel: 071 736 3388

Photography

Kodak Ltd, PO Box 66, Station Road, Hemel Hempstead, Herts, HP1 1JU. Tel: 0442 61122

Specialist pencil and felt tip suppliers

C. W. Edding (UK) Ltd, Merlin Centre, Acrewood, St. Albans, Herts, AJ4 0JY. Tel: 0727 34471

Royal Sovereign Ltd, 6/7 St George's Industrial Estate, White Hart Lane, London, N22 5QL. Tel: 081 888 7029

Textiles

Whaleys (Bradford) Ltd, Harris Court, Great Horton, Bradford, W Yorkshire, BD7 4EQ. Tel: 0274 576718

Suppliers of multi-cultural arts and crafts resources

Jackson Contra-Banned, Unit 2, Gatehouse Enterprise Centre, Albert Street, Lockwood, Huddersfield HD1 3QD. Tel: 0484 530855

Useful addresses

Children's Book Foundation, Jean Egbunike, Book House, 45 East Hill, London SW18 2QZ. Tel: 081 870 9055

Crafts Council, 12 Waterloo Place, London, SW1Y 4AU

Regional Arts Association (CORAA), Litton Lodge, 13a Clifton Road, Winchester, Hampshire, SO22 5BP. Tel: 0962 51063

NSEAD (National Society for Education in Art and Design), 7a High Street, Corsham, Wiltshire, SN13 0ES. Tel: 0249 714825

Schools Library Association, Executive Secretary, Valerie Fea, ALA, Liden Library, Barrington Close, Liden, Swindon, Wiltshire, SN3 6HF. Tel: 0793 617838

Group For Education in Museums, Care of Regional Convenor, Museum of London, London Wall, London EC2Y 5HN

For reference purposes, the programme of study and Attainment Targets are set out below for Key Stage 2. Alongside these are printed the accompanying examples, which are non-statutory. You will also find a chart showing in outline how the sections of the book meet the requirements of Key Stage 2. The general requirements for programmes of study are also included.

For general purposes it is worth mentioning here some of the key features of Art in the National Curriculum, as follows:

- There are no levels of attainment for National Curriculum Art, and no statutory requirement for formal assessment.

- There is a need to provide a balanced programme of art, craft *and* design activities. You will find that *Blueprints: Art* meets this need.

- Children should work in two and three dimensions and have opportunities to meet a wide range of art styles. For the first time children are required to see examples of art from around the world and from across the whole history of art. This is an important new dimension to primary art, which forms the core of AT2: Knowledge and understanding.

- Art skills are now an essential part of primary art, as embodied in AT1: Investigating and making.

- The two ATs need to be continuously integrated in the work provided and the emphasis should be laid most heavily on AT1: Investigating and making.

Programme of study

Art should be interpreted as 'art, craft and design' throughout.

Pupils' understanding and enjoyment of art, craft and design should be developed through activities that bring together requirements from both **Investigating and Making** and **Knowledge and Understanding**, wherever possible.

- **1.** Pupils should be given opportunities to experience different approaches to art, craft and design, including those that involve working individually, in groups and as a whole class.

- **2.** In order to develop visual perception, pupils should be taught the creative, imaginative and practical skills needed to:

    a express ideas and feelings;

    b record observations;

    c design and make images and artefacts.

- **3.** In order to develop visual literacy, pupils should be taught about the different ways in which ideas, feelings and meanings are communicated in visual form.

- **4.** Throughout their work, pupils should be taught about visual and, where appropriate, tactile elements, including:

    a the use of pattern and texture in designing and making;

    b how colour is applied and experienced in images and designs;

    c different qualities of line and tone in images;

    d how shape, form and space are presented in images and artefacts.

- **5.** Pupils should be introduced to the work of artists, craftspeople and designers, *eg drawing, painting, printmaking, photography, sculpture, ceramics, textiles, graphic design, architecture,* in order to develop their appreciation of the richness of our diverse cultural heritage. The selection should include work in a variety of genres and styles from:

    a the locality;

    b the past and present;

    c a variety of cultures, Western and non-Western.

- **6.** Pupils should be taught to use materials, tools and techniques for practical work safely and in accordance with health and safety requirements.

Investigating and Making

■ **7. Pupils should be given opportunities to:**

a **record responses, including observations of the natural and made environment;**

b **gather resources and materials, using them to stimulate and develop ideas;**

c **explore and use two- and three-dimensional media, working on a variety of scales;**

d **review and modify their work as it progresses;**

■ **8.** Pupils should be taught to:

a develop skills for recording from direct experience and imagination, and select and record from first-hand observation;

b record observations and ideas, and collect visual evidence and information, using a sketchbook;

c experiment with ideas for their work suggested by visual and other source material;

d experiment with and develop control of tools and techniques for drawing, painting, printmaking, collage and sculpture, exploring a range of materials, including textiles;

e experiment with and use visual elements, *eg pattern, texture, colour, line, tone, shape, form, space*, to make images and artefacts for different purposes, using the range of media in 8d;

f reflect and adapt their work in the light of what they intended and consider what they might develop in future work.

Knowledge and Understanding

■ **9.** Pupils should be taught to:

e **develop understanding of the work of artists, craftspeople and designers, applying knowledge to their own work;**

a identify in the school and the locality the materials and methods used by artists, craftspeople and designers;

b identify how visual elements, *eg pattern, texture, colour, line, tone, shape, form, space,* are used in images and artefacts for different purposes;

c recognise ways in which works of art, craft and design reflect the time and place in which they are made;

f **respond to and evaluate art, craft and design, including their own and others' work.**

d compare the ideas, methods or approaches used in different styles and taditions;

e express ideas and opinions, developing an art, craft and design vocabulary, and the ability to use knowledge to support views.

PROGRAMME OF STUDY COVERAGE OF THE TOPICS ▶

A black circle indicates considerable coverage. A white dot indicates more limited coverage.

AT	Pupils should be taught to:	Ancient Egypt	Ancient Greece Rome	The Sea	Colour and light	Food and farming	Advertising	Lines and shapes	Seasons and weather
1a. Record responses etc	a. Develop skills for recording what has been experienced, etc.	●	●	●	●	●	●	●	●
1b. Gather resources etc.	b. Record observations, use sketchbook etc.	○	●	○	○	●	●	○	●
	c. Experiment with ideas from source materials etc.	○	●	●	●	●	○	○	●
1c. Explore and use 2 and 3 D etc.	d. Experiment and develop control of tools and techniques etc.	●	●	●	●	●	●	●	○
	e. Experiment with visual elements, e.g. pattern etc.	●	●	●	●	●	○	●	●
1d Review and modify etc.	f. Reflect on and adapt what they have done etc.	●	●	●	●	●	●	○	○
2e. Develop understanding of the work of artists etc.	a. Identify in the school and locality the work of artists; materials and methods etc.	●	●	●	●	○	○	●	○
	b. Identify visual elements, e.g. pattern etc.	●	●	○	●	●	●	○	○
	c. Recognise ways in which works of art reflect time/place etc.	○	●	○	●	○	●	●	●
2f. Respond and evaluate etc.	d. Compare the ideas in different styles/traditions	○	●	○	●	●	●	○	○
	e. Express ideas and opinions etc.	●	●	●	●	●	○	●	○

PROGRAMME OF STUDY COVERAGE OF THE SKILLS ▶

A black circle indicates considerable coverage. A white dot indicates more limited coverage.

AT	Pupils should be taught to:	Art History	Ceramics	Design	Drawing	Modelling	Painting	Print-making	Textiles
1a. Record responses etc	a. Develop skills for recording what has been experienced, etc.				●		●		
1b. Gather resources etc.	b. Record observations, use sketchbook etc.			○	●		●	●	○
	c. Experiment with ideas from source materials etc.	○	○	○	●	●	●	●	●
1c. Explore and use 2 and 3 D etc.	d. Experiment and develop control of tools and techniques etc.	○	●	●	●	●	●	●	●
	e. Experiment with visual elements, e.g. pattern etc.	○	●		●	●	●	●	●
1d Review and modify etc.	f. Reflect on and adapt what they have done etc.		●		●	○	●	●	
2e. Develop understanding of the work of artists etc.	a. Identify in the school and locality the work of artists; materials and methods etc.	●	○		●		●		
	b. Identify visual elements, e.g. pattern etc.	●	○		●	●	●		
	c. Recognise ways in which works of art reflect time/place etc.	●			●		●		
2f. Respond and evaluate etc.	d. Compare the ideas in different styles/traditions	●	○		○	●	○		
	e. Express ideas and opinions etc.	●	●	○	●	●	●	●	●

TOPICS AND SKILLS INDEX

Blueprints: Art is structured around eight topics but ideas within it can be used to resource a far wider range of other topics. The index below shows you, by activity number, how ideas within the books can be used to resource a wider range of overlapping topics. You will find that *Blueprints: Art Key Stage 2* will provide you with many links to History and Geography work and these are listed below. You will also find listed below activities which allow children to study and work in the style of famous artists. These are listed by name under artists. You should also refer to the section on Art history pages 75–85 for activities of this kind. You will also find an easy-reference index for all the skills in the book.

TOPICS INDEX ▶

SKILLS INDEX ▶

ANCIENT EGYPT

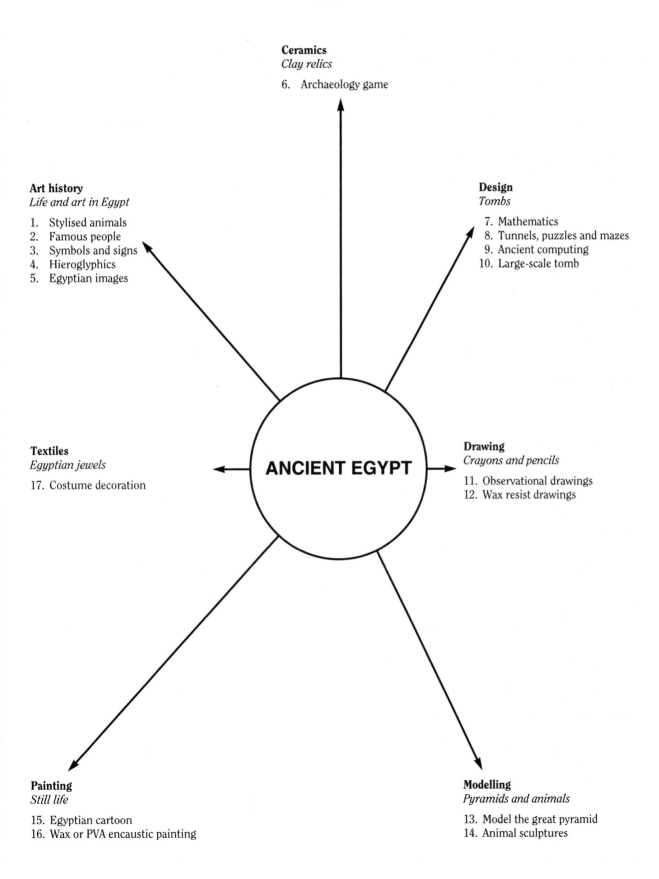

Ceramics
Clay relics

6. Archaeology game

Art history
Life and art in Egypt

1. Stylised animals
2. Famous people
3. Symbols and signs
4. Hieroglyphics
5. Egyptian images

Design
Tombs

7. Mathematics
8. Tunnels, puzzles and mazes
9. Ancient computing
10. Large-scale tomb

Textiles
Egyptian jewels

17. Costume decoration

ANCIENT EGYPT

Drawing
Crayons and pencils

11. Observational drawings
12. Wax resist drawings

Painting
Still life

15. Egyptian cartoon
16. Wax or PVA encaustic painting

Modelling
Pyramids and animals

13. Model the great pyramid
14. Animal sculptures

1

CROSS-CURRICULAR LINKS ▶

Design and technology Designing and making models, problem-solving, use of pulleys
Drama and dance Home corner as a pyramid or burial chamber, dance like an Egyptian, mime of ceremonies
History Study many aspects of ancient civilisation
Language Signs and symbols, the development of simple languages for codes, writing up facts and imaginative writing

Mathematics Plane and solid shapes, measuring distances in metres and centimetres, scale
Music 'Walk like an Egyptian'
RE Discussion of afterlife and the weighing of the soul against a feather
Science Problems of preservation, change in state of material

ABOUT THIS TOPIC ▶

General points

Art in ancient Egypt was very different to modern, western art. Egyptian art was understood by the whole of society whilst western art is so individual that it can mean something different to everyone. It had an agreed, symbolic meaning, unlike western art which is prized mainly as a way of personal expression.

The Egyptians had a very sophisticated understanding of science and art, both of which were enmeshed in the heart of their religion. Their art united science and religion in a way that the whole of society understood. Its function was spiritual, to promote a consciousness of superhuman realities. The incredible engineering and mathematical feats that produced the great pyramids, the artistry of the majestic symbolism of the Temple of Luxor, and the empathy that these early humans felt for wildlife were all expressions of an integrated culture.

Numbers and mathematics fascinated the Egyptians and so we are impressed by the harmony and orderliness of their compositions. As artists they were remarkable people who had developed exceptional technical and artistic skill. They were clear and logical thinkers, systematic in all that they did, and remarkably accurate in executing plans, being by no means satisfied with 'near enough'.

This topic will allow good coverage of graphic, sculptural and architectural forms of Egyptian art. At the same time it provides plenty of opportunities to develop your pupils' skills with a variety of media. Many of the exciting art activities described in this topic will involve symbols and signs. To deal with these satisfactorily you will need to consider the differences between signs and symbols and to understand what symbolism meant for the ancient Egyptians.

Symbolism

You can introduce discussion about symbolism by getting your children to make a collection of contemporary signs and symbols. Include pictures of John Bull (the archetypal Englishman), owls and donkeys (wisdom and stupidity); road signs, pub signs and supermarket motifs. Discuss the meanings of such graphic images and how languages might be formed by using them in combinations and sequences. You will often find that contemporary symbols are more like designs or logos than the symbols of ancient Egypt. A real symbol stands for something else. Understanding the original meaning of a symbol requires more than the superficial glance we give to a road sign. Also the same object may have distinctly different meanings for different societies. The owl for example is a symbol of stupidity in China whilst in the west it stands for wisdom. Generally people use symbols to express essential aspects of their culture and religion. Signs are more everyday things used as a visual shorthand to give information easily.

The symbolism of ancient Egypt was different, it was sacred and a science. The core of Egyptian myth is given concrete expression in images of dogs, snakes, cats and birds. The Egyptians chose those subjects to be recreated as symbols most carefully. A bird for example represented the volatile forces of 'spirit', and the stork, a bird that returns to its own nest, is a uniquely migratory creature and is chosen as the symbol of the 'soul'. These examples are enough to link class discussion to a real empathy with the characteristics of animals and other

Signs and symbols

2

living creatures that the children may wish to use as symbols. Work on signs and symbols will be a useful introduction to further work on logo designs in the topic on 'Advertising' (pages 48–54).

Displays and resources

If you have a museum loan service near at hand try to borrow as many artefacts as possible. These may include replicas of cats, hedgehogs, lions, hippo heads, grasshoppers, Rosetta stones, scarab beetles and replica eyes of Horus. You may also be able to get hold of reproductions from *The Book of the Dead*. These are particularly useful as they contain some superb examples of hieroglyphics in full colour. You can add to displays as the topic progresses. Models of pyramids, paintings of King Tutankhamen and clay sculptures will all bring life and freshness to your original exhibits. Remember to collect relevant books from your library service.

Display items

STARTING POINTS

- Visit to the Egyptology section of a museum
- Discussion about the spiritual characteristics attributed to birds, animals and plants. Talk about the Christian symbols of the lamb and the dove, the Islamic symbols of pigeons, date, milk and bread and the Hindu symbols of the cow and rice

- Discussion about signs and symbols
- Discussion about such different forms of visual language and codes as Morse Code, sign language for the deaf and the use of colours for traffic control.

ANCIENT EGYPT ACTIVITIES

C1 –11

 ## Life and art in Egypt

You need

Illustrations, posters, books, artefacts, magnifying glasses, pencils, paper, **Copymasters 1–4**, illustrations of mazes.

Activity 1: Stylised animals

Use books and replicas to examine early forms of representing animals, in both two and three dimensions. Get your children to make drawings and notes. Use **Copymaster 1** and **2** as a quiz about the types of animals portrayed. Get your children to make their own designs in the same style for cows, whales and reindeer.

Activity 2: Famous people

Look at the encaustic wax portraits on the mummies. The artists tried to make them very realistic. Why? Did everyone who died have their portrait painted on their tomb? Who did? Get your children to collect and sort images of famous contemporary people who could be immortalised on a sarcophagus. Use cut out photographs to make a chart of who might be immortalised and who would not.

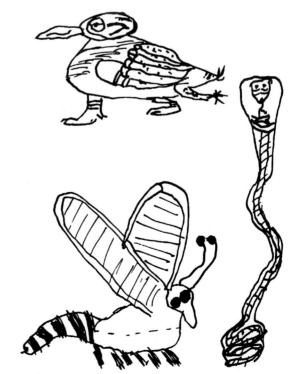

Child's animal drawings

3

Activity 3: Symbols and signs

Collect examples of contemporary signs and symbols and compare them with those of ancient Egypt. Discuss the differences between signs and symbols. **Copymaster 3** contains a range of different symbols from various cultures and periods. What do they have in common? Are they all flat shapes? Are they all silhouettes? Are they all simple? Are some abstract? What does abstract mean? Make a list of related words and define them by using a dictionary. Include:

● signs: icon, mark, character, emblem, poster, token
● symbol: example, drawing, image, figure, statue, idol
● logo: brand, mark, emblem, seal, stamp, trade-mark, representation
● design: pattern, device, figure, motif, outline, blueprint, draw, paint, depict, shape.

Activity 4: Hieroglyphics

Copymaster 4 contains examples of hieroglyphics from the oldest written document, *The Book of the Dead* (sometimes more correctly called *The Book of the Coming into Light*). Get your children to use the simple key and translate small portions. Make up a simple language with ten different characters. Combine them to make a simple vocabulary.

Activity 5: Egyptian images

Discuss the purposes and methods of image-making in ancient Egypt. Aspects to include:

● the scale of different work from colossal sculptures to small toys, from large wall paintings to detailed portraits
● the media and techniques used, including sculpture, modelling, carving, imprinting, painting with wax and with tempera (on canvas, wood, limestone and papyrus)

● the subjects depicted, such as scenes from everyday life, realistic portraits (death masks), closely detailed paintings of wildlife and plants, schematic designs portraying the afterlife, images of gods and ceremonies
● the importance of symbols abstracted from realistic images.

Clay relics

Activity 6: Archaeology game

Divide the class into groups of five or six children. Through discussion introduce the idea that the children are to play the parts of ancient Egyptians and archaeologists. The children will play both parts at different times. As Egyptians the children are given the task of working in groups to produce artefacts which will represent and symbolise their culture in a specific way. The artefacts should include items that are in the form of a visual language, sculpture and graphic images. Children could make a clay 'Rosetta stone' which could be broken into two halves (the key being on one part and the message on the other), canopic jars and jewellery. The collection should give clues to everyday life and may also include information about what happened to the ancient people. Once the collection of artefacts is complete they are to be hidden and then 'discovered' by the archaeologists. Then, as archaeologists, it is the groups' job to interpret their findings and to give a presentation to the class who will then evaluate the whole activity. Use the art history activities as an introduction. **Copymasters 3** and **4** will be useful.

The children should make designs for their own 'ancient artefacts' before using clay to model them in 3D. Once the artefacts are completely dry use PVA-based paints to colour and decorate them.

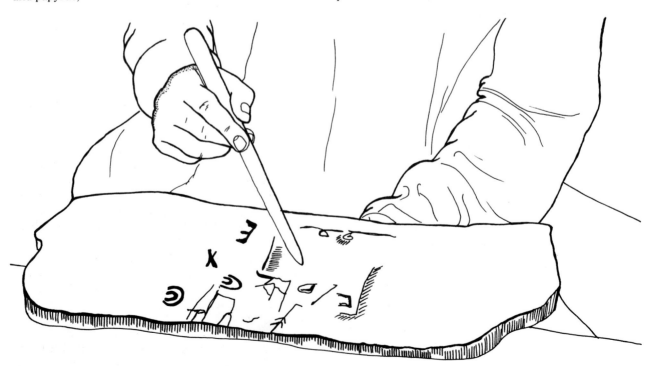

Making a Rosetta stone

You need
Modelling tools, PVA paints, brushes. (Coloured slips and a kiln are optional). Clay (either natural or self hardening), rolling pin, water paints, texture making tools, strong adhesive. Designs of scarab beetle, eye of Horus and examples of hieroglyphics (**Copymasters 3 and 4**).

 # Tombs ▷

Activity 7: Mathematics
Discuss the use of mathematical shapes in Egyptian designs and architecture. Make a list of commonly used shapes and solids. Use compasses, rulers and pencils to construct triangles and solids of planned sizes and shapes.

Activity 8: Tunnels, puzzles and mazes
Enormous trouble was taken to protect the burial chambers of the Pharaohs and their queens. **Copymaster 5** contains examples of how rectangles can be divided and cross sections of tombs with layouts of burial chambers. Use these to encourage discussion about ways of hiding the true routes through pyramids to the inner sanctuary. Make a list of methods of making tunnels and passageways through a solid that can be defended against thieves.

Children's tunnel drawings

Activity 9: Ancient computing
Based on the art history activities, get your children to use a computer program such as Paintbox to design the layout of a tomb. Discuss the ancient Egyptians ideas about proportion, symmetry and beauty. **Copymaster 5** contains simple mathematical ways to divide up rectangular shapes and sketches of how the original tombs were often laid out. These can be used to stimulate the work of organising space in a considered way. The procedures to be covered should include changing the scale of simple shapes, moving, copying and printing. Print the children's computer designs as a record. The prints can be coloured by hand according to a key devised by the children.

You need
Computer, printer and software such as Paintbrush®, Paintbox® or Artist®, **Copymaster 5**.

Child's computer design

Activity 10: Large-scale tomb
As your topic progresses you can introduce this activity which draws diverse strands together. The task is for the class to co-operate to produce a well-finished large scale 'ancient Egyptian' tomb for a Pharaoh. First ask the children to research and make notes, sketches and rough designs for an inner tomb. Their designs for constructing the inner tomb should include hieroglyphs, wall decorations, sculptures, canopic jars, jewellery and paintings. When made up, these will be placed to accompany the mummified Pharaoh.

Try to get a hold of a large freezer transit carton as the basic structure for the tomb. Once the designs are complete they can be scaled up to suit the carton (a finished rectangular cuboid size of approximately 1 metre by $1\frac{1}{2}$ metres by about $1\frac{1}{2}$ metres high). A door can be cut into the carton and hinged. Once this is done children can get inside to fit it out and finish the decoration. The internal wall decorations can be produced on large sheets of white paper that are then

5

Children working on the tomb

fixed carefully to the cardboard surface. The sarcophagus can be constructed from corrugated card and the mummy made up from scrap materials bandaged and painted with PVA paints. The portrait of the Pharaoh can be painted with molten wax crayons as described in Activity 16. Statuettes of cats and other animals, clay sculptures of fruit and food can be made from clay which is either glazed or painted.

You need
Large freezer carton, **Copymasters 1** to **5**, corrugated cardboard, paper, pencils, paint brushes, clay.

 **Crayons and pencils** ▷

Activity 11: Observational drawings
Prepare well prior to visiting a museum. Contact the museum education officer and check whether they have a variety of Egyptian items in the museum (such as, images of Anubis, Bast, scarab beetles or mummies). Remember to ask for any preparatory packs that the museum may have for visiting school parties. It is sensible to be aware of any children who may be nervous about 'spooky' things so that they are not frightened by the visit or the prospect of such a visit. Go through a range of suitable books with your children which

include items similar to the ones in the museum. This preparation will help to make the visit purposeful. The children will be looking for particular things and the chances of the visit providing merely ephemeral and random experiences will be reduced. Use worksheets at the museum if they are available. Use **Copymaster 7** to set specific tasks such as: 'Make an accurate drawing of the most interesting item in the collection. Make notes on why you found it interesting, note any colouring.' Children may find that using squared paper (**Copymaster 6**) will help them to be accurate. Make sure that pencils are sharp!

On returning from the museum your children can make larger drawings by simply scaling up from the existing squared up drawing on to a larger grid.

Finally, using tracing paper, your children can produce a well-finished drawing of their chosen subject. This can be coloured according to the notes they made at the museum. These activities are very valuable as they encourage links between thinking about what they will see, looking carefully, recording their observations and using their memory later (prompted by their notes). They also teach the useful, technical exercises of drawing to scale, enlarging, tracing and using colour descriptively.

You need
Sketch pads, squared paper **Copymasters 6** and **7**, tracing paper, pencils, coloured felt tip pens, brushes and water-based paints.

Activity 12: Wax resist drawings

The fact that wax does not mix with water is used in numerous artistic techniques. Here your children can produce dramatic images from their observational drawings. Using the sketches and notes made during the museum visit, get children to use white, chunky wax crayons on white or very light paper. The drawing will need to be very simple with plenty of open and filled areas. When complete, simply wash over the whole of the paper with black ink or Brusho dye®.

You need
Observational sketches from the museum, white paper, white wax crayons, dark or black ink or Brusho dye®, brushes.

Pyramids and animals

You need
Use **Copymaster 6** to make 1 cm grid card, paper, pencils, rulers, PVA glue, double-sided Sellotape®, paper clips, cotton, plasticine, protractors. A range of mathematical solids or nets; a ready cut out net for a pyramid for demonstration purposes. **Copymasters 8** and **9** and hardboard bases, paint and brushes. You will need papier mâché for the animal sculpture. (See the Modelling skill section on p 111.)

Activity 13: Model the great pyramid

Talk with the children about the way that the Egyptians valued mathematics as a perfect way to plan perfect structures. Discuss the mathematical solids that the children already know about. Ask questions about how high their models are going to be and how they are going to construct them so that they can work on the

Making up the pyramid

insides as they make them, and how they can see the inside once the pyramid is fixed.

First get the children to do a sketch of how the pyramid should look when finished. From this they can make a rough, small-scale net on paper. Cutting out, creasing and folding this rough model will introduce questions about the geometry of a pyramid. How tall should the apex be above the centre of the base? What should the angle of the faces be? How do you measure an angle? What is an isosceles triangle?

Now the children should be in a position to use **Copymasters 8** and **9** to make their own nets based on the plans given. Try to ensure that the children do not become too ambitious about the finished size of the pyramid. About 35 cms high is about the maximum when using thin card. Also make sure that the sticking tabs are not too small and flimsy. About 1 cm width is about right. Once the basic net is complete, the three faces can be stuck in position leaving the front face open as access for fitting out the inside.

Internally a complicated maze of tunnels can traverse the pyramid. (Try to make a system of interconnecting paths down which a ball of plasticine can roll to entomb or squash some unfortunate grave-robbers.) Make up the resting place of the Pharaoh or queen. Model the sculptures to scale and invent a way of viewing the interior once the final face has been sealed.

Activity 14: Animal sculptures

Make up sufficient papier mâché (follow the method on p 111). Give each child a baseboard and let them build slowly, step by step, a sculpture of their chosen subject. If they are going to produce a big piece of work, for example the head of a sphinx, then use a cardboard box upon which to build the papier mâché. When complete allow the sculptures to dry out thoroughly. They can then be painted and finished with a coat of clear PVA to give a semi-gloss finish. This activity will be built upon later, with the introduction of simple armatures which are covered with the papier mâché.

You need
Papier mâché, junk materials, illustrations.

Still life

Activity 15: Egyptian cartoon

Use **Copymaster 10** to show the way the Egyptians represented everyday activities and a sequential series of events. Emphasise the way of using schematic and symbolic language and ask your children to make a 'cartoon' of linked episodes of someone's life.

Things to include might be:

- Going to the shops
- Watching a favourite TV programme
- Eating
- Sleeping
- In the garden.

Child's cartoon

Activity 16: Wax or PVA encaustic painting

As children progress through Key Stage 2 the use of melted crayons can be tried as a way to approximate the ancient techniques from the Upper Egyptian region.

Ask the children to consider why most paintings on sarcophagi are contained within an oval shape. Some paintings were made directly on to the surface while others were painted with tempera on to small pieces of canvas which were then applied to the surface and fixed with glue. For their own work they can choose a famous person to immortalise. To paint with molten wax you need to melt wax crayons in small old saucepans or, for preference, a double boiler. Use bristle hair brushes to apply the wax to the surface. Use pinks, yellows, white tints and black for faces. Paint the under colours and gradually build up to a final coat. Allow only older children to use molten wax and supervise them carefully. Cover the work place with plenty of newspaper to mop up spills. Alternatively your children can use thin layers of PVA paints to build up an impression of encaustic work. Each layer of paint must be allowed to dry thoroughly before the next layer. As the idea is that colours should shine through subsequent layers your children need to discuss the order of applying colours to achieve the result they want. When dry apply a coat of thinned PVA medium to protect the surface.

You need
Paper, felt tip pens, pencils, wax crayons, paints and brushes, clear PVA. Magazine pictures of famous people. Illustrations of the Egyptian paintings found on the sarcophagi.

Egyptian jewels

Activity 17: Costume decoration

Seals of this famous mythical symbol were widely used in ancient Egypt. Discuss the origin and use of the seals. Using **Copymaster 11** transfer the detailed outline drawing of the eye of Horus on to a piece of newsprint (either by tracing or by freehand). This design needs to be about 10 cms long. Then roll out some clay into rolls of about 1 cm and 5 mm diameter. Place the rolls of clay in position on the design and model it to form a smooth, flowing profile. Cut out eye lid shapes as shown and fix in place. Around the finished eye build a small thin wall of clay. Mix a small quantity of plaster of Paris and pour this into the reservoir. Allow to 'go off'. Once the plaster has set you can turn turn over the plaster and the clay eye, and pick out all of the clay. Let the plaster dry for a few days then wash it with water and a tooth brush. This mould can be used to make impressions of the eye of Horus into clay tablets of hieroglyphs. These impressions can be trimmed and finished to make broaches or pendants.

You need
Clay (natural or self-hardening), **Copymaster 11**, flat pieces of wood, shapes for impressing, flat working surface, (cover plastic surfaced tables with newsprint, hessian or hardboard this will reduce mess as clay dries and flakes). Small, thin pieces of clear Perspex (approx 20 cms square), old shirts for children to wear as protective smocks.

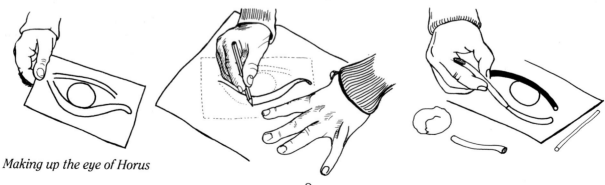

Making up the eye of Horus

ANCIENT GREECE AND ROME

Ceramics
Pots and plaques

26. Army pots
27. Patterned tiles
28. Pressed red gloss plaque

Art History
Classical worlds

18. Labours of Hercules
19. Minotaur
20. Collecting classics
21. Pictures on pots
22. Mosaics
23. Wallpaintings
24. Roman roads
25. Figures in sculpture

Design
Cool designs

29. Masks for *The Chicken*
30. Plaster relief
31. House for a hot climate

ANCIENT GREECE AND ROME

Drawing
Gods and wax

32. Gods
33. Museum objects

Textiles
Colour and pattern

43. Pad printing textile borders
44. Clothing and colour
45. Town appliqué

Print-making
Borders and grapes

41. Vine stencils
42. Antique patterns

Modelling
Figures and faces

34. Cycladic figurines
35. Aristophanes' masks
36. Oil lamp
37. House model

Painting
Ships and mosaics

38. Greek fire
39. Class mosaic
40. Plaster bed mosaic

CROSS-CURRICULAR LINKS ▶

Design and technology Making models of hypocausts, roads and villas, problem solving about keeping homes warm or cool

Drama and dance Masks, Greek plays

Environmental studies Looking for influences of Classical life, buildings, patterns, formal gardens

History Birth of civilisation, study of artefacts

Language Reading and other research for the topic, writing up facts, reportive writing of visits, imaginative writing

Mathematics Geometry (Euclid), patterns, symmetry, measuring, proportion, golden section, classical ideals

Music 'The Trojans' by Berlioz, film scores from *Ben Hur* and *Jason and the Argonauts*, Nana Mousskouri's 'Alexander the Great', music by Olivier Messiaen based on classical Greek poetry, 'The Planets' by Holst

RE The Pantheon of gods, start of Christianity

Science Triremes, producing heat by reflecting and focusing the sun's rays with mirrors

ABOUT THIS TOPIC ▶

General points

The Hellenistic world view was one of light and assurance, in which gods were more beautiful, powerful versions of humans. The gods mixed with humans to teach serenity and reason. Our civilisation inherited this image of the world from the Greeks of 500 BC. The Greek and Roman empires, died of exhaustion but their influence has remained and, at certain times, been a dominant force. Classical revivals in Florence and Rome and later in France, and the Palladian influence in England are all important. The influence can be seen all around us today. Theatre and cinema design, patterns, advertisements and the English countryside are littered with references. Besides the Roman towns of London, Cirencester and Bath there are many other sites that may be worth a visit.

Claude Lorrain and Nicholas Poussin represent the flawless combination of the real and ideal that typifies the classical worlds of Greece and Rome. For many

children their experience of watching the Walt Disney classic, *Fantasia*, is a great starting point. The Arcadian landscapes are matched with classical architecture and, of course, a whole host of gods, centaurs, mythical beasts and some legendary performances of classical music. Mathematics, physical perfection, theories of beauty and a grand union of architecture and countryside underlie our notions of those civilisations. The Pantheon of gods, a rich mythology and the calendar of celebrations has, to some extent, been taken over relatively recently by the Christian religion.

Displays and resources

In addition to paintings by Poussin and Claude, you may be able to collect a range of other illustrations and artefacts to display. These could include reproduction costumes (either full-scale or miniature), models of architectural features, pottery sherds and replica sculptures.

STARTING POINTS ▶

- Discussion about myths and Gods
- Reading simple translations of comedies such as *The Chickens* by Aristophanes
- A debate about the issues involved in the 'Elgin' marbles
- Looking at the range of art produced by the ancient civilisations
- Talk about the legend of Romulus and Remus and the saying that 'Rome was not built in a day'
- Walt Disney's *Fantasia*
- A display of classical images. Include paintings such as: *The Gathering of the Ashes of Phocian* by Nicolas Poussin, *The Embarkation of the Queen of Sheba* by

Claude, *The Ideal Town* by Piero della Francesca and Raphael's *School of Athens*.

Examine the importance of women and female deities, include Athena, Demeter (goddess of harvest), Hera and Aphrodite, find images on **Copymaster 13** and in the following paintings: *Diana* by Renoir, *Venus and Mars* by Sandro Botticelli (and also by Piero di Cosimo), *The Origin of the Milky Way* by Tintoretto (the bedroom of Hera and Zeus), *The Judgement of Paris* by Rubens (Aphrodite winning the apple) this painting is interesting for the way the defeated Graces responded to the judgement, *The Toilet of Venus* by Velazquez, *The Reconciliation of Cephalus and Procris* by Claude.

ANCIENT GREEK AND ROMAN ACTIVITIES

 ## Classical worlds

Activity 18: Labours of Hercules

Discuss the pantheistic religion of classical times and the relationship between gods, goddesses and humans. **Copymasters 12, 13** and **27** depicts members of the Greek and Roman Pantheons. Discuss the labours of Hercules and ask your children to illustrate one of the labours as a cartoon. Before starting, get them to sketch the characters that they will use and select the right kind of colours and materials. Using text in cartoons can be much easier if your children follow the example shown in the illustration below. Always write the text before drawing a speech bubble around it.

You need
Copymasters 12, 13 and **27** paper, paints, inks and pencils and pens.

Cartoon bubbles

Activity 19: Minotaur

Many artists have produced images of the minotaur. Picasso's etchings and drawings are remarkable. Show reproductions of Picasso's work and discuss the kind of sympathy shown for this poor, mutant creature.

Children are fascinated by mazes. Collect a number of different designs of mazes that can stimulate children's own work. Children can produce their own small models of minotaurs using clay and they can produce a maze for the minotaur's home using cardboard boxes, papier mâché, paint, glue and brushes. (Refer to p 111 for the papier mâché recipe.)

You need
Illustrations of minotaurs (particularly those by Picasso), clay, glazes, papier mâché, scrap materials and cardboard boxes, paints and brushes, illustrations of mazes.

Child's Minotaur

Activity 20: Collecting classics

Get your children to collect and sort all kinds of images that relate to classical times – old and contemporary. Look at:

- illustrations of classical architecture
- images of classical life as portrayed by Poussin and Claude
- the influence of classical life on the Georgians
- the use of classical imagery in 20th century advertising
- the cinema and pseudo classical, mutant buildings.

Organise a trip around the centre of town and pay particular attention to cinema and theatre facades and architectural details including columns, pediments, podiums, ornamental vases and fountains in parks and garden statues. Make a record of contemporary classical use of images. These can include patterns such as the Greek key, fluted and non-fluted columns, reproduction fireplaces, art work in magazines, television adverts with classical overtones, Roman typefaces, classical pottery shapes.

You need
Magazine and newspaper illustrations, sketch books, reproductions of classical architecture and paintings, pencils, felt tip pens.

Activity 21: Pictures on pots

Prior to a museum trip get your children to study illustrations of pictorial ceramics. Pay particular attention to red and black Greek ceramics and such famous pictorial Roman glassware as the Portland vase. Discuss the sophisticated technology that flourished in Roman times which could not be matched successfully for many years until the work by Thomas Wedgwood. **Copymasters 18, 19** and **77** contains typical designs from pottery. Get your children to use sketch books on their trip to the museum and make notes on the shapes and colouring of the vases. Point out that many of the beautiful designs on Greek ceramics show everyday activities such as fighting, eating and drinking, while some show the influence of the gods on their lives. On returning to class, your children can produce finished illustrations of plates and vases based on their notes.

You need
Sketchbooks, pencils, felt tip pens, paints, brushes and tracing paper, books containing pictures of ceramics and glassware, **Copymaster 18, 19** and **77**.

Activity 22: Mosaics
Study the use of animal and human figures in Greek and Roman mosaics. Discuss the relationship between the sizes of the tesserae and the detail in the pictures. Use a magnifying glass to examine the 'mosaic' way colour television pictures and magazine images are made up. Look at **Copymasters 14–16** which contain simple outline designs of a mosaic.

You need
Copymasters 14–16, sticky paper, scissors, paints, brushes and mixing pallets.

Activity 23: Wallpaintings
Study the wallpaintings of Pompeii and ancient Greece. Discuss the way everyday activities were portrayed and the decorative use that was made of foliage and vines. **Copymaster 17** contains detailed outline drawings of parts of wallpaintings. Encourage the children to use this as a guide to composing their own designs. Ask them to make a list of the contemporary everyday activities that they could include in a wallpainting for their own bedroom. Give your children a piece of A3 paper and, after having made some sketches in their sketchbooks, get them to make their own designs for a wallpainting. They could take photographs of the local environment to use as a source for their designs.

You need
Cameras, **Copymaster 17**, illustrations of wallpaintings, sketchbooks, pencils, felt tip pens.

Activity 24: Roman roads
First discuss the importance of communications for the Roman Empire and the need for good roads. The Roman roads were generally straight and constructed so thoroughly that evidence of them is clear even today. Discuss the way that roads are made today with layers of different sized stones and hard-wearing surfaces. Discuss the problems of making sure that roads go in the right direction and join in the right places. Set the task of making a small cross-section model of a roman road. To make the models your children will need to collect coarse sand, small gravel and other fine stones to simulate the different stones used in the original construction. Children working in groups, can form bases for their models from layers of papier mâché (or plaster) set inside the base of an old, cut down cardboard box. Extra layers of papier mâché can be built up on either side of the 'road' and the cross-section can be shown by layering the different stones and sands correctly. The stones and sand can be fixed with PVA glue and the surface of the 'road' finished with a smooth

mixture of papier mâché. Mark the papier mâché carefully to show the outlines of stones and finish by painting carefully.

You need
Old cardboard cartons, papier mâché (see page 111 for recipe), paint, brushes, PVA, grits, sands, sandpaper.

Activity 25: Figures in sculpture
Early Greek sculptures of animals and human beings were very simple. Their soft, fluid shapes had much in common with some recent western sculptures (for example, the work of Henry Moore, Gaudier-Brzeska, Modigliani and Picasso). The techniques of the Greek sculptors progressed enormously in only a few hundred years. Give each child a copy of **Copymaster 25** which contains pictures of sculptures from different periods in ancient Greece. Get the children to put the sculptures in chronological order and then discuss them as a class.

You need
Copymaster 25, illustrations of sculptures from different periods.

Pots and plaques ▷

Activity 26: Army pots
The Roman armies in Britain were constantly in need of food supplies. Milling food was a problem, one way of overcoming this was by using a special kind of pottery. Mortaria pottery was made by producing rough bowls, the inside of which was covered with a rough surface of grit embedded in the clay. (Consider the meaning of pestle and mortar.) The Roman soldiers simply put their ration of cereal inside the bowl, ground it up against the rough surface, made some porridge and marched on. Give each child sufficient clay to make a pinched pot and surface the interior with grit. Ask the children how thick the walls of the pots should be? What is the best shape for such pots? How big should they be? Fire the pots and try out the method of making porridge using a pestle and mortar technique to grind cereal down.

You need
Clay, grit, cereals, pestle.

Activity 27: Patterned tiles
Using a craft knife and thick card cut out patterns selected from those on **Copymasters 18** and **19**. Make up a frame from 1 cm square wood to fit exactly around the template. With the card template in position as shown in the illustration opposite, press and roll clay to form a tile. Allow to dry, remove the card and frame. Dry thoroughly and biscuit fire the tiles. (Alternatively, before biscuit firing, you can make up coloured thick slip and fill in all the indented areas. Let these dry and then fire the tile.) Glaze in the usual way after biscuit firing. Always work with clay on an absorbent surface; using polythene or working directly on laminated surfaces always creates a mess and can be a health hazard. See the ceramics skill section (page 89) for details about drying, glazing and firing.

Pot shapes

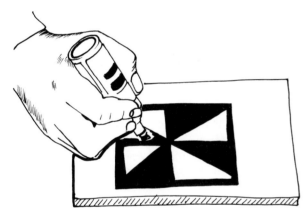

1. Cut a design from thick card.

2. Press clay to form a patterned tile.

Making patterned tiles

You need
Red clay, designs produced in Activity 42, card, craft knives, wooden battening, rolling pin, fabric or newsprint to cover the work surfaces and overalls **Copymasters 18** and **19**.

Activity 28: Pressed red gloss plaque
Typical of Roman ceramics are 'fast wheel' pots and mould-pressed red gloss ware. This activity will give your children experience of moulded ware. Give each child some Plasticine®, waxed cord and a small frame (15 cms × 10 cms) and a sheet of card. Place the frame on the card. On the inside of the frame get them to make simple relief models of animals, people or a scene. Cut strips of cord and use these as decorative borders. The height of the modelling should not exceed about 7 mm. When the design is complete, mix and pour plaster into the frame covering the plasticine modelling to a depth of 1 cm. (Use scrim and plaster to reduce the amount of plaster required – see the 'Modelling' section, pages 111–12, for more information.) Let the plaster go off and harden. When the mould is hard remove the plasticine and cords entirely from the mould. Roll out a slab of red clay to a thickness of about 1 cm. Place this on the thoroughly dry mould and press it evenly so that it takes a perfect impression from the mould. Trim the edges and let the clay dry sufficiently to shrink away from the plaster. The plaque can be fired and glazed.

You need
Clay, plaster, cord, Plasticine®, modelling tools, card, wood for the frame.

 Cool designs ▷

Activity 29: Masks for *The chicken*
For many mask-making activities, your children will find it useful to use **Copymaster 26** which contains a guide to drawing a standard head shape. Read Aristophanes' story, *The Chicken*, which is very funny and simple enough to put on as a class or school production. The masks for the chickens can be made in the following way. Mark out the shape of the mask on the corner of a cardboard box which has been painted white. Use the Copymaster to position the width from ear to ear and other features. Cut out the mask and the

nose, mouth and eyes as shown in the illustration. Using the same box, cut out the top part of the beak as shown, so that it fits the main mask shape properly. Make the beak whatever length you like. The lower beak needs to be a bit smaller and it is cut out in the same way. The lower beak will be hinged to the bottom part of the main mask shape and needs to have holes pierced in it to fix through similar holes in the main mask shape. Now fix the top part of the beak to the main mask shape. Fix the under beak with a strip of cloth tied through the holes and tucked down. The bird's feathers are made by cutting up coloured paper and sticking them in layers to the forehead part of the main mask. Use different coloured feathers and build them up around the eyes and behind the mask. The mask can be fitted to the head by an elastic thread. The mask itself can be decorated by being painted and the eyes can be embellished in a number of ways. For the performance, the lower beak can be moved if it is attached to a large lolly stick and operated by hand.

You need
Pencils, felt tip pens, cardboard boxes, craft knives, scissors, elastic thread, paints, brushes, coloured paper (or coloured feathers), large lolly sticks and **Copymaster 26**.

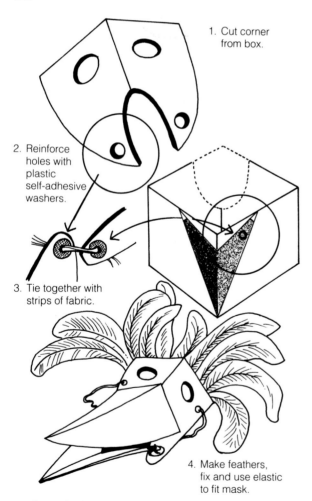

1. Cut corner from box.

2. Reinforce holes with plastic self-adhesive washers.

3. Tie together with strips of fabric.

4. Make feathers, fix and use elastic to fit mask.

Making chicken masks

Activity 30: Plaster relief
Collect and sort illustrations of Greek sculptures, particularly relief sculptures such as the Parthenon.

Give your children some thin, coloured card and first get them to make a sketch of the fragment that they are going to use as a design. Once they have made the sketches get them to do an outline drawing on the card. Mix up a small quantity of plaster. (Use a little washing up liquid in the mixture to slow down the going off process.) Work quickly and apply the plaster carefully inside the outline drawing. As each thin layer is made, draw into the drying plaster to re-establish the main details of the drawing. Carefully build up the thickness of the relief model. Using the washing up liquid will give your children the opportunity to smooth features and put in details as well. For further information about managing plaster work, see the 'Modelling' section (pages 111–12) of this book.

You need
Coloured card, pencils, felt tip pens, wax crayons, plaster, mixing bowl, washing up liquid and a tool to apply the plaster, source books.

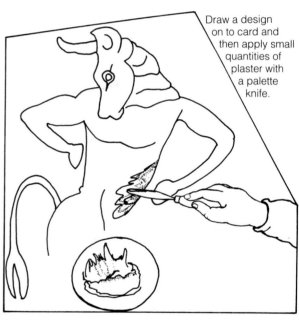

Draw a design on to card and then apply small quantities of plaster with a palette knife.

Making a plaster relief

Activity 31: House for a hot climate
Examine and study how towns were laid out in ancient Greece (see **Copymaster 24**) and Rome. The city states of ancient Greece were protected by strong walls and included temples, market places and living accommodation. The houses often had a central courtyard area that included a shrine where offerings were made to the family god. The houses fitted together organically and when combined they gave an enclosed structure to the town.

In this activity, your children are to work as architects, producing house designs for clients in ancient Greece. The materials available include marble, ceramics, stone and wood. The main design requirement is that the house should provide a cool place to live throughout the day as the sun moves its position.

Brainstorm the issues involved in designing a house for a hot climate. Divide the class into pairs. Give each pair a copy of **Copymaster 24** which contains a map of an ancient town with numbered building sites and drawings of typical types of plans of houses. Each pair can be allocated a particular site. The position of the sun and other features (such as trees) will need to be considered in making the house design.

The plans should be on a scale of 1 : 50. Each building site is 160 square metres approximately and only 50% can be built on, the rest has to be garden or patio. The shape of the plan should not be rectangular, as most houses were poleodomic (designed to fit together according to the shape of the land, to provide a wall around the dwellings). Each pair will need a copy of **Copymaster 6** which contains a grid for working out the plan and scale of the building. Coloured card can be cut into strips and stuck on to the grid to produce the walls, courtyards, rooms and any ponds or religious shrines. **Copymasters 18** and **19** contain abstract designs used in the decoration of buildings.

You need
Coloured card, rulers, pencils, scissors, **Copymasters 6**, **18**, **19** and **24**, glue.

Gods and wax

Activity 32: Gods
Give each child a copy of **Copymaster 27**. The task is for your children to copy the outline drawing of Zeus as accurately as possible. Their drawings should be the same size and proportion and have the same line qualities. When everybody has finished, give each child a piece of tracing paper. Trace the Copymaster accurately. Then place the tracing over the children's drawings and get them to see where their drawings are inaccurate. Ask them to correct their drawings.

You need
Copymaster 27, tracing paper, pencils and erasers.

Activity 33: Museum objects
If you are able to arrange a museum visit get your children to sketch and make notes on any domestic objects such as vases, shoes, combs, oil lamps or jewellery. Back in school, these sketches can be used as the basis for colourful wax and wash designs. Give your children sheets of tinted paper or thin card, light-

Wax resist oil lamp

coloured wax crayons and a range of coloured inks. Make large designs based on their drawings using the wax crayons. These will be more effective if they are linear rather than solid blocks of wax. When the wax crayon drawings are complete, use a brush to wash over the whole of the drawing with a chosen colour of ink. The wax will resist the ink and will produce a strong silhouetted design.

You need
Sketches made on museum visit, tinted card or paper, wax crayons, waterproof inks, brushes.

Figures and faces

Activity 34: Cycladic figurines
Look at illustrations of Cycladic sculptures. Compare these simple shapes with those of Miro, Gaudier-Brzeska and Henry Moore. Give each child a small amount of clay and some coloured slips. Get them to make their own versions of chosen sculptures, taking care to concentrate on the size and form of the pieces. When the clay is leather hard use the coloured slips to complete the replicas.

You need
Illustrations of sculptures, clay, modelling tools, coloured slips, brushes.

Activity 35: Aristophanes' masks
Copymasters 28 and **29** contain line drawings of two famous masks. Give each child a copy of either one of these drawings copied on to card. Cut out the profiles and outlines to make templates. Use a slab of clay rolled out to about 1 cm and trace the outline shape of the face. Cut away the waste and build up the face using the drawing as a guide. When the work is nearly complete turn it over carefully and hollow out the back. Pierce two holes for the eyes as shown and two more holes for a string. The masks can be fired and wall mounted.

You need
Copymasters 28 and **29**, clay, modelling tools, prepared work surfaces for clay.

Activity 36: Oil lamp
The illustration overleaf shows a design for a Roman oil lamp. Modelling a replica will involve your children in making two or three parts and joining them together.

- make a simple design on paper (include decoration)
- draw a simple egg shape (about 9 cms by 7 cms) on to a piece of thin card and cut out as a template
- roll out two small slabs of clay about 10 cms × 8 cms and about 7 mm thick
- trace two egg shapes on to the slabs
- use one as the base and the other as the upper part of the lamp
- model the base, draw up the edges of the base so that it forms a hollow shape
- form the upper part in a similar way
- using a plastic straw or a piece of plastic pipe cut holes through the upper part.

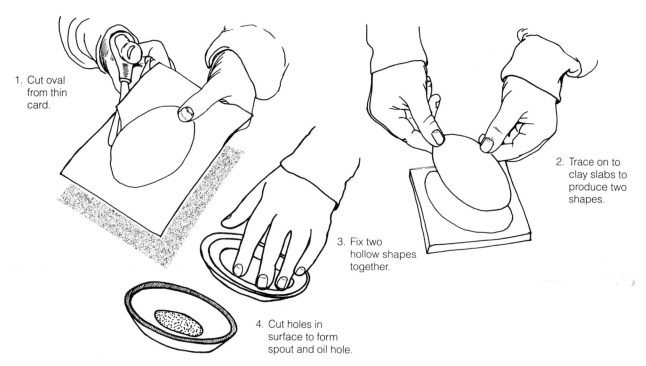

1. Cut oval from thin card.

2. Trace on to clay slabs to produce two shapes.

3. Fix two hollow shapes together.

4. Cut holes in surface to form spout and oil hole.

Making oil lamps

When both parts have been shaped check the profiles by using the template and modify if necessary so that they fit together. Turn over the upper part so that it is the right way up again. Join both parts together by using slip. Smooth the joining edges, form a little handle and fix to the upper end as shown. Decorate the lamp and allow to dry. Fire it. Vegetable oil is poured into the large hole and a wick placed through the small hole.

Activity 37: House model
The pairs who worked together to make a scale design of a house for a hot climate (Activity 31) can now continue in three dimensions. The transfer of designs should be all to the same scale so that the models can be mounted together to produce a town. Your children will need to think about how thick walls should be for a model that is made on a scale of 1 : 50. A variety of cards, glues and finishing materials will be needed. The various surfaces of marble, tile, stone and wood will need to be treated differently. Points to consider: how much of the interior of the houses will need to be shown? Will it be necessary to have a removable roof? When the models are complete the architects are to present their designs and review their work with the rest of the class. Which are the best and why?

Other modelling activities could include designing and making a Roman hypocaust, chariot, or an articulated Roman helmet.

You need
Various sheet modelling materials, coloured card, rulers, pencils, scissors, glue.

 ## Ships and mosaics ▷

Activity 38: Greek fire
Scientific reconstructions have shown that the account of how Greek soldiers set fire to an invading fleet by directing and focusing the sun's rays from a host of their mirrored shields on to the ships' sails may well be true. This could provide an exciting stimulus for a large-scale painting. Describe the story, get your children to make notes and sketches before setting to work on an imaginative composition. Discuss the sketches: Where should the focus of attention be? How can sunlight be shown? Can perspective be used to dramatic effect?

You need
Sketches, paints, pencils, large sheets of white paper.

Child's painting

Mosaics

There are very many types of mosaic found in Greek and Roman periods. There is no need always to use images of Caesar as a starting point. Consider the geometrical patterns with impressions of shadows, images of great hunts, 'Unswept dining rooms', the 'Battle of Alexander the great and Darius', and the bikini-clad girls in the famous 'ten girls pavement' mosaic.

Making mosaics can be approached in a number of ways. Both making mosaics with sticky paper and using plaster with fragments of pottery are described here. Common to both approaches is the need to get your children to arrange the fragments in such a way that they follow the general lines and flow of the designs. Introduce the ideas through Activity 22 and the use of **Copymasters 14–16**. (**Copymaster 15** is a mosaic of a dog.)

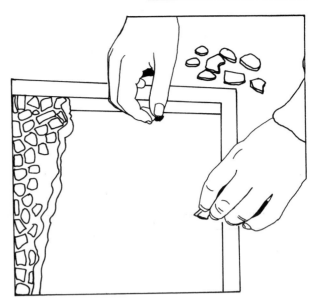

Making plaster bed mosaic

Activity 39: Class mosaic

To produce a class mosaic, first divide the class into groups. Use a very large piece of background paper (approximately 70 cm by 1 m). Collect and sort pieces of coloured sticky paper or torn up pieces of coloured magazine illustrations. Get the first group of children to square up the paper and transfer a design either from **Copymasters 14–19**, or from their own small design. Then each group in turn selects and sticks small pieces of paper in place until the mosaic is complete.

You need
Copymasters 14–19, coloured fragments of paper, a large sheet of background paper, scissors, glue, pencils.

Activity 40: Plaster bed mosaic

To produce a small mosaic using fragments of coloured pottery is more demanding but very rewarding. This activity can be undertaken by a group of about five children working on their own in an area of the class especially prepared for messy work. The size of the mosaic will define the amount of materials required. Collect and sort the right colours of ceramic fragments (old cups and saucers can be smashed up in a heavy sack). Get each child to make a simple wooden frame the same size as a prepared design that has been carefully executed in colour. Mix up a small quantity of plaster which contains a little washing up liquid. Using a plastic knife, spread a small quantity of plaster into the top part of the frame. Place the tesserae carefully in position. Work progressively downwards until the design is complete, making small quantities of fresh plaster as the work continues. When the design is complete, squeegee a fairly liquid mixture of plaster over the whole surface so that the gaps between the fragments are completely filled. When the plaster has hardened, polish the tiles so that they are clean and show their colours properly.

You need
Ceramic fragments, plaster, frames, prepared work surfaces.

 Borders and grapes ▷

Activity 41: Vine stencils

It may help your children to produce cleaner, more controlled wall paintings (as in Activity 23) if they have stencils with which to print part of the designs. Use the vine stencil on **Copymaster 30** to produce a card stencil to use in wallpaintings or as part of a decorative pattern on fabric.

You need
Copymaster 30, thin card (oiled manila for preference), craft knives, safety rulers and cutting boards.

Activity 42: Antique patterns

Repeating patterns are often based on designs made in a square. **Copymasters 18** and **19** contain examples of Greek and Roman patterns and show how they were constructed. Compare these with those on **Copymasters 20–23** which show the geometrically based Islamic and Anglo Saxon patterns and their methods of construction. Give your children a piece of A4 paper and get them to divide it into 15 squares. In the left hand column of five squares, get them to make five separate designs which can then be continued across the page to produce five strips of repeating patterns. The colours to be used for each pattern should be a maximum of two plus white. (These designs may be used later in Activity 47 for printing textiles.)

You need
Copymasters 18–23, paper, rulers, pencils, sets of compasses, paints, brushes or felt tip pens.

 Colour and pattern ▷

Activity 43: Pad printing textile borders

Copymasters 18 and **19** contain a few traditional shapes and patterns that can be used to produce a concertina greaseproof paper stencil for pad printing textile borders. See the 'Textiles' section (pages 126–8) for details of this method.

You need
Greaseproof paper, dye pads, fabric (cotton), scissors, **Copymasters 18** and **19**.

Activity 44: Clothing and colour

Study the changes in clothing styles from the 7th century BC when dresses were relatively simple and decorated with geometrical patterns, through to the diaphanous flowing robes of later periods in Greece. Discuss the kinds of colours which were available in Rome. The colour of a person's clothes often denoted their rank. Purple was used by emperors. Get your children to research the colour of clothes and complete the clothing styles on **Copymaster 13**.

You need
Books, visual aids, **Copymaster 13**.

Activity 45: Town appliqué

Use the work on towns as a starting point for making a class appliqué based on the designs. Choose colours and textures of fabrics to suit each particular area. Children can work in groups on sections of the overall design.

You need
Scrap fabrics, needles, thread, hessian backing panel.

THE SEA

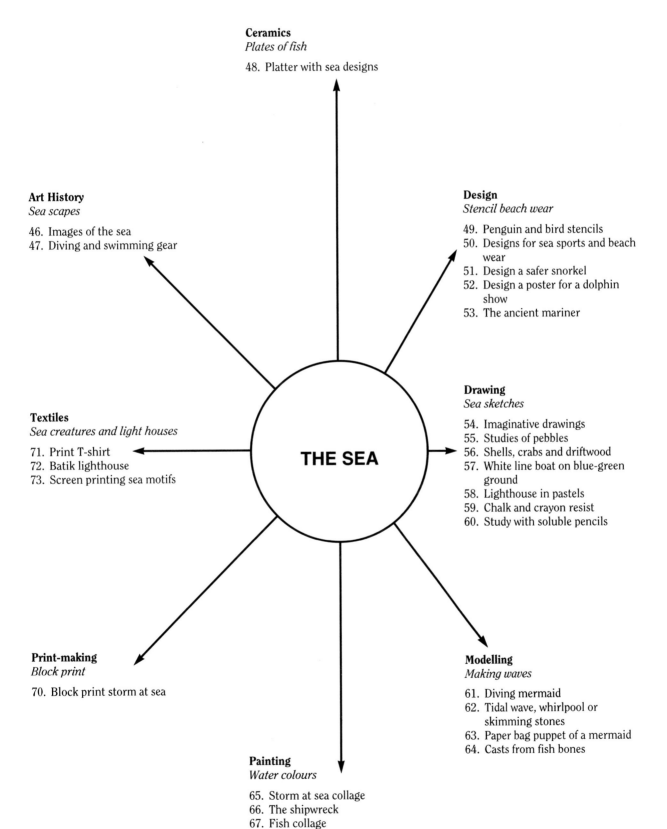

Ceramics
Plates of fish

48. Platter with sea designs

Art History
Sea scapes

46. Images of the sea
47. Diving and swimming gear

Design
Stencil beach wear

49. Penguin and bird stencils
50. Designs for sea sports and beach wear
51. Design a safer snorkel
52. Design a poster for a dolphin show
53. The ancient mariner

Textiles
Sea creatures and light houses

71. Print T-shirt
72. Batik lighthouse
73. Screen printing sea motifs

THE SEA

Drawing
Sea sketches

54. Imaginative drawings
55. Studies of pebbles
56. Shells, crabs and driftwood
57. White line boat on blue-green ground
58. Lighthouse in pastels
59. Chalk and crayon resist
60. Study with soluble pencils

Print-making
Block print

70. Block print storm at sea

Modelling
Making waves

61. Diving mermaid
62. Tidal wave, whirlpool or skimming stones
63. Paper bag puppet of a mermaid
64. Casts from fish bones

Painting
Water colours

65. Storm at sea collage
66. The shipwreck
67. Fish collage
68. Under sea collage
69. Blues and greens

CROSS-CURRICULAR LINKS ▶

Design and technology Designing and making a boat or raft to float and carry one lego man involves the choice of materials. Waterproofing materials

Drama and dance Puppet and mimed stories and poems, rhythmic movement of various sea-creatures

Environmental studies Importance of water to global health, ways water is used, sporting activities and safety

History Water transport, water supplies; carriers and early supplies such as from London Bridge

Language Listening, imaginative and reportive writing, *Treasure Island*, *Moby Dick*, 'The Rime of the Ancient Mariner'

Mathematics Measuring capacity of containers

Music Making 'water' sounds, listening to music such as: 'Singing in the rain'; *The Pastoral* by Beethoven, 'Yellow submarine', 'Fingal's Cave' by Mendelssohn, '*La Mer*' by Debussy, The Flying Dutchman

RE Stories from the Bible, baptism, Muslim ablutions, Hindu scattering of ashes on the Ganges, washing of the hands

Science Origin of life in water, changes in state: solid, liquid, gas, the water cycle, floating and sinking

ABOUT THIS TOPIC ▶

General points

The sea is a mysterious force, the source of life, full of changes, calm one minute and violent or swamped in fog the next. For explorers and artists the sea has posed many questions about its capriciousness, its vastness, colour and light. Artists can find it a vehicle for their moods, designers can draw upon the imagery of sea-life and mythology to decorate fine fabrics for fashion or as a backdrop to product image and advertising.

If you can arrange a visit to the *Victory* or *Marie Rose*

your topic may get off to a flying start. For such a visit try to resist the temptation to do everything. Sitting quietly for half an hour will be worth a whole day of unstructured activities.

Displays and resources

Reproductions of paintings and drawings, shells, starfish and other sea-creatures; flotsam and jetsam found on sea-shores; models of ships, cross-sections of the seabed, diving gear and beach wear.

Children by an anchor

STARTING POINTS ▶

- The sea in paintings
- The sea and weather
- Famous journeys by sea or under the sea
- Pollution and the sea

- Food from the sea
- Islands and other geographical features such as fjords, deltas

THE SEA ACTIVITIES

Sea scapes

Before you start

The sea is an extremely important element in nature, covering some two thirds of the earth's surface. It is indifferent or full of cruel moods. No great artist has reflected these hostile, violent moods so well as Turner. Although the most easily available images of the sea are reproductions of famous paintings and drawings, do not ignore other media such as ceramics decorated with fish, or films and videos. Try also to keep a balance between observed images and those from imagination. The range of images of the sea is quite vast. The list below includes expressionist, impressionist, European, Asiatic, ancient and modern examples of work.

The Bayeaux tapestry (1080); Botticelli (1444–1510), *The Birth of Venus*; Boudin (1824–98), *Beach Scene*; Canaletto (1697–1768), various marine scenes combined with architecture. Particularly good is *Bacino di S. Marco looking east*; Cappelle (1624–79), Coastal scenes; Claude (1600–88), *Embarkation of the Queen of Sheba*; Courbet (1865), *Normandy Coast*; Cotman (1782–1842), *Seashore*; 'Cretan' fresco of dolphins (in the bathroom of the temple of Knossos, Crete); Daubigny (1980), *The Ferry*, (painted from floating studio); Degas (1834–1917), *A Beach Scene*; Dufy (1877–1953), *Deauville, Drying the Sails*; Gericault (1791–1824), *The Raft of Medusa*; Hoitsu (1761–1828), Wave paintings; Hokusai, Katsushika (1760–1849), *Fuji Seen Through the Waves off Kangawa*; Kandinsky (1866–1944); Leonardo (1452–1519), *The Deluge*; Loutherbourg (1740–1812), *Battle of the Nile*; Lowry (1887–1976), *Yachts* (1920), *The Sea* (1963), *A Ship* (1965); Manet (1832–83), *Combat of the Kearsage and Alabama* (1864); Monet (1840–1926), *Terrace at the Seaside near le Havre, Beach at Trouville*; Nash (1889–1946), *Dead Sea* (Totes Meer); Okyo (1733–95), *Fire and Flood, Typhoon*; Ruisdael (1628–82), many seascapes; Seurat (1859–91), *Boats, Low Tide*, Grandcamp (1885); Sickert (1860–1942), *The Bathers, Dieppe* (1902); Turner (1775–1851), *Seascape with storm coming on, Snow storm, Steamboat off a harbour's mouth making signals in shallow water, and going by the lead*. (The artist was in this storm on the night the *Ariel* left Harwich); Utamaro (1754–1806), *Young Women Visiting Seashore*; Van de Velde (1591–1630), *Dutch Man of War, other vessels in breeze*; Van Goyen (1596–1656), many seascapes; Viking carved boats; Vlaminck (1876–1958), *Sails*, a woodcut (1913), *Boats at Low Tide* (1938); Vroom Hendrick (1566–1640), *The Battle of Gibraltar*; Wadsworth (1889–1949), *The Beached Margin*; Wallis (1855–1942), *Schooner under the Moon*; Whistler (1834–1903), *Green and Gold, The Great Sea, The Blue Wave, Biarritz*.

Activity 46: Images of the sea

Ask your library for help in collecting a good range of different ways to represent the sea. Try to arrange a slide show. Look at the differences between Turner's brushstrokes and the deliberate methods of the Dutch school. Look at the graphic realism of Hokusai and the expressive power of Vlaminck. Look at the symbolism of Wadsworth and the contemporary fabric designs that feature sea life. Ask your children to write about their favourite work. Why do they like it? Try to focus on colour, movement, feeling and pattern. Get your children to do their version of their favourite picture using whichever media they prefer.

You need
Selection of images, notebooks, slides, sketchbooks, charcoal, paints, brushes, pen and ink, pencils.

Activity 47: Diving and swimming gear

Collect and sort illustrations of swimming costumes, beach wear and diving equipment. Try to borrow Victorian or Edwardian swimming costumes and illustrations of old fashioned swimming scenes (including postcards). Cut out illustrations from magazines and make a class collage of the history of sea fashions.

You need
Costumes, artefacts, illustrations.

Plates of fish

Activity 48: Platter with sea designs

To help give your children ideas about slip decorating plates you may be able to borrow examples of work by local potters. Your museum service may be able to lend you work by Colin Cafell and other contemporary ceramicists who often decorate plates and vases with images of fish and marine life. (See illustration.) Get your children to make some sketches of shells, fish and

Sea designs and plates

21

other sea creatures or mythological figures such as Neptune. Cut out a few circles of tinted card. From the sketches make up simple two-colour designs on these circles of card. Try out different colour combinations. Use fluid, rhythmic brush strokes. Make up platters (see Activity 117), paint or dip the platters in a coloured slip. While the slip is drying use a paperclip or pointed modelling tool to draw the outline of the subject through the slip into the clay. Encourage your children to use flowing graceful lines. Complete the design using another coloured slip to make dots, fine lines and patches of colour. Again, it would be possible to draw additional details through the second colour. Allow the platter to dry, biscuit fire it and use clear or transparent glaze to finish the design.

You need
Sketches of fish or marine subjects, clay, slip, glazes, brushes, tinted card, paints and mixing palettes.

 Stencil beach wear ▷

Activity 49: Penguin and bird stencils
Using books for reference get your children to make outline drawings of a penguin or a bird. The drawings should be about 10 cm high. Give the children some tracing paper and trace the line drawings. Transfer the image from the tracing paper to thin white card. Converting the penguin drawing into a stencil will be relatively simple. First, use a thick felt tip pen to redraw the traced image and fill in the black areas of the penguin. Your children should consider how to keep the design simple but still 'penguin like'. It will be necessary to leave certain pieces of card uncut to tie the stencil in place. See the illustration. Making a bird stencil is more complicated but requires the same procedure. These stencils can be used in Activity 71 for printing T-shirts

Make sure that ties are not so thin that the stencil breaks.

tie

tie

Ties on penguin stencils

or beach wear. **Copymaster 31** contains a number of options for designs of penguins and birds.

You need
Illustrations, pencils, felt tip pens, thin card, tracing paper, craft knives, cutting mats, **Copymaster 31**.

Activity 50: Designs for sea sports and beach wear
Collect and sort illustrations from fashion magazines and newspapers. Ask your children to bring in their swimming costumes. (You may be able to arrange a visit to your school by a fashion design student or an assistant from a boutique.) Discuss with your children what kind of images, colour and style they should use for this particular kind of product design. As a general rule, simple shapes and bright colours will complement a summery feel. The design should be made so that it can be used on clothing accessories. A T-shirt, bathing costume and a beach bag should all feature in the final design sheet. First of all your children will need to produce sketches and mix colours. Only when they are confident should they transfer their work to a good quality piece of paper and finish it neatly. It will be appropriate to spend some time on figure drawing.

You need
Illustrations, examples of existing beach wear, pencils, felt tip pens, tracing paper, coloured pencils or paint, good quality white paper for the fashion sheet.

Activity 51: Design a safer snorkel
Get your children to bring in snorkels from home. Discuss the safety problems of all snorkel designs. Are any safe? How can they be tested? Make mock up designs. Invite a safety officer to judge their attempts and point out dangers. (Children should not, of course, actually use these.)

You need
Paper, snorkels, paints, brushes, pencils, scrap materials, glue, scissors, craft knives, cutting mats and safety rules.

Activity 52: Design a poster for a dolphin show
This activity introduces simple grid layout work. **Copymaster 32** contains a grid that is suitable for organising posters that are in A4 proportion. Explain to your children that the graphic design work that they see around them has, very often, been composed using guidelines and rules which help to organise the display of information in a balanced and creative way. A poster for a dolphin show should include: dolphin(s), some text including dates, prices of tickets and venue. Get your children to rough out positions for the text and the graphic image using the copymaster. Encourage the children to discuss their rough designs in class before drawing up the selected grid on the poster paper. The text could be produced by computer word processor and handwork and then be pasted into position. The image

of the dolphin will need to be handled carefully, to keep it both simple and evocative.

You need
Illustrations, examples of typefaces, poster paper, **Copymaster 32**, tracing paper, pencils, paints, brushes, scissors, glue.

Activity 53: The ancient mariner
Coleridge's poem, *The Rime of the Ancient Mariner*, is full of evocative images of the sea. Ask your children to choose specific passages to illustrate. Restrict the media to pen and ink. The illustrations should not be bigger than 10 cm by 10 cm. First, draw the picture with a light, soft pencil, making modifications with an eraser. When the work is ready, work over it using a pen and waterproof ink. The introduction of waterproof ink will mean that your children have to be more careful and a good procedure is to work from the top of the picture down so avoiding smudges. It is also a good idea to use a piece of blotting paper under the palm of the hand to keep the work clean. When the ink has dried rub away the pencil lines.

You need
The Rime of the Ancient Mariner, pencils, paper, pens, and waterproof ink.

 Sea sketches ▷

Activity 54: Imaginative drawings
Show and discuss the way that Leonardo made his drawings of the deluge, sea foam and whirlpool. Compare these with Miro's drawings. Here are just a few suggestions to stimulate imaginative drawings: catching fish under the sea; a tidal wave; skimming stones on the beach; flying fish; an octopus turning over a ship; the moment when Ahab looks at his ship as Moby Dick strikes. Different subjects will require different materials. A tidal wave may best be drawn using charcoal on its side. Wax cutting will produce a range of colours and fine lines suitable for the flying fish. A mixture of pen, ink, charcoal and pencil could be combined to show Ahab's anguish. By using solid graphite sticks on their side your children will be able to produce sweeping shapes and impressions of movement. Graphite powder (produced by scraping the side of a graphite stick with a knife) can be applied with fingertips to sketch in the general forms of the drawing.

You need
A range of drawing materials (including graphite sticks), different coloured papers and tinted cards.

Before you start
As a warm up to the next activity get your children to use **Copymaster 33** and complete Activity 258 in the 'Drawing' section.

Activity 55: Studies of pebbles
Collect and sort a range of pebbles from a beach. Try to have dark, medium, light, textured, smooth and variegated examples. Let each child choose their own pebbles. Arrange the classroom so that the pebbles could be placed on the table with light falling from one side. Put the pebbles on a light (but not white) paper or card. Demonstrate using the blackboard how shadows and marks on the pebbles vary in tone. This technical exercise should build your children's awareness of tonal values and manual skills in drawing. First, insist that the children observe the shape of the pebble carefully. Plot the outline using consecutive dots. Point out to your children that they are not to outline the shape but simply to build up areas of varying tone against each other to produce the round form of the pebble. Do not allow smudging as the point of this exercise is to develop the ability to make and control tones positively by using a pencil tip or pen. The drawing should be no bigger than 10 cm across. Slowly, using a fine felt tip pen build up areas of light and dark. A good way of checking how dark or light a particular part should be is by punching a small, round hole into a piece of paper and looking at different parts through the hole in isolation.

You need
Pebbles, paper, pencils, fine black felt tip pens (0.1 cm), erasers, **Copymaster 33**.

Activity 56: Shells, crabs and driftwood
Talk about the texture and surface markings on the flotsam and jetsam objects in your display. Give your children a range of drawing materials and ask them to make detailed studies of shells, crabs and driftwood. Your children should pay particular attention to the differences in the surfaces, and choose the media carefully.

You need
A variety of media, paper, objects from the beach.

Child's drawing of driftwood

Activity 57: White line boat on blue-green ground
If you are able to arrange a visit to the seaside or a port get your children to make line drawings of boats, cranes and people on the beach. When you return to school give your children some large pieces of tinted paper or thin card to work on. If they have blue paper show them how to paint areas of green or different blues on to the sheet to make the surface more interesting. Let the paper dry thoroughly. Now use sharply pointed white or silver wax crayons to produce a line design based on one of the sketches made at the seaside. Line drawings of boats or crayons are very effective. Using reds and purples as additional background colours will give the impression of different times of day.

You need
Sketchbooks, pencils, wax crayons, tinted paper or card, paint and brushes.

Activity 58: Lighthouse in pastels
Look at illustrations or models of lighthouses. Discuss the feelings of loneliness, isolation and the fierce weather that lighthouse-keepers experience. Give each child a piece of tinted sugar paper (let them choose from a range of blues, greens and greys), pastels and soft pencils. The drawings can be of the lighthouse during fog, with the beams of light just breaking through, or of the isolated sentinel standing quietly in the surrounding sea. Review the drawings with the class and discuss whether or not the feelings have been well expressed. This activity can be extended by providing papers that have a textured surface. Using pastels on rough surfaces can produce some interesting results. Also pastels can be wetted with a brush and the effects made much more smooth.

You need
Books, illustrations, models, sugar paper, pastels, soft pencils.

Activity 59: Chalk and crayon resist
This activity is an extension of Activities 57 and 58. Give each child a small piece of light-coloured sugar paper, chalk, wax crayons, inks and brushes. Based on either sketches made on the seaside trip or the picture of the lighthouse get your children to do a simple linear design in chalk across the whole surface of the paper. Where the paper shows through, use a variety of different coloured wax crayons to fill in the shapes thickly. When complete choose the ink colour and paint over the whole surface of the picture with the ink. The chalk will pick up the ink colour while the wax areas will resist it. Blot up the excess ink. The chalked lines will have the colour of the ink while the wax is bright and stands out. Your children may use two colours of ink in bands from top to bottom. (This technique is very good for townscapes, field patterns and stained glass.)

Activity 60: Study with soluble pencils
The sea is an ideal subject for using water-soluble pencils. They can be used wet or dry and on smooth, rough and textured papers. For a seascape the main colours will be blue and green although the opportunity to experiment with mixing subtle tints from combinations of yellows, reds, blues, greens, purples and oranges must not be missed. Before making a finished drawing get your children to experiment with the pencils, smudging, using them dry and with water.

You need
Paper, water-soluble pencils (or pastels), brushes.

 # Making waves ▷

Activity 61: Diving mermaid
This activity describes how to make models of diving mermaids, it could equally well be used to make a water skier or a diver seeking treasure. Get your children to make a sketch of how they imagine a mermaid might dive back into the sea from a pirate's ship. Give them a small lump of clay to roll out a slab and cut out two pieces, which when combined will produce the splash that will in turn support the figure of the mermaid. When the splash is ready start work on the mermaid with another piece of clay. She should be made so that her arms and head can fit into the splash and be supported. Finish the tail and eyes and hair carefully. (Use an old toothbrush or nail brush and modelling tools.) Once all the parts are dry biscuit fire. Glaze and use as part of your display.

You need
Sketches, clay, glazes, brushes, kiln.

Mermaid

Activity 62: Tidal wave, whirlpool or skimming stones
Imaginative claywork is often best based on sketches or drawings. Your children may well have made pictures of a tidal wave, whirlpool or themselves skimming stones on a beach. Let them choose which subject to work on in clay. The tidal wave may involve the swamping of a small town; the whirlpool a ship being sucked under; the skimming stones may involve a small section of a beach. Get your children to work on a small scale, on a clay board about A4 size. Use fingers, modelling tools and various materials to texture the clay. Dry, fire and glaze.

You need
Sketches, clay, clayboards, modelling tools, glazes, brushes.

Activity 63: Paper bag puppet of a mermaid
Protect your work surface with plenty of newspaper. Paint a piece of newspaper with PVA glue and roll it around the end of a giant lolly stick. Press the paper against the stick so that it is well glued to it. Put the newspaper ball inside a strong paper bag and fill in any spaces with more PVA covered newspaper. Tie the bag around the neck with a piece of cotton. Roughly shape the head and paint the whole surface with a diluted PVA solution. Let it dry. Build up the face with papier mâché (with a little PVA added). Leave to dry thoroughly, paint with PVA colours. Make a costume from scraps of fabric, fix hair made from wool.

You need
Giant lolly sticks, PVA, PVA paints, brushes, newspaper, papier mâché (recipe on page 111), scrap fabrics.

Activity 64: Casts from fish bones
Ask your fishmonger for the skeleton of a large cod or similar fish. Boil the skeleton to clean it thoroughly. Make a smooth surfaced thin slab of clay large enough to accommodate the skeleton. Gently press the skeleton half way into the clay. Remove, build up a cottle (a temporary plastic wall tied with string) around the slab. Mix plaster and pour on to the clay, use scrim to build the strength of the plaster cast. When the plaster has hardened carefully remove the cottle and the clay. When the plaster is thoroughly dry, paint around the cast skeleton of the fish to make it stand out.

You need
Large fish skeleton, plaster, clay, material to make up cottle (sheet plastic/hardboard), paint.

Water colours

Before you start
Use paintings and drawings from the list on page 21 to introduce the range of imaginative subjects in the area of study. Compare the different ways artists have tackled the sea. The work of Turner and the romantic, Gericault, should be included. Some artists use thick, heavily carved paint, others use flat stylised techniques. Each style has its place.

Activity 65: Storm at sea collage
Collect and sort images from magazines of boats, ships and marine life. Get your children to choose images and cut them out. These will be the central pieces of their compositions. Using a variety of colours get your children to produce marbled paper that can be used as part of their collages. Cut out swirling storm-like areas from the marbled sheets. Combine this to surround the printed images of boats in a convincing storm. The collage can be added to by using paint or other media.

You need
Previously marbled paper (grey, blues and greens), mounting background paper, cut out illustrations of ships and boats.

Children going on board the Victory

Activity 66: The shipwreck

Show the amazing painting by Gericault of *The Raft of The* Medusa. The frigate, *Medusa*, foundered and 149 survivors were put on to a raft which was towed by sailors in the pinnaces (large rowing boats). The sailors became tired and decided to cut the towing ropes leaving the passengers to drift to an almost certain death. Amazingly, some survived and Gericault dedicated himself to researching carefully, sketching from all kinds of sources to produce a masterpiece describing the horrific ordeal. Give your children large pieces of paper and ask them to do their own version of the raft. Alternatively, get your children to record a contemporary event at sea (from newspapers, TV or film) in their own compositions. Debussy's *La Mer* contains a number of different passages that describe, musically, the conflict and union between the sky and sea. This piece could be used to stimulate a mood painting.

You need
Reproduction of Gericault's *Raft of the* Medusa, paints, brushes, Debussy's *La Mer*.

Activity 67: Fish collage

Rip up illustrations from colour magazines or scrap coloured paper into pieces about 1 cm square. Give each child a piece of sugar paper to use as a support for the collage. Using **Copymaster 34**, or drawing directly on to the sugar paper, get your children to outline the shape of a fish. Arrange the torn pieces of paper to build up a realistic image of a fish (use source books for information about colouring). When your children are happy with the arrangement they have made, glue the pieces into place.

You need
Torn up coloured paper, sugar paper, **Copymaster 34**, pencils, glue, source books.

Activity 68: Under sea collage

Using tissue paper and reflective materials get your children to make an imaginative submarine world. Lay tissue paper in place and use diluted PVA to fix in place and to add to the transparency of the paper. Overlay pieces to give new colours, use fish, octopus and other sea creatures as part of the composition.

You need
Sugar paper, tissue papers, reflective materials, PVA, scissors.

Activity 69: Blues and greens

On a visit to the seaside or port get your children to make direct colour pictures of a chosen subject. If possible get them to use paint directly, searching for strong simple shapes.

You need
Sketchbooks, paints, felt tip pens.

Block print

Activity 70: Block print storm at sea

Lino printing is an extremely good activity. There are some easy-to-cut blocks of lino available from NES Arnold which make it safer than previously. Page 125 describes in detail how to produce single and multicolour lino prints. The kinds of images that your children can print will need to be simple. Make the drawing exactly the same size as the finished print and trace it. Using carbon paper transfer the image to the lino block. Continue the procedure as described in the skills section. The block can be used to print on card, paper or fabric.

You need
Lino blocks, tools, paper, tracing paper, pencils, ink, rollers and an ink slab.

Sea creatures and lighthouses

Activity 71: Print T-shirt

Make a simple design, for example the sun, a yacht and wavy lines for the sea, on a piece of paper the same size as the finished print. Trace the simple shapes and transfer each colour to a separate sheet of newsprint or screen stencil material. (It is much cheaper to use newsprint.) Follow the guidance in the 'Print-making' section for registering and printing on the T-shirts. Use a general purpose ink such as Sericol-Texiscreen. Wash and iron the T-shirts before printing and follow the manufacturer's instructions for fixing the colours.

You need
Tracing paper, newsprint, screens, squeegees, inks, T-shirts.

Activity 72: Batik lighthouse

Prepare the fabrics to be dyed before sketching the designs on to it with chalk. Dark and light colours will be needed in this work and it is a good idea to plan the sequence of dying in advance. Using batik tools or a brush, paint the areas that are to remain undyed with wax. Follow the procedure given in the 'Textiles' section for batik work. Your children will probably need to use a dark blue, bright yellow and perhaps a red in their composition. It will be very important to double or treble dye some areas to get the right colours and effects.

You need
Cotton or silk, batik tools or brushes, wax double boiler (or old saucepan), cold-water dyes, salt, dye baths, an iron, newsprint.

Activity 73: Screen printing sea motifs

The screen printing techniques on page 129 include direct painting of stencil medium on to a screen as a blocking system. Use the drawings that the children have done of shells, starfish and other marine creatures and look at the designs produced by contemporary fabric designers based on similar themes. With a piece of paper the same size as the screen draw simple silhouettes from the sketches. These shapes will be the first colour to be printed on to the fabric. Transfer these shapes by painting a stop out medium underneath the screen. After letting this dry, print on the fabric and on some pieces of paper. The next colour can be worked out on the paper printed images and the new stencil painted on to the screen in the same way. Two or three colours should be the maximum used in this activity.

You need
Screens, stop out medium, inks, fabrics, paper, illustrations from fashion magazines, squeegees.

COLOUR AND LIGHT

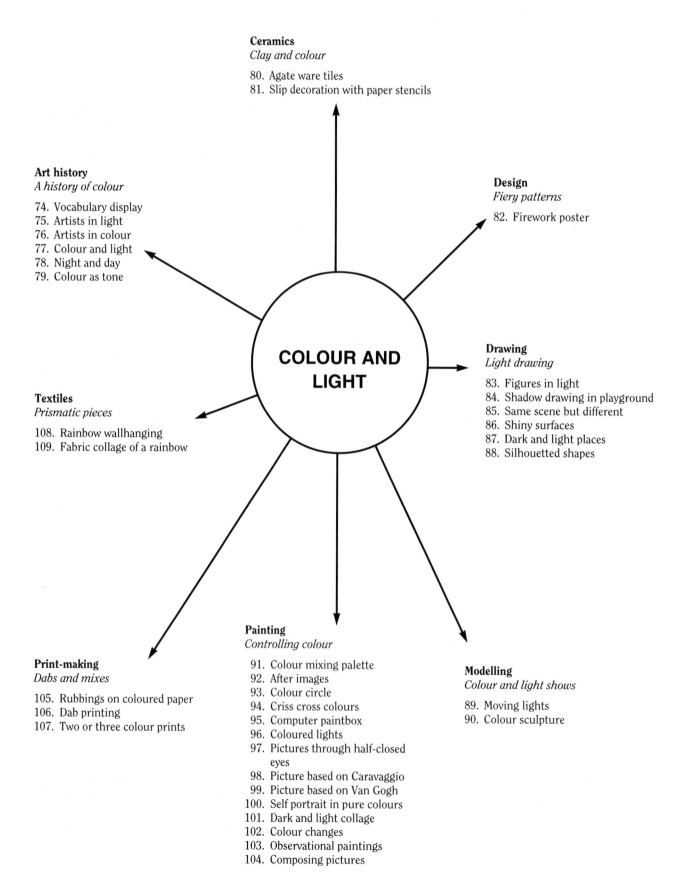

Ceramics
Clay and colour

80. Agate ware tiles
81. Slip decoration with paper stencils

Art history
A history of colour

74. Vocabulary display
75. Artists in light
76. Artists in colour
77. Colour and light
78. Night and day
79. Colour as tone

Design
Fiery patterns

82. Firework poster

COLOUR AND LIGHT

Drawing
Light drawing

83. Figures in light
84. Shadow drawing in playground
85. Same scene but different
86. Shiny surfaces
87. Dark and light places
88. Silhouetted shapes

Textiles
Prismatic pieces

108. Rainbow wallhanging
109. Fabric collage of a rainbow

Print-making
Dabs and mixes

105. Rubbings on coloured paper
106. Dab printing
107. Two or three colour prints

Painting
Controlling colour

91. Colour mixing palette
92. After images
93. Colour circle
94. Criss cross colours
95. Computer paintbox
96. Coloured lights
97. Pictures through half-closed eyes
98. Picture based on Caravaggio
99. Picture based on Van Gogh
100. Self portrait in pure colours
101. Dark and light collage
102. Colour changes
103. Observational paintings
104. Composing pictures

Modelling
Colour and light shows

89. Moving lights
90. Colour sculpture

CROSS-CURRICULAR LINKS ▶

Design and technology Designing and making houses, vehicles, lighthouses
Drama and dance Fiery, colourful dances of China
Environmental studies Colours from natural materials
History The search for valuable minerals, black tulip
Language Colour adjectives, reflections
Mathematics Colour patterns, charts (data collection), sequencing patterns, hair colour survey, most popular colour car survey
Music 'Yellow submarine', Firebird, *Pastoral suite*, Pictures from an exhibition
RE Joseph's coat of many colours
Science Types and uses of materials

ABOUT THIS TOPIC ▶

'Colour', 'Colour and light' or 'Colour and shape' are popular topics throughout Key Stage 1 and Key Stage 2. Colour was introduced in *Blueprints: Art Key Stage 1*, here, in *Key Stage 2*, it is developed with the additional theme of light. If you have a copy of *Blueprints: Art Key Stage 1* then you will be able to use many of the colour activities given there. These include making colours for cave painting; colour and clouds; a simple introduction to the impressionists and expressionists; colours and shapes; colour and our environment; colouring pots; colour and lettering; colour schemes for a doll's room; firework night; colour spinners and coloured glasses or visors; coloured masks; autumnal leaves; colour rainbows; mood paintings; music paintings; warm and cool colours; colours from stories and poems; changing colours; and monotype colour prints and wallhangings based on drawings.

This topic considerably extends children's knowledge of colour and light. It includes work using computer graphic packages and children basing their work on that of significant artists.

Vocabulary
The first names for colours were linked to sources of pigments. Early colours made from earths have been extended to a point where we now have over 7,000 names for colours in the UK. There are many activities that you can set up to run throughout the topic. These will include collecting and sorting colour charts (from commercial paint manufacturers) and coloured illustrations from magazines. Additionally you can focus on vocabulary as an activity in its own right as described below in Activity 74. Use these words carefully: hue, chroma, tone and density.

General points
Besides concentrating on seasonal or obviously 'art' activities to do with colour and light you should not forget to include coverage of multiple images (kaleidoscopes), moving images (zoescopes), video, photography and computer paint programs. Art history activities offer very good links to many practical activities.

Displays and resources
Besides the reproductions of paintings and sculptures listed below try to have photographs that show effects of light, such as shadows thrown by slatted seats; have images of different periods of day; twilight (Atkinson Grimshaw), dawn, sunsets, clouds with light shining through; and weather conditions such as fog, drizzle, snow, and the strong contrasting shadows cast by strong sunlight. Include flexi mirror, objects that reflect, materials with different surfaces, transparent materials and objects such as nylon, lace, voile, tissues, leaves, feathers and plants such as 'honesty'.

Try to make your displays simple and clearly focused. Carefully collect and sort visual resources, materials and tools. Although you will need plenty of resources don't overdo it as your children may be overwhelmed. A simple display may be made by suspending a long strip of flexi-mirror at eye level all the way along one wall of the classroom. Perhaps you could oil some autumn leaves and mount them on the windows so that light can pass through them. You could make a table display based on one colour or you could mount a bright comparative display of multi-coloured objects and light them with two or three strongly coloured lights. Place the objects on sheets of white and grey paper, then study the shadows.

You will need to have some equipment readily available. Include an overhead projector, slide projector, computer with paint-type package, video machine and TV, cellophane and theatrical coloured gels, blank cheap glasses frames, directional lights (flexi desk light), torches, candles, reflective surfaces and mirrors, magnifying glasses, kaleidoscopes, viewfinders and cropping frames.

STARTING POINTS ▶

Compare historical paintings which are primarily colour and others which are strongly tonal. Examine the way sources of light are portrayed (the candles of de La Tour, *The Sun* by Van Gogh, Claude and Poussin, interiors by de Hooch, Vermeer and Caravaggio and Wright of Derby).

29

- Examine the way colour has been used historically by sculptors, solid body colour, transparent materials, painted metal
- Discuss the way light can change our perceptions
- The contrasting psychological impacts of light and dark
- From your display, use the vocabulary of colour and light or concentrate on one colour at a time
- Stories and poems featuring seasonal subjects, plus direct references to colourful subjects
- How colours were first made and used, grinding and mixing colours from natural materials

- Painting from landscape, still life, portraits, mixing from primaries, warm and cool colours
- Colour from other cultures, batik work
- Colour of festivals, Chinese New Year, Caribbean festivals
- Colour of food
- Colour and shapes, tessellations, spinners
- Colour and our environment, landscapes and townscapes, churches, buildings, natural and made building materials, signs and symbols, lettering and legibility.

COLOUR AND LIGHT ACTIVITIES
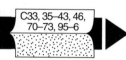

C33, 35–43, 46, 70–73, 95–6

A history of colour ▷

Before you start

The way that artists have used colour and light has changed throughout history. Some have tended to produce images that are primarily tonal, relying on the effect of light to produce rounded forms through shadow and light. Others, particularly the impressionists, have focused very much on the way pure colours can be used to produce impressions of scenes and people. Colour has also been used because of its perceived value or meaning. Gold, for example, has been used decoratively and symbolically in many cultures and at different periods. Colours have always held special significance: for example, red, the colour of blood, is full of meaning and is perhaps pre-eminent amongst colours in many cultures. Colour vocabulary is fascinating and could introduce this topic by itself.

The following list of artists and works is by no means exhaustive yet it contains a good range which easily satisfies the requirements of the National Curriculum. Although it is impossible to say that one artist works exclusively tonally whilst another is a colourist, there is a key included to give you rough guidance. * = colourist *Albers, Bellini (1431–1516), *Madonna with the Saints* (1505); *Bonnard (1867–1947); Breugel the Elder (1530–1569) *A Country Wedding*; Caravaggio (1573–1610); Cassat (1844–1926); Cezanne (1839–1906); Correggio (1494–1534) *The Holy Night* (1530); *Degas (1834–1917); *Gauguin (1848–1903); Giorgione (1478–1510) *The Tempest* (1508); *Van Gogh (1853–1890), Drawing of: *View of Saintes-Maries* (1888) a fantastic impression of sunlight from a black and white drawing; Grimshaw, A (1836–1893) *View of Heath Street, Hampstead by Night* (1882); *Kandinsky (1866–1944) *Sketch for Composition iv* (1910); *Kokoschka, O (1886–1980) *Large Thames View* (1926); La Tour (1593–1652); Lautrec (Toulouse) (1864–1901) (Posters); Manet (1832–1883); *Matisse (1869–1954) *La Desserte* (1908); *Mondrian (1872–1944) *Boogie-Woogie*; *Monet (1840–1926); *Morisot (1841–1895); Neer, van der (1603–1677), specialised in moonlit scenes around Amsterdam; *Picasso (1881–1973), blue and pink periods; *Pissaro (1831–1903); *Pollock (1912–1956); Rembrandt (1606–1669); *Renoir (1841–1919) *A Dance at the 'Moulin de la Galette'* (1876); *Seurat (1859–1891), compare conté drawings with finished paintings, *Rue Saint Vincent, Montmartre* (1884); *Signac (1863–1935); *Sisley (1839–1899); *Titian (1487–1576) *Madonna and the Saints* (1528), *The Young Englishman* (1540); *Turner (1775–1851) *Steamer in a Snow Storm*; *Vlaminck (1876–1958); Whistler (1834–1903), tonal images: *Nocturnes – Westminster Palace* (1870) in blue and silver, *Chelsea Snow* in grey and gold, *Chelsea Rags* in brown and gold, *The Falling Rocket* in black and gold; Wright of Derby (1734–1797) *An Iron Forge* (1772).

What you need

The following list includes everything that may be needed for all the activities. You need papers of all kinds (rough and smooth, white, black, grey, tinted, newsprint, card, corrugated card), magazines and newspapers, paints (PVA, tempera, oil-based and water-based printing inks), pencils, charcoal, pastels, graphite sticks, inks, felt tip pens, water-soluble colour pencils, brushes, mixing palettes, scissors, craft knives, cutting mats, safety rules, junk materials (tubes, boxes, cylinders, fabric scraps), Sellotape® or masking tape, clay and glazes.

Activity 74: Vocabulary display

Make a list of words that describe kinds of light and colour. Include: cloudy, colourful, crystal, dark, dazzling, deflected, delicate, dim, dingy, dirty, dismal, dusky, expressive, flashing, flickering, foggy, frosted, fuzzy, glaring, gleaming, glimmering, glisten, glittering, gloomy, glowing, hazy, intense, lightless, limpid, lively, misty, murky, nebulous, obscure, overcast, powerful, reflected, scintillate, shaded, shadowy, shimmering, shining, silhouetted, smoky, sombre, sparkling, dappled, steamy, striking, strong, tenebrous, tinged, tinted, toned, translucent, twinkling, unilluminated, vague, vaporous, varied and vivid.

Your children can work in groups and search for images that represent chosen words. If they cannot find photographs or illustrations then they can find scenes around the school and make their own pictures. The words and images can be combined as part of your changing display.

Activity 75: Artists in light

Compare the way that different artists have approached light. For example look at the following pairs of artists or schools. Compare Caravaggio (or Wright of Derby or La Tour), who worked almost exclusively from interior settings that featured one single source of directed light, with Vermeer who often bathed his interiors with a more even, glowing light. Caravaggio, like Rembrandt, used the tonal effects of chiaroscuro (effects of light and dark) to produce paintings which were predominantly dark. The contrast and balance between dark and light areas gave impressions of projected parts of the picture out in front of the picture plane. Compare the luminous light of the warm, southern Claude Lorrain with the colder more 'realistic' images of Dutch painters such as Hobbema.

Compare the way that tonal values were produced in the etchings of Rembrandt with the charcoal drawing of Kathe Kollwitz and Seurat.

Directional light

Activity 76: Artists in colour

Compare how effects of light and colour were produced by impressionists and how feelings were shown through the raw use of colour by the Expressionists and Fauves (wild animals!).

Compare how colour and shapes were treated differently by Mondrian, Miro, Klee, and Jackson Pollock. Contrast the fore planning of Mondrian that resulted in his formal geometrical designs with the immediate action painting of Pollock.

Activity 77: Colour and light

Compare the way that Van Gogh used colour to sculpt and blaze images in a new and intense way and the way he used marks and lines to show with equal vividness the effects of light and sunshine, particularly the fantastic drawing, *View of Saintes-Maries* (1888), in which an impression of sunlight is given from a black and white drawing.

Activity 78: Night and day

Look at a range of different images of night and day. Discuss how colours change at night. Give each child a copy of **Copymaster 35** and ask them to mix a range of colours to complete the pictures for day and night comparisons. (Colours that are mixed with others to produce subtle dark tones are called broken colours. These predominate at night time when everything tends towards black.) When complete, discuss the paintings and ask whether or not your children have looked closely at night-time colours.

You need

Images of night and day, include examples of Van Gogh's, Whistler's, Grimshaw's and van der Neer's night scenes, **Copymaster 35**, paint, brushes.

Nightscape

Activity 79: Colour as tone

Compare the paintings of Atkinson Grimshaw and those of Whistler. Both artists used colour in a descriptive tonal way. The tonal use of colour is often associated with a limited or even monochrome palette. Examples of work to consider are: *View of Heath Street, Hampstead by Night* (1882) by Grimshaw and paintings by Whistler (1834–1903) such as: *Nocturnes, Westminster Palace* (1870) in blue and silver, *Chelsea Snow* in grey and gold, *Chelsea Rags* in brown and gold and *The Falling Rocket* in black and gold. Get your

31

children to copy their favourite picture with a very limited palette of colours.

You need
Illustrations, paper, paints, pencils, brushes, mixing palettes.

Clay and colour ▷

Activity 80: Agate ware tiles
Give your children two pieces of clay with contrasting body colours. Fold them together while retaining the separate colours. Make up some small tiles as described in the 'Ceramics' section on page 88. Once the clay has been rolled out, clean the surface with the side of a metal ruler. This should reveal a clear marbled effect produced by the two colours of the clay. Dry, fire and glaze. As children's co-ordination develops this method can be used on the wheel to produce agate vases.

You need
Clay (two or more colours), glazes, work area, protective clothing, rolling pins, brushes, kiln.

Activity 81: Slip decoration with paper stencils
Get your children to make pots or tiles. Let these dry almost to the leather hard stage. Cut stencils (positive or negative) the right size to suit the tiles or pots. Fix to the damp piece of pottery and either dip into slip or paint with a brush. Remove paper stencil after a short while. Repeat with different colours. Use **Copymaster 46**.

You need
Clay (two or more colours), glazes, work area, protective clothing, rolling pins, brushes, kiln, **Copymaster 46**.

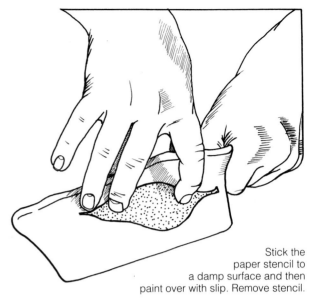

Stick the paper stencil to a damp surface and then paint over with slip. Remove stencil.

Stencils on a pot

Fiery patterns ▷

Activity 82: Firework poster
This is a graphic design activity. Look at and discuss good examples of posters including those by Lautrec and examples of Japanese block prints. Give your children pieces of paper and tracing paper about A4 size. The task is to make a design for a poster that is equally good when produced in black and white or in colour. Start by producing memory drawings based on what was seen on firework night. Trace elements from these on to the tracing paper. Simplify the elements and make provision for text. Transfer the design to a piece of white paper. Get your children to complete the design using

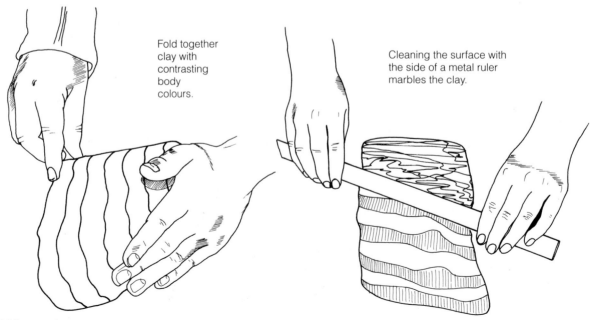

Fold together clay with contrasting body colours.

Cleaning the surface with the side of a metal ruler marbles the clay.

Making agateware

colours in flat areas. Now trace another version on to another piece of paper, discuss what changes will be needed to produce a black and white image that will still be suitable to advertise a firework show. These designs can be used as the starting point for single or multi-coloured print-making activities.

You need
Sketches, paper, tracing paper, paints, brushes, pencils, mixing palettes.

Light drawing ▷

Activity 83: Figures in light
Drawing folds in cloth on a figure is an important technical exercise. It could be either very boring or a lot of fun. Use **Copymaster 36** which contains examples of shading techniques. Arrange the classroom so that everyone can see where the model is posing. Or work in groups of five or six. In either case, as the first exercise, get the models to stand with a sheet completely covering them. Give your children charcoal and large pieces of white paper to work with. Light the figure strongly from one side. Get your children to concentrate on the simple contrasts in tone when drawing the hanging fabric. Get the model to pose first for five minutes, then ten minutes, then change the model and do a more lengthy pose of 15 minutes. Follow this up with a model lying on the ground with their hair spread on a sheet of white paper. This time use a combination of charcoal and fine felt tip pens. Finally, get your children to make studies of the model's face when lit from below and then from above.

Concentrate on the shadows without trying to make the face look real. For further exercises in figure drawing, please refer to the 'Drawing' section, pages 104–106.

You need
Paper (rough, smooth and white and tinted), charcoal, chalk, pastels, charcoal, erasers, **Copymaster 36**.

Activity 84: Shadow drawing in playground
A simple activity for a sunny day is to get the children to work in pairs. Go into the playground first thing in the morning and choose a place to draw around their partner's feet with chalk. At the same time, trace around the edge of the shadow cast by the sun. At regular intervals throughout the day get the children to go back to the same places and trace around the new shadows. At the end of the day, discuss with the class what happened and possible reasons for it.

You need
Chalk and a sunny day.

Activity 85: Same scene but different
Give your children a variety of materials and objects and go into the school grounds or on a short trip from the school to an interesting visual environment. With a variety of media, get the children to make comparative studies of the same scene but through the different viewers (use round, square and irregularly shaped ones) and materials.

You need
Various types of viewing devices and materials (coloured glasses, piece of voile, telescope, tubes), pencils, pens, felt tip pens, brushes, paints.

Different views

Activity 86: Shiny surfaces

Get your children to collect and sort shiny materials and objects. These should include spoons, mirrors, (shaving, ordinary and tinted), shiny foils, flexi-mirrors, various coloured bottles, tins with their wrappers off. Let each child choose a reflecting object or mirror. Before starting to draw they should examine the reflections that can be produced until they are happy with the view chosen. Using grey, black and white pencils, charcoal and paint get the children to study the reflections with particular attention to any patterns or textures. Working on grey paper can be helpful as the grey can be used for some of the mid-tones.

Reflected images

Activity 87: Dark and light places

You may already have used **Copymaster 33** to introduce the idea of making carefully controlled areas of tone using different materials. If not, you should remember to stress the need to make areas of tone evenly and to try to keep within the areas allocated for each tonal block. At this point it is easy to introduce the idea of producing a flat area of tone that is, for example, 30 or 90 per cent of black. You can talk about what a mid-tone is or how many tones are needed to make a picture of a dark subject, or a light subject. You can also raise questions about whether or not the white paper is white enough to stand for the brightest or lightest area of a scene or view. Punch a small, round hole into a piece of grey paper and check the area of lightness against the white paper. Very often the white paper is not as light as the lightest area of the subject and in fact all tonal values have to be compromises.

After completing this exercise get your children to use viewers to find dark and light scenes around the school as subjects for drawings. Use the work on the copymaster as a guide and reference for judging tones.

As an addition to the usual drawing materials children can combine torn up newspapers with drawn elements on white or grey paper. If your children are using grey paper as the base for a drawing of a medium or dark subject then they will need to use white chalk or pastels to highlight the lighter tones.

You need
Grey and white drawing paper, **Copymaster 33**, pencils, charcoal, chalk and pastels, paints (black and white), brushes, mixing palettes.

Activity 88: Silhouetted shapes

Arrange two similar collections of interesting natural materials, twigs with leaves, bulrushes, cereals, grasses. Place one collection so that it is lit from the side by natural light. Place the other so that it is lit from behind (for example, on a table in front of a window). Get your children to study both arrangements and to select interesting elements to draw. From drawings of the back lit display get your children to transfer outline drawings on to black or dark coloured paper. Cut out the shapes and mount on a light background paper.

You need
Pencils, charcoal, black, coloured and white paper, glue, scissors.

Back-lit and side-lit objects

Colour and light shows

Activity 89: Moving lights

There are many types of viewers and moving picture devices that rely on light and what is known as the 'persistence of vision', that is, the ability of the brain to retain (for an instant) images which can then be linked in a sort of cerebral animation.

Copymasters 37 and 38 contain detailed designs for producing kaleidoscopes and zoescopes. Get your children to make up examples using card and scrap materials. Discuss their workings and success.

You need
Card, paper, pencils, felt tip pens, cardboard, scissors, craft knives, cutting mats and safety rulers, biscuit tin, mirrors, **Copymasters 37** and **38**.

Activity 90: Colour sculpture

Get your children to select junk materials and tubes from which to make a sculpture. Get them to paint the materials with primary or secondary colours. Use a flat, solid piece of painted cardboard as a support, then fix other objects in place with glue. The object of this activity is to compose an abstract three dimensional design using strongly coloured objects.

You need
Scrap materials, cardboard, paints, brushes, glue, cutting mat, safety rule, craft knives.

Controlling colour

Before you start

Discuss how light can change the way things look. Use coloured sunglasses to look at the colour display. Get your children to describe the way colours are changed. Make up coloured sunglasses using cardboard and coloured acetate. Black out the room and look at a model dressed in bright clothes under different coloured lights, blue, yellow, red and combinations of lights. What changes? Look at leaves displayed against the window. How do they compare with those lying in piles in the playground or park? How does distance change colours? Are mountains really purple? Is the roof of a distant house the same colour as the one across the road?

Activity 91: Colour mixing palette

Give each child a copy of **Copymaster 39**. From the six primary and secondary colours plus black and white get them to complete the mixing exercises. Use good quality paints and ensure that small equal quantities of the required colours are used for mixing. Get your children to describe the resulting colours. Can they find similar colours on any commercial paint charts?

You need
Paints (the primary and secondary colours plus black and white), brushes, mixing palettes, **Copymaster 39**.

Activity 92: After images

If you look hard at bright orange and then transfer your gaze to a plain white sheet you will probably see a brilliant blue-green 'after-image'. This is produced by over exposing the eyes to a strong colour. After-images are complementary in colour and tonal value to the colour first seen. So a dark blue will produce a light yellow/orange image, and black will produce a brilliant white one. Give each child a copy of **Copymaster 40** and get them to experiment and complete the chart carefully.

You need
Paints, brushes, mixing trays, **Copymaster 40**.

Activity 93: Colour circle

Following on from Activity 91 give each child a copy of **Copymaster 41**. This diagram should be completed carefully with paints of a thin creamy consistency. Make sure that the work is produced neatly as this will improve your children's manual control.

In the perimeter band the colours will be absolutely pure. As small quantities of complementary colours are added to each of the pure colours towards the centre bands, the colours will change. In theory the central band should be a continuous neutral grey but it is likely that the colours will simply be rather muddy yellows, reds, greens, blues, violets or blues. Discuss the tonal values of pure colours with your class. For example, lemon yellow is a very light colour whereas monastral blue is very dark. How can they be made to be the same tonal value. One way is to add sufficient white to the blue until it is as light as the yellow. Alternatively a little violet could be added to the yellow to darken it. Use **Copymasters 42–3**, **95** and **96** with this mixing exercise. You will also find that very light colours such as tints of blue, violet and red can be combined nicely with yellow, oranges and light greens with the William Morris designs on **Copymasters 70–73**.

Using the chosen colours, get the children to paint the bands carefully in an attractive way (see Robert Delauney's *Manege de Cochons*, and Sonia Delauney's *Electric Prisms*).

You need
Good quality paints, brushes, mixing dishes, **Copymasters 41–3**, **70–73** and **95–6**, illustrations of Delauney's paintings.

Activity 94: Criss cross colours

Give each child a large piece of white paper and PVA paints and a large soft brush. Get your children to mix up some watery mixtures of the six primary and secondary colours in mixing dishes with clean water. Get them to paint bands of colour in sequence across the paper so that they have six equal strips in all. Let this paint dry and repeat the exercise across the width of the paper to produce a series of 36 squares of variegated colours.

You need
Large pieces of white paper, paints, mixing dishes, large soft brushes.

Activity 95: Computer paintbox
Computer programs for painting and drawing can be used for a variety of tasks. After introducing the work of Mondrian, get your children to try to produce a computer image that links colour and shape in a positive way. Print the images and keep as a record and for assessment.

You need
Paint or draw programme, colour printer.

Activity 96: Coloured lights
Set up a still life with familiar objects such as oranges, coloured telephones and a variety of brightly painted bottles and tubes or boxes on a white cloth. Using theatrical gels and flood lights illuminate the still life so that an interesting range of shadows and changes to the coloured objects are produced. Give your children white paper, good paints and brushes to paint a representational study of the still life. Discuss with the children why certain shadows are produced and the differences between the additive theory and the subtractive theory of colour for pigments and light. Pigments, dyes, inks and paints when mixed together make new hues according to the subtractive system. It is called subtractive because each individual colour of the mixture subtracts a segment from the light absorbed. Primary pigments are red, yellow and blue. In theory, when these are mixed together they should produce a neutral grey or black. Coloured lights, however, mix according to the additive system. Here primary colours, when projected together, produce pure, white light. Use a prism and daylight to produce a rainbow of coloured lights from white light.

You need
Colourful still life, magenta, cyan and yellow gels, flood lights, paints and brushes, prisms, white cloth.

Activity 97: Pictures through half-closed eyes
Colours become blurred and changed when viewed through half-closed eyes. Working in pairs, get your children to concentrate on producing a portrait (head and shoulders) of their friend, painted as they look at them with half closed eyes. If the children wear brightly patterned shirts or jumpers then the results will be more striking.

You need
Paints, paper and brushes.

Activity 98: Picture based on Caravaggio
Choose a figure group painting by Caravaggio. Arrange part of your classroom so that you can control the lighting. You may need to black out some windows. Dress some children as models and have props set out. Project a single source of bright light from the upper right hand side to mimic the effect in the painting. Set your children to make their versions of the dramatic scene. For the paintings get your children to use two or three tones of the same colour (red ochre) as 'under-painting'. This will give the pictures strong tonal qualities.

You need
Reproductions of paintings by Caravaggio, paint, brushes, paper and still life objects and a costume for the children to wear as models.

strong directional light

some parts of figures picked out with light

Caravaggio set up

Activity 99: Picture based on Van Gogh
Look at some of the paintings produced by Van Gogh and discuss the way he used colour. Set up a similar subject to one of the paintings (*The Postman, Room with Chair* or *Sunflowers*) and ask your children to use pure colours applied in small carefully controlled dabs or strokes to imitate Van Gogh's style. Add the paintings to your display.

You need
Reproductions, paint, mixing palettes, brushes, paper, suitable subject.

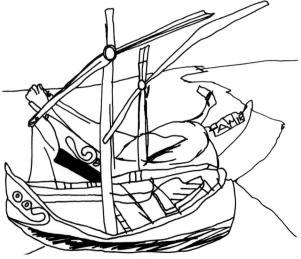

Child's work based on Van Gogh

36

Activity 100: Self portrait in pure colours
Vlaminck, Kokoschka and Matisse are all artists who used bright colours to express their feelings. Provide your children with primary and secondary colours but no black or white. Get them to paint self portraits without mixing any colours at all. Compare the results with examples produced by the famous artists mentioned above.

You need
Reproductions, paints, brushes, paper.

Activity 101: Dark and light collage
This should follow Activity 86. Divide the class into groups of about six. Each group will use different tonal materials. One will have a selection of newspaper images from which to cut and sort a range of tones from white to black. The other groups will use charcoal and graphite sticks on white, black and grey paper; black and white wax crayons on black, grey and white paper; a range of felt tip pens and black markers on black, white and grey paper; paints (black and white plus water) on the same three types of paper. The collages should be abstract arrangements of tones and shapes. Review the work with your children and discuss the kinds of tones and the feel of different materials that they have used.

You need
White, black and grey paper, pastels, wax crayons, felt tip pens and markers, paints, brushes, mixing dishes, water, charcoal, graphite sticks.

Activity 102: Colour changes
Lighting effects change the appearance of objects. Pebbles that are pastel coloured when dry often achieve a deeper and more vibrant range of colours when wet. Torchlight gives a dramatic impact to faces and interiors. The weather or coloured neon lights change the way buildings and shop displays look. Get your children to compare the changes in a chosen subject. Make the studies as meticulous as possible.

You need
Pebbles, torches, paints, charcoal, brushes, mixing palettes.

Activity 103: Observational paintings
Collect together a range of interesting natural and made objects. Include mammals, birds, feathers, fungi, seeds, leaves, bottles, baskets and pieces of fabric with coloured patterns. Work with a finely pointed pencil initially to examine the structure and colouring patterns of the chosen subjects closely. When the drawings are good, carefully apply strokes of colour with fine brushes to complete the observed study. Alternatively, water-soluble coloured pencils can be used.

You need
Pencils, white paper, paints, water-soluble pencils.

Activity 104: Composing pictures
Discuss with your children events or remembered images that are strongly linked to colour or light. Such events might include: bonfire night (from sketches),

playing in the snow, kite flying on a windy day, clouds, trees in blossom or during autumn, sun and sea related subjects. Get your children to use their sketchbooks to make notes and drawings before starting their compositions. Discuss different ways of organising a picture. Different artists have used different methods for composing pictures. Rectangles, curves and other geometrical shapes have often formed a skeleton for pictures. Discuss these ideas with your children, using the abstract colour and shape patterns in **Copymasters 42** and **43**.

You need
Sketchbooks, paints, pencils, **Copymasters 42–3**.

Child's snow painting from memory

 Dabs and mixes ▷

Activity 105: Rubbings on coloured paper
The way that impressionists combined colours by juxtaposing small dabs of pure colour alongside each other or painting on a coloured background can be reinforced by the simple activity of using coloured wax crayons and taking rubbings from textured surfaces on to contrasting coloured paper. For example your children could use red crayon on yellow, white crayon on blue, yellow crayon on purple. Holding the results a distance away will give the impression of a mixed colour.

You need
Wax crayons, tinted papers.

Activity 106: Dab printing
Following on from Activity 105 your children can use open textured pieces of foam rubber or sponge to dab print pictures with pure colours. By making small marks alongside each other and overlaying, many combinations can be achieved when using two, three, four or five colours together.

You need
Pieces of sponge, paints, paper.

Activity 107: Two or three colour prints
You will find detailed information about making block prints and lino prints in the 'Print-making' section of this book. Follow the general guidance about designing a print and the technical aspects of registering colours properly. The task here is to use transparent inks over each other to achieve a desired effect. Set a subject that will tie up with the time of year, autumn leaves, blossoming trees, etc. Make the initial drawing the same size as the block and proceed in the usual way but using transparent inks such as magenta, cyan and yellow. Your local printer may let you have small quantities of lithographic process inks in these colours.

You need
Process inks, paper, lino blocks and cutters, tracing paper.

Prismatic pieces

Activity 108: Rainbow wallhanging
Working in groups of three or four, get your children to make wallhangings from scraps of coloured fabric. The wallhangings should progress from yellows through to the deepest purples and blues at the other end. As a variation on this some children could make a padded appliqué.

You need
Scraps of cloth (sorted according to colours of the rainbow), needles, threads and backing paper.

Activity 109: Fabric collage of a rainbow
Collect and sort a spectrum of scraps of fabrics. Cut up small sections and complete a colour and tonal picture based on the theme. Your children will be able to work more easily if they make a sketch of the design on the backing fabric first with some chalk. Just outline the various elements. Place colours in position before finally fixing.

You need
Backing fabric, scraps of coloured fabric, glue, scissors.

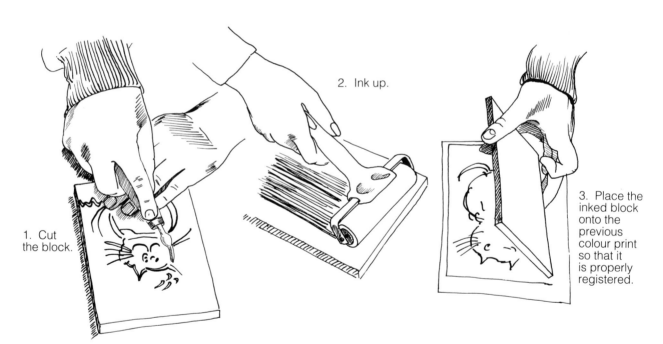

2. Ink up.

1. Cut the block.

3. Place the inked block onto the previous colour print so that it is properly registered.

Child making lino print

FOOD AND FARMING

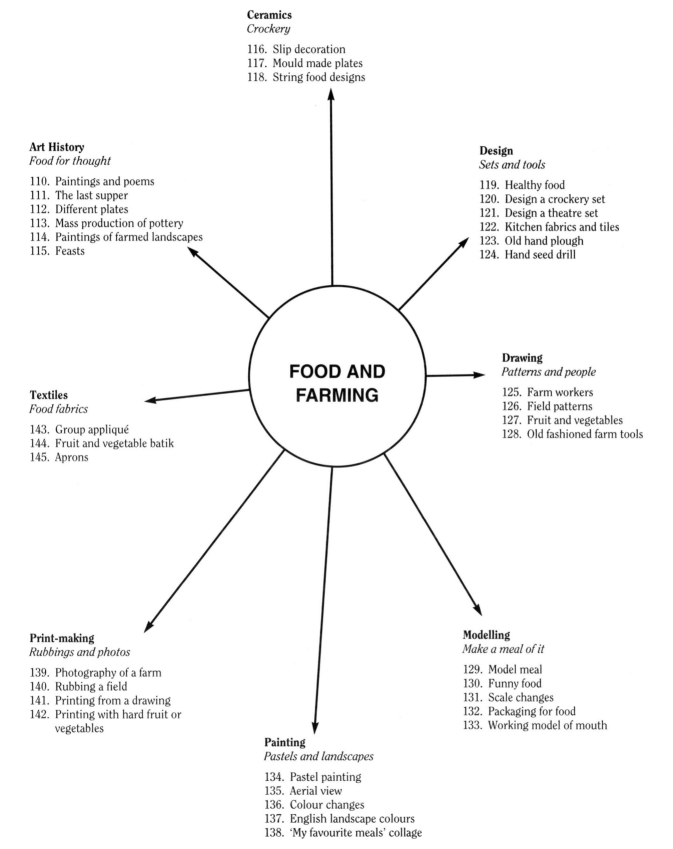

Ceramics
Crockery

116. Slip decoration
117. Mould made plates
118. String food designs

Art History
Food for thought

110. Paintings and poems
111. The last supper
112. Different plates
113. Mass production of pottery
114. Paintings of farmed landscapes
115. Feasts

Design
Sets and tools

119. Healthy food
120. Design a crockery set
121. Design a theatre set
122. Kitchen fabrics and tiles
123. Old hand plough
124. Hand seed drill

FOOD AND FARMING

Drawing
Patterns and people

125. Farm workers
126. Field patterns
127. Fruit and vegetables
128. Old fashioned farm tools

Textiles
Food fabrics

143. Group appliqué
144. Fruit and vegetable batik
145. Aprons

Print-making
Rubbings and photos

139. Photography of a farm
140. Rubbing a field
141. Printing from a drawing
142. Printing with hard fruit or vegetables

Modelling
Make a meal of it

129. Model meal
130. Funny food
131. Scale changes
132. Packaging for food
133. Working model of mouth

Painting
Pastels and landscapes

134. Pastel painting
135. Aerial view
136. Colour changes
137. English landscape colours
138. 'My favourite meals' collage

CROSS-CURRICULAR LINKS ▶

Design and technology Design and make irrigation systems, seed drills, working model of windmill or watermill
Environmental studies The changing landscape, conservation issues, effects of pesticides and fertilisers
Geography Exploring ponds and the local environment
History The history of farming, preserving foods
Language Notes and record keeping, descriptive writing, Aesop's fable of the fox, the stork and the jug of wine

Mathematics Measuring growth of plants, class members, etc, presenting information as graphs, pie charts
Music and dance Growing movements, *Rite of Spring*
RE Kindness, cruelty, caring, selfishness, harvest festivals
Science Senses, cooking, health and hygiene, botany, biology

ABOUT THIS TOPIC ▶

Food and farming is a topic that relies very much on elements of the landscape. Paintings and drawings of the earliest times show how farming and food production have changed the landscape. Country life has often been romanticised by artists such as Palmer and the pre-Raphaelites. Others, who knew something of the hardship that work in the fields meant, were much truer to the dull, routine and often painful lifestyle. Food is often linked to religion, celebrations and specific times of the year. Do not forget the multi-cultural diversity of foods that we are lucky to have.

Displays and resources
A full list of works of art which relate to food and farming is given in the introduction to art history. As many early paintings of religious themes contain detailed and historically accurate images of the landscape, quite a number of these are included. Different schools of art and significant individual artists have made their own contributions and you should try to have representative reproductions available for your display. It is unlikely that you will be able to (or need to) get examples of all the titles given. With this list, however, you will be able to ask for specific titles thereby making your search easier. Quite a few of the examples in the list are held by the National Gallery in London so you should be able to get slides, posters or postcards of a range of images.

Agricultural artefacts and models, posters, food packaging and, of course, a rich supply of relevant books are all important.

STARTING POINTS ▶

- A visit to a farm or the countryside
- A visit to an open air market or shopping centre
- Multi-cultural foods
- Religious festivals such as Ramadan, Harvest Festival, Christmas, Easter
- Discussing the times and lives of agricultural workers
- Stories (including multi-cultural stories about famine and plenty) and poetry
- Cookery
- Art history
- Advertising
- Healthy and unhealthy food.

FOOD AND FARMING ACTIVITIES ▶

 Food for thought ▷

Before you start
Collect as many images as you can of farming and food, including photographs and as many as possible of the works of art listed below.

Farming
Breugel, Pieter (1530–1569) *Winter the Dark Day, Return of the Herd, The Fall of Icarus*; Cezanne, Paul (1839–1906) *The Mont-Sainte-Victoire*; Cima, Giovanni (1459–1517) *St. Jerome in a Landscape*; Claude (1600–1682) *The Reconciliation of Cephalus and Procris*; Constable, John (1776–1837) *The Cornfield, The Vale of Dedham*; Corot (1796–1875), various country scenes with animals; Gogh, Vincent van (1853–1890) *Market Gardens* (June 1888), *The Sower* (October 1888); Hobbema, Meindert (1638–1709) *The Avenue, Middleharnis*; Konink (1619–1688) (An extensive landscape with a hawking party); Millet (1814–1875) *The Gleaners* (1857), *Peasants, The Death*

of the Pig; Monet, Claude (1840–1926) *Farmyard*; Palmer, Samuel (1805–1881) *Hilly Scene, The Early Ploughman, Morning of Life*; Potter, Paulus (1625–1654) *The Bull*; Poussin, Nicolas (1594–1665) *Summer*; Rubens, Peter-Paul (1577–1640) *Le Chateau de Steen*; Unknown (C 1415) *Occupation of the Months*; Werden, The master of (late 15th century), *The Conversion of St. Hubert.*

Food
Arcimboldi, Giuseppe (16th century) *The Gardener* (a fanciful painting of a man made up from fruit and vegetables); Bonnard, Pierre (1867–1947) *Corner of the Table*; Braque, Georges (1882–1963), Series of still life with food; Caravaggio (1573–1610) *Boy with a Basket of Fruit*; Courbet, Gustave (1819–1877) *Still Life: Apples and Pomegranate*; Leonardo Da Vinci (1452–1519) *The Last Supper*; Gogh, Vincent van (1853–1890) *Still Life with Coffee Pot* (May 1888), *The Potato Eaters*; Snyders, Frans (1579–1657) *Still Life*; Teniers, Davis the younger (1610–1690) *Le Roi Boit.*

Activity 110: Paintings and poems

They are numerous poems that can be linked with paintings of the period and seasons of the year. For example the poem, 'The Gleaner', by Jane Taylor (1783–1824) can be linked to *The Gleaners* by Millet:

Before the bright sun rises over the hill,
In the cornfield poor Mary is seen,
Impatient her little blue apron to fill,
With a few scattered ears she can glean.

She never leaves off, or runs out of her place,
To play, or to idle and chat;
Except now and then, just to wipe her hot face,
And fan herself with her broad hat.

'Poor girl, hard at work in the heat of the sun,
How tired and hot you must be;
Why don't you leave off, as the others have done,
And sit with them under the tree?'

'O no! for my mother lies ill in her bed,
Too feeble to spin or to knit;
And my poor little brothers are crying for bread,
And yet we can't give them a bit.

'Then could I be merry, and idle, and play,
While they are so hungry and ill?
O no, I would rather work hard all the day,
My little blue apron to fill.'

The sentimental feeling of this poem can be contrasted with paintings by Millet, Courbet and Van Gogh that are much more earthy in reflecting the way peasants and farm workers lived.
    Other poems to consider include:
'The Watercress Seller' by Thomas Miller; 'Invitation to the Bee' by Charlotte Smith; 'The Cow' by Robert Louis Stevenson; 'The Jam Fish' by Edward Abbot Parry.

Activity 111: The last supper

Food is used symbolically in many religions. Images of The Last Supper by Leonardo and other artists are very carefully composed. **Copymaster 44** contains details of how Leonardo planned to arrange his famous composition. Get your children to use this copymaster to plan their own modern version of the last supper. When they have finished their plan get them to draw class members for their finished painting.

You need
Paints, reproductions of various last suppers, **Copymaster 44**, pencils, paper for final painting, brushes.

Activity 112: Different plates

Make a collection of plates for your display and also slides of famous decorated plates. Discuss the decoration used on plates and get your children to make an analysis of forms, functions and decoration.

You need
Collection of plates, illustrations, sketchbooks.

Activity 113: Mass production of pottery

Hire or borrow a video which shows the methods of making crockery in Staffordshire. Get your children to make notes which can then be discussed and compared with their own methods of production.

You need
Video.

Activity 114: Paintings of farmed landscapes

Look at paintings showing farmed landscapes and get your children to discuss how farming has changed and developed. Artists to include are Constable, Breugel and Millet.

You need
Reproductions, notebooks.

Activity 115: Feasts

The 'good life' is often represented by celebrations and feasts. Use **Copymaster 45** which contains a line version of Archimboldi's famous face. Get your children to

Child's picture of food face

colour this and design and colour their own fantasy faces. Look at *Les Très Riches Heures*, Breugel's Harvest and still lives by Caravaggio, Cezanne, Braque, Pieter Claesz and Kalf. Are there any common features to the paintings? How have things changed? Are there any differences in the use of colour? Are some paintings of food more realistic? Which ones are true to life and why?

You need
Reproductions, **Copymaster 45**, paints, felt tip pens, pencils.

Crockery

Activity 116: Slip decoration

Slip can be used in a number of ways to decorate leather hard ceramics. Pieces of pottery can be dipped into coloured slip, then the wet slip can be decorated with the use of simple wooden combs. Similarly a dipped piece of pottery can have slips trailed over the still wet background and, by shaking or twisting the clay board, the slips run into each other and produce marble effects. Thick liquid clay can simply be brushed on to leather hard clay. Stencils and pads of foam rubber can also be used to apply coloured slip. Coloured slip can be applied in lines from a home made icing bag. Give your children a copy of **Copymaster 46**, this contains plenty of help in slip decoration.

You need
Clay, coloured slips, icing bags, brushes, **Copymaster 46**.

Activity 117: Mould made plates

You can buy ready made moulds for producing regular ceramic plates. Alternatively you can make your own. Take a large plastic plate and set it the right way up on a table as shown. You need to fix a cottle firmly around the plate so that the plaster will not leak through. Mix and pour in sufficient plaster of Paris to make a substantial mould. Let it dry and then remove the cottle and the plaster from the plastic plate carefully. Let the plaster mould dry out thoroughly. Get your children to roll out a slab of clay sufficiently large to cover the mould. Place the clay on to the mould and press it down carefully so that it has an even thickness. Trim off the excess from around the edge. The dry plaster will readily absorb the water from the clay which can be removed from the mould. Allow to dry thoroughly and decorate it with slip if required. The plate can then be fired and glazed. For further information see pages 88–9 of the 'Ceramics' section.

You need
Clay, hump mould (or plaster of Paris, plastic plate), material for cottle, brushes.

1. Cut strips of thin plastic or waxed card.

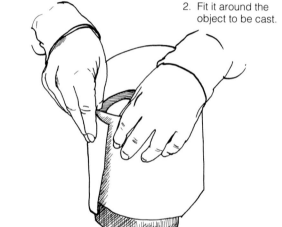

2. Fit it around the object to be cast.

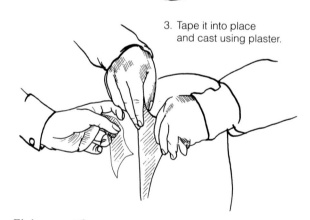

3. Tape it into place and cast using plaster.

Fixing a cottle

Activity 118: String food designs

Get your children to make detailed line drawings of cross-sections through fruit and vegetables. With a small piece of thick card and string make up a string printing block based on the drawings. Roll out slabs of clay and, using the string blocks, press into the clay to produce four different tiles. These tiles can be decorated with slip or fired and glazed.

You need
Drawings of fruit and vegetables, string, card, clay, slips, glazes.

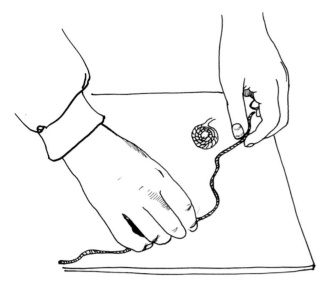

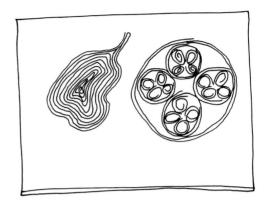

Making up a string block

Sets and tools ▷

Activity 119: Healthy food

Get the class to discuss their ideas about healthy food. Collect and sort advertisements about healthy food and fast food. Record TV commercials. Working in pairs get your children to design a packet for the healthy food of their choice.

You need

Advertisements, paper, card, food packets, TV commercials, paint, pencils, rulers.

Activity 120: Design a crockery set

Collect illustrations of different designs for household pottery. Discuss your children's likes and dislikes. Give each child some tracing paper, good quality white paper, pencils, felt tip pens and paints. The task is for them to design a crockery set with matching decoration. Include a plate, bowl, jug, cups and saucers.

You need

Paper, tracing paper, compasses, paints, brushes, mixing palettes, illustrations, pencils and felt tip pens.

Activity 121: Design a theatre set

Read *Bringing the Rain to Kapiti Plain* (Macmillan, 1986) the African folk tale of drought and rains. Discuss the farming problems in other countries. Explore and use colours to produce theatre set designs for a dramatisation of *Kapiti Plain*.

You need

Copies of *Kapiti Plain*, paints, paper, pencils, source books.

Activity 122: Kitchen fabrics and tiles

Bring illustrations of kitchen decoration and design into school. Discuss with your children the types of images that can be used for the different kinds of products. A simple stencil type of design of about 8 cms square will be most suitable. Give each child a copy of **Copymaster 47** which contains a variety of types of kitchen designs. Refer to the 'Print-making' section (pages 124–9) for a range of methods for printing on fabrics and paper. Simple designs can be applied to tiles by using stencil techniques and slips. Points to consider include colour, repeating patterns and co-ordination.

You need

Illustrations, tracing paper, stencil paper, **Copymaster 47**.

Children's designs

Activity 123: Old hand plough

Provide a range of images of old and contemporary hand ploughs. Can your children design a different one? Get them to make their designs to scale. Then using stick and string and other junk materials get them to make up their designs. This activity will help them to understand how people started to use and develop tools.

You need
Sticks, string, paper (gridded), card, paint, brushes, glue, craft knives, junior hacksaws.

Activity 124: Hand seed drill
Try to include museum artefacts such as models of ploughs, combine harvesters, original seed drills, and countrymen's clothes in your display. Get your children to make detailed drawings of a seed drill. The drawings should be to scale so that another person could use them to make up a seed drill without ever having seen a real one. The designs could be tested out by dividing the class into two groups.

You need
Seed drill (or similar simple farming machine), paper, pencils, rulers.

Old hand seed drill

Patterns and people

Activity 125: Farm workers
Making a trip to a farm will provide exciting opportunities for sketching, photography and, on return to school, drawing from memory. Have examples in class of drawings of farm workers by Millet and Van Gogh and paintings by Breugel. Get your children to use their own photographs and sketches to make their own compositions for paintings. **Copymaster 48** contains an impression of the way Millet drew peasants, get your children to make their own drawings of contemporary farm workers on this sheet. Discuss and compare their work.

You need
Sketches, photographs, reproductions of paintings and drawings, paper, pencils, coloured pencils, pastels, **Copymaster 48**.

Activity 126: Field patterns
Try to visit a hilltop that overlooks a farming landscape. From here your children can explore the patterns and colours created by fields and crops. This is an ideal situation for observational drawing and offers the chance to compare their own work with that of great artists. These drawings will be most useful as preparatory information for fabric work. The drawings can also be used as the basis of decorative designs (try working on a circular piece of paper), or as a starting point for making up block prints.

You need
Paper, pencils, coloured pencils or pastels.

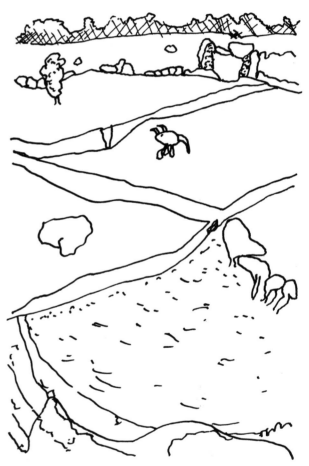

Child's drawing

Activity 127: Fruit and vegetables
Cut some fruit and vegetables in half. Oranges, pomegranates and cabbages are good. Draw your children's attention to ways that lines and shapes are linked. Give them white paper and soft pencils to make careful studies of the sections, taking particular care to relate the internal lines and patterns to the overall shape.

You need
Fruit and vegetables, soft pencils, paper.

44

Activity 128: Old fashioned farm tools

Give your children large sheets of grey paper, charcoal, white chalk and soft pencils. Get them to make drawings of old fashioned farming tools from your display. Texture and feelings of solidity and roundness are important here. Using grey or black paper will help provide the 'midtones' while the white chalk or pastel will introduce highlights.

You need
Old fashioned farming tools, charcoal, soft pencils, white chalk or pastels, grey paper.

Make a meal of it ▷

Activity 129: Model meal

Get your children to make sketches of different kinds of prepared food from magazine illustrations or, better still, from a school meal. Ask them to model their chosen meal in papier mâché or clay. When the models have dried thoroughly, paint or glaze can be used to decorate and finish their meals. Put the meals on plastic or paper plates as part of your display. (See page 111 for instructions to make papier mâché.)

You need
Papier mâché or clay, illustrations, sketches, glazes, paints, brushes.

Activity 130: Funny food

Modelling directly from the imagination should be encouraged as well as that which is well planned. Give your children a choice of modelling: bad fruit with worms wriggling out, surprise fruit (with funny things inside), elephants climbing over pieces of cheese, mice sitting in egg cups.

You need
Clay, papier mâché, brushes, paint, slips, glazes.

Funny food

Activity 131: Scale changes

Get your children to make large scale versions of small food items, such as chocolate digestives, slices of tomato, a chicken drumstick. Make them at least twice as big. Ask questions about how a change of linear scale will affect the amount of material required to make the models. Colour the finished models with glazes or paint.

You need
Examples of food, clay, papier mâché, brushes, paint, slips, glazes.

Activity 132: Packaging for food

Advertising and packaging of delicate or perishable goods is problematic. Bring bananas, eggs and other foods into school. Get your children to design a container to transport four eggs or a hand of bananas. The container will, of course, need to be nicely decorated to add to the impact of the produce at the point of sale. The effectiveness of the designs can be tested by visiting a local supermarket and asking the staff. The protection afforded by the packages can also be tested by dropping the items from a specific height.

You need
Delicate foods, paper, felt tip pens, card, cardboard, paints, glues, scissors, craft knives and cutting mat.

Activity 133: Working model of mouth

Working in pairs first get your children to make studies of each other's mouths. Sketches of mouths open, closed and in the process of being opened will be needed. Using scrap materials, boxes, papier mâché, string and glue get them to make working models of a mouth (with tongues that move). See page 111 for information about papier mâché.

You need
Scrap materials, glue, paint, brushes, scissors, craft knives, papier mâché.

Pastels and landscapes ▷

Activity 134: Pastel painting

Give your children a choice of coloured papers for pastel work and pastels with which to record the variety of colours seen in a landscape. Pastels can be used dry or wet with a brush and water. When water is added the pastels act like a thickly mixed paint and can be blended easily.

You need
Pastel papers, pastels, brushes, water.

Activity 135: Aerial view

If you are able to make a trip into the country take some paints with you so that your children can make a painting of a farming landscape exploring hues of green. If you provide your children with a grey-green piece of paper they will find it easier to mix and match the various greens which they can see. Some greens can be

45

mixed from yellow and black, others broken with additions of red, violet, blue, white, orange or combinations of more than one basic colour. If your children use PVA paints then they can apply these in thin coats so as to build up transparent glazes (in which case it will be better to work on white paper).

You need
Paints, brushes, mixing palettes, water (covered jam jars for mobile use), pencils or charcoal.

Activity 136: Colour changes
Get your class to document the changing colours of the landscape by repeating photographs and paintings. Make paintings and take photographs from similar positions at the beginning and end of term. (Autumn is particularly good.) Alternatively you can arrange for different classes to paint the same scene throughout the year. Try to ensure that all other details of the pictures are the same so that it is the changing colours which are highlighted.

You need
Paper, paints, cameras, brushes, water, pencils.

Activity 137: English landscape colours
The colours of the English landscape are markedly different from those found abroad. Collect illustrations of farmland in France, Italy, Germany and other countries. Using these photographs get your children to make their own pair of paintings that typify the English landscape and that of another country.

You need
Paints, brushes, water, paper, illustrations.

Activity 138: 'My favourite meals' collage
Make a collection of illustrations of food from magazines. Also show and discuss some of the paintings of food given above (include Arcimboldi's *Gardener*; some of Braque's still lives with food and Caravaggio's, *Boy with a Basket of Fruit*). Cut up pictures from the magazines supplemented with torn up fragments of coloured paper. Give each child a large piece of sugar paper. (Let them choose the colour.) After sketching out a rough design of a meal on a plate with white chalk, get your children to place fragments of torn paper so as to make up a good impression of their favourite meal. When they are happy with the result they should carefully stick all the pieces in place.

You need
Illustrations from magazines, torn up fragments of coloured paper, sugar paper, white chalk, glue, scissors, illustrations of works of art.

Rubbings and photos ▷

Activity 139: Photography of a farm
Please refer to the 'Print-making' section for information about taking and printing photographs. On your trip to a farm get your children to take photographs that will document the farm visit,

particularly at work. It is sensible to plan well before taking the photographs. A good way to reduce wastage of film is to prepare a shooting list. Simply discuss with the children what would be good subjects to photograph and what technical problems might present themselves (for example, indoor photography). Use **Copymaster 49** to plan the shooting with notes about any special requirements. The photographs will be useful for many other practical activities.

In addition to photographing the farm your children can use a camera to record patterns and textures in farming landscape from an aerial viewpoint.

You need
Cameras, film, **Copymaster 49**.

Activity 140: Rubbing a field
Give your children pieces of lining paper or newsprint and heavily grained wooden boards. Using wax crayons make a rubbing of a particularly roughly grained piece of timber on the lower part of the paper. (This will stand for the ploughed fields.) Now use a different, less rough, piece to make rubbings for the sky. Alternatively a separate piece of paper can be marbled on blue ink to be the basis of the sky. Marble only the top section as in the illustration. The paper can be used as a background to a number of different farming scenes that can be drawn with wax crayons.

You need
Paper, wax crayons, grained wood.

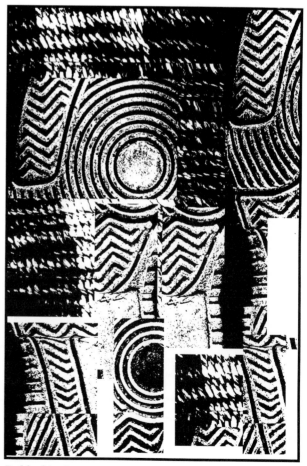

Rubbed textures

Activity 141: Printing from a drawing
Use the cropping aids on **Copymaster 50** to select, in a critical way, a section of one of your children's drawings. Make the selected element about 15 cm by 10 cm. From this get your children to make up a printing block by sticking string on to a thick piece of cardboard. The printing block can be the same size as the section of drawing for repeat printing or enlarged to make a one off print. This activity can be extended by producing more than one printing block and over-printing with different colours.

You need
Cardboard, string, scissors, glue, paper, printing ink and rollers, **Copymaster 50**.

Using a cropping aid

Activity 142: Printing with hard fruit or vegetables
Carrots, potatoes, cabbages and apples can all be used for printing. Carrots and potatoes can be cut in half and simple patterns can be cut on to the circular surface. Cabbages can be cut in half with a large, sharp knife and pad printed in the same way as the other vegetables. Fabrics can be printed using a dye pad against which the vegetable printing surface is pressed and then placed firmly on the fabric to make a print. Regular patterns on fabric can make them attractive as useful tea towels or an apron.

You need
Carrots, potatoes and cabbage, knives, dye pads, cold-water dyes, paper, cotton.

 Food fabrics

Activity 143: Group appliqué
Using the drawings that the children have made of field patterns, design a landscape textile wallhanging. The original design needs to be in the form of a map composed of a number of regular or irregular fields which fit together. When the design has been agreed for everybody, give the children a range of fabrics, scraps, needles, threads, sequins and decorative buttons or beads and scraps of wool. Each child is to produce a field using appliqué and embroidery techniques (including drawing with water-soluble pencils or dyesticks). When all the fields are complete they will be brought together and co-ordinated into a wallhanging.

You need
Fabrics, scraps, needles, thread, woollen scraps, scissors, glue, water-soluble pencils and dyesticks, sequins, buttons.

Activity 144: Fruit and vegetable batik
Prepare the cotton fabric for the batik in the way described in the textile skills section of this book (page 133). Get your children to sketch out, on the fabric, the lines and patterns for the first dying. Combine lines with more detailed textured areas. Then use the wax to complete this first stage. Crunch up the fabric and dye it in the first colour. Rinse, flatten out and iron between sheets of newsprint to remove the wax. Repeat the process until the required effect is achieved. Pay careful attention to the colours used and try to make sure that some areas are retained as white.

You need
Cotton, wax, tjanting and brushes, wax double boiler, cold-water dyes, chalk, dye baths, iron, newsprint.

Activity 145: Aprons
Using the technique of printing with hard fruits or vegetables, your children can design, print and make aprons for a butcher or a greengrocer. If the pattern that your children want to make cannot be fitted on a carrot or a potato, then they can use the string block prints or lino block as described in the 'Print-making' section of this book (pages 124–5). When designing the aprons, your children should consider what kind of features are necessary. A large strong pocket and a stout tie will be necessary and the garment will need to be hemmed properly.

You need
Pieces of stout cotton, fabric suitable for ties, cotton, needles, dye pads, prepared printing blocks.

ADVERTISING

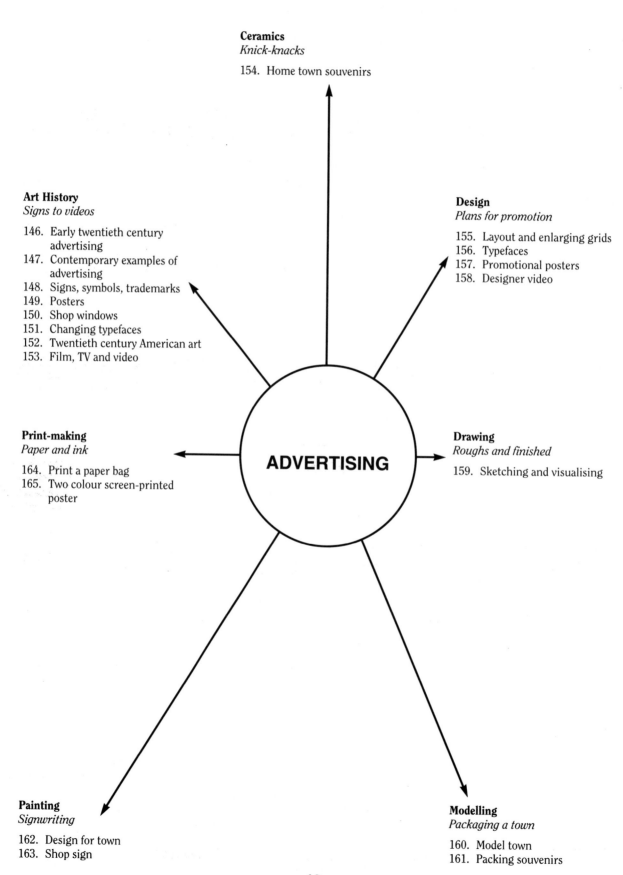

Ceramics
Knick-knacks

154. Home town souvenirs

Art History
Signs to videos

146. Early twentieth century advertising
147. Contemporary examples of advertising
148. Signs, symbols, trademarks
149. Posters
150. Shop windows
151. Changing typefaces
152. Twentieth century American art
153. Film, TV and video

Design
Plans for promotion

155. Layout and enlarging grids
156. Typefaces
157. Promotional posters
158. Designer video

Print-making
Paper and ink

164. Print a paper bag
165. Two colour screen-printed poster

ADVERTISING

Drawing
Roughs and finished

159. Sketching and visualising

Painting
Signwriting

162. Design for town
163. Shop sign

Modelling
Packaging a town

160. Model town
161. Packing souvenirs

48

CROSS-CURRICULAR LINKS ▶

Design and technology Design and make models, efficient use of materials, design and make point of sale dispensers, Computer assisted design
Geography Many links specifically to NC environmental issues
History Local studies, research old documents and use for artwork
Language Reportive, imaginative and technical writing. Writing script for video and catch-phrases for adverts
Mathematics Measuring, planning the use of space, grids
Music For video, jingles
RE The morality of advertising, questions of needs and wants

ABOUT THIS TOPIC ▶

The overall theme of this topic is to work on producing a positive image for you children's home town. This image should point to the strong aspects of the town and should promote its touristic, recreational and industrial sides. Since you will be working from your own environment it has not been possible to identify specific subjects for work. The Art history activities give a broader background to this closely focused topic.

Displays and resources
Collect and sort as wide a range of examples of advertising materials as possible. These could include enamel signs, posters, leaflets, corporate videos, magazines and examples of work by graphic and fine artists, material on your town and region. Artists to include are Toulouse Lautrec (1864–1901), Stuart Davis (1894–1964), Roy Lichtenstein (b. 1923), *Wham, Sunset* (1965), *Standing Explosion* (1965), *Drowning Girl* (1963), Rauschenberg (b. 1925) and Andy Warhol (1926–87).

STARTING POINTS ▶

- Your local council should be able to provide existing advertising materials
- Write away to other towns and some twin towns on the continent to see their ideas
- Art history, using styles of famous artists
- Existing TV adverts

- Brainstorming session with your children
- Survey of some members of public about the image of the town
- American Pop art, including Stuart Davis (1894–1964), Roy Lichtenstein (b. 1923) *Wham*, Rauschenberg (b. 1925) and Andy Warhol (1926–87).

ACTIVITIES   C6, 8, 32, 51–8 ▶

 ## Signs to videos ▷

Activity 146: Early twentieth century advertising
Your children may well have product catalogues in their homes. Ask them to bring some in to compare with the way that the Victorians and Edwardians advertised their products. **Copymaster 51** contains a number of different pieces of graphic art used for advertising. Compare the use of images and language.

You need
Copymaster 51.

Activity 147: Contemporary examples of advertising
Adverts are produced for all kinds of products. Collect examples of printed adverts for cars, electrical goods, tourism (including hotels, restaurants and leisure facilities), baby clothes, nursery equipment and toys, toys for older children, fashion, industrial equipment, sports equipment, music, travel (including air, road, sea and rail). Examine the way that colour, images and language are used. Are any kinds common to more than one type of product or service. Which look the most modern? Which are serious? Which are fun or cool?

You need
Printed adverts of all kinds sorted into types.

Activity 148: Signs, symbols, trademarks
The old guilds and trades were early users of pictures to advertise their wares. Besides visual messages traders often called out their adverts in the street. **Copymaster 52** contains a number of different signs and symbols used by trades and guilds. Get your children to complete the quiz. Get them to think about suitable colours for

49

Signs and symbols

the images and to finish each with colour. This activity can be used to introduce ideas about style, image and logos.

You need
Copymaster 52.

Activity 149: Posters
Consider the way that different artists have made lively and colourful posters. Lautrec had a very fluid elegant style, the LNER posters used flat areas of colour in most evocative ways. **Copymaster 53** contains these different styles of posters. Using either Lautrec's or LNER (London and North Eastern Railway) style get your children to make up their own design for a contemporary version of the subjects portrayed.

You need
Copymaster 53 (of different styles based on the transport posters of LNER, etc. and those of Lautrec), source books.

Activity 150: Shop windows
In shopping malls there is an awful sameness about shop windows. Give your children a copy of **Copymaster 54** and make a trip around town. Look for shop windows which are interesting because of the colours and designs. Make sketches of these.

   You may find examples such as the special tiles manufactured for butcher shops or other trades. On return to class discuss the merits or defects of the windows observed.

You need
Copymaster 54, pencils, felt tip pens, clipboards.

Activity 151: Changing typefaces
Typefaces have changed to match technological advances and general trends in art and style. Lettering alone is often the advertising symbol for products. Coca-cola® is probably pre-eminent. **Copymaster 55** and **56**

Poster styles

contain two common typefaces that will be useful source material for your children. Get your children to sort out adverts that make particularly strong (or exclusive) use of lettering. **Copymaster 57** contains some impressions of familiar brands including the powerful image of the competitive Pepsi-cola®.

You need
Copymasters 55–7, collection of sorted printed adverts.

50

Pop art images

Activity 152: Twentieth century American Art

Modern advertising in all its forms has to a large extent been influenced by twentieth century American art. This has celebrated the American dream of luxury, plenty, glamour and consumption. Brilliant graphics, neon light, TV and video all play parts in this excessive drama. Get examples of paintings by Stuart Davis, Roy Lichtenstein, Warhol and Rauschenberg. Include images in your display of billboards and other brilliant promotional materials. Discuss how advertising images have been used to persuade people to imagine themselves differently. What about the morality of advertising? Could your children imagine themselves producing a positive image for cigarettes when everyone knows about the damage they cause to health?

You need
Illustrations.

Activity 153: Film TV and Video

Many children find TV adverts more compulsive viewing than Blue Peter. Discuss which adverts the children like most. Record and play a selection of suggested adverts. Ask which are the favourites and why. Is it because an image or jingle is repeated frequently, the colour, the music or some silly catch phrase? Ask about specific adverts and how they change your children's views of the products on offer. Discuss how making a video could help promote your home town or aspects of it.

You need
Video equipment, props.

 # Knick-knacks

Before you start
This is the first of the practical activities linked to promoting or advertising your town. In all of them your children will need to research and think about your town. When designing promotional material try to have examples from other towns to discuss. Look for strengths and weaknesses in terms of product, styling and fitness to purpose.

Activity 154: Home town souvenirs

Many seaside and historic towns have the most ghastly souvenirs for visitors to buy as keepsakes or to give to luckless friends. Collect a few examples and try to find out why they are often so aesthetically poor. Is it because there is no link between the subject and the actual town? Is it the style (or lack of) of the souvenir, or the colour? Is it quite likely that your children will admire some particularly 'naff' souvenirs. They may see qualities which you do not, so have an open mind in this discussion. Look at examples which you consider to be good, and have a degree of style. What is style? Examine similar kinds of products which are not 'touristic' such as ordinary, good quality cups and saucers. Get your children to brainstorm ideas for ceramic souvenirs that will suit your particular town. Consider the main feature or character of your town and try to embed it in any product designs. After sketching out and discussing a range of ideas give your children some clay to make the souvenirs. The Ceramics skill section contains technical information to help with making and decorating the products. Remember that mass production might require the use of moulds and slip casting techniques.

You need
Examples of souvenirs, clay, plaster of Paris.

Children's souvenirs

Plans for promotion ▷

Before you start
This topic is strongly weighted in design activities. Design is an essential ingredient for graphics, products and typography. Computers will be used increasingly as they cut out many old trades. Nevertheless the artist's eye and manual skills will always be retained as these are the key to appreciation and knowledge and therefore to future developments. Class teaching about grids and their applications will be balanced by a considerable amount of individual work and work in pairs.

Activity 155: Layout and enlarging grids
Newspapers, posters, leaflets, promotional packaging and other forms of advertising have a hidden ingredient in common: grids. These organise the layout, the placement of pictures, text and open spaces, and are perhaps the most essential tool for designers. Your children need to consider how to organise space in all the activities in this topic. **Copymaster 58** contains a number of different standard grids for the layouts that your children may wish to achieve. Get your children to work out what kind of grids are used for magazines, newspapers and posters. Mark up the lines. **Copymaster 8** shows how to enlarge sketches up to any size for finished artwork. Using the Copymasters, discuss how paper can be used efficiently, can be made to look luxurious, scientific and free or jazzy. You will find a full analysis of the use of grids in the Design skill section of this book (pages 93–4).

You need
Copymasters 8 and **58**, examples of page layout from magazines, newspapers, brochures, leaflets and posters, rulers, felt tip pens, pencils.

Activity 156: Typefaces
Having given your children copies of the typefaces on **Copymaster 55** and **56** ask them to decide what kind of typeface they would like to use for their posters and other promotional material. Perhaps they wish to design a special typeface for the first letters of text. These could perhaps be combined with word-processed letters available on your computer. Will the chosen typeface be coloured? Will specific letters be a particular colour? Get your children to try out different combinations until they are happy. Get your children to use fine brushes and a light mixture of poster paint to paint the letters carefully.

You need
Copymasters 55 and **56**, fine paint brushes, tinted papers, poster paints, pencils, rulers.

Activity 157: Promotional posters
Some of your children may wish to plan a mini poster and menu for a new local restaurant or a leaflet for a museum. In either case it will be essential to visit the venue and either take photographs or make some sketches on site. Your children can rough out some layouts using these references after they have

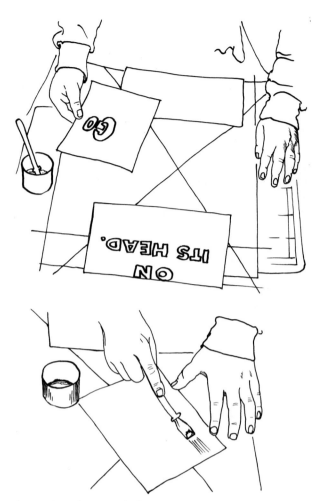

Arranging elements before gluing them in place

considered the options on **Copymasters 32** and **58**. Encourage your children to keep their messages short and to the point. Leave plenty of open spaces, but try to leave balanced and considered spaces. Get your children to make up a full size version with the same proportions as the selected grid. Make up sketches or photographs to the finished size and mock up text blocks as shown in the illustration. Cut out all the elements and position them on the grid until their final positions are agreed. Glue them down and keep these roughs for future assessment.

You need
Examples of existing promotional material, paper, **Copymasters 8, 32** and **58**, photographs, sketches, glue, pencils, rulers.

Activity 158: Designer video
Set the task of producing a three to five minute promotional video or advertisement for your town. Before making a video you will have to arrange for a small group of three or four to work together, with the option for others to do so later in the topic. You will almost certainly need a helper with a video camera for this activity. Get the group to discuss what they want to show in the video. Make a list and then work out the sequence of shots that will be needed. The model from Activity 160, making a model of your town, can be a useful prop for the video. Besides a shooting list your

children will need to write a simple script for the talk over. Use smooth movements when video-recording; pan and zoom in on special features. When every group has made their video (at the end of the project) invite your local councillors to visit your school to view the results.

You need
Video camera and player, sketchbooks, notebooks.

Roughs and finished

Activity 159: Sketching and visualising
Drawing activities will most often be concerned with sketching and visualising ideas to use in designs or posters. Encourage your children to change their ideas, to try new angles or approaches and not to hold too firmly to their initial ideas.

Sketch and finished graphic

This is an important exercise in building a new, more mature, confidence in your children. One way to do this is to help your children to select a sketch and redraw it using something like a thick, black felt tip pen (with or without tracing paper). Discuss how the new drawing looks more cartoon-like or more dramatic or graphic. Compare these images with commercial designs and graphics in magazines.

You need
Examples of commercial graphics and cartoons, felt tip pens, tracing paper.

 ## Packaging a town

Activity 160: Model town
Models are often used in exhibitions to give a sense of scale and quality to a promotion. Start this activity by using contour maps of your area to build up a layered surface as a base for the model. Discuss with your children how to make models to scale. Then, using card, scrap materials, glue, scissors and other modelling tools, work on the individual buildings and layout for roads and open areas of parks and golf courses. Papier mâché can be used to smooth the surface of the landscape which can be finished with different textures to imitate grass and stone. Make trees from pipe cleaners and scraps of foam rubber. Paint the buildings before fixing them into place. The model can be completed by including model cars and street furniture.

You need
Contour maps of your area/town, sheets or cardboard, papier mâché, finishing surfaces (sand, fine grits and grass effects), card, scraps, paints, glues, brushes, scissors, craft knives, cutting mats, safety rules, pencils, felt tip pens.

Use a contour map to build up a layered surface.

Make scale models using scrap materials.

Making the model town

Activity 161: Packaging souvenirs

Having made some souvenirs it will be necessary to package them safely and attractively. If possible get a postman and marketing officer or manager from a local leisure, industrial or tourist centre to visit your school to advise on packaging requirements. The images on packaging will normally need to follow the style of the range of products. A small image plus a small amount of text will probably be needed. First make up a rough net for the container from cartridge paper. Will the souvenir need internal support? How will this be made? Once this mock-up and internal packing have been tested and refined the package can be transferred to card. Your children should paint (or print) the outside with the required image before making up the final package. Make up the container by sticking any tabs down cleanly and firmly. Ask local shops what they think about the results.

You need
Existing commercial examples, souvenirs from Activity 154, card, paints, brushes, glues, scissors, craft knives, cutting mats, safety rules.

Signwriting

Activity 162: Design for town

Many towns are twinned with towns in other countries. Get your children to design a sign that can be used at the entrances to the town and used on official notepaper. The designs should be in one or two colours and utilise silhouetted images worked together with text, for example 'The Historic town of Bleagden, wool, rubber and prosperity'. **Copymasters 6**, **8**, **32** and **58** of the layout grids will be useful for planning the layout of such signs.

You need
Copymasterss 6, **8**, **32** and **58**, sheets of cardboard (previously painted white as a background), sketches of the town's features, carefully selected colour combinations.

Activity 163: Shop sign

On your tours around town make notes about interesting shop signs. Note the size, proportions, colours and images. Your children can work in groups using large sheets or prepared white cardboard to plan out and produce their designs for specific shops. Your children will need access to source books relevant to the shopkeepers' trades. Draw out the designs carefully with light yellow chalk. Using thick and thin brushes your children should work carefully to finish their designs. Paint around the outline of letters or images with a fine brush first, and then fill in. When the designs are complete invite local shopkeepers to judge the results.

You need
Notes, sketches, cardboard, chalk, fine and large brushes, paints, mixing palettes.

Paper and ink

Activity 164: Print a paper bag

Using the logos which have been designed for your town get your children to use either lino-blocks or screen process printing to produce paper bags to advertise your home town. Examine the nets of existing paper carrier bags and consider how they have been manufactured. Make up paper bags and then print on both sides. See pages 125–9 for full technical details about block printing and screen printing.

You need
Sample paper carrier bags, paper, glue, scissors, lino blocks, cutters and inks or screen equipment.

Activity 165 Two colour screen-printed poster

Not all posters need an obvious grid, although the need to divide up space in a controlled way is clear. The balance of elements pictures, text and open space, is more easily achieved with a grid. Your children are probably going to produce simple posters with a small amount of text. In such a case a simple solution would be to centre the text top and bottom as shown in the illustration. The grid for this style is simply the diagonals across the finished paper size with a vertical and horizontal divider.

When the design is complete, separate the colour by tracing the image on to two sheets of tracing paper. Transfer the two separate colours on to separate stencil sheets. Carefully cut out the stencils with a craft knife. Print the two elements in the normal way using screens and ink. See pages 128–9 of the 'Print-making' section for technical guidance.

You need
Screens, squeegees, inks, stencils, tracing paper, paper for printing on.

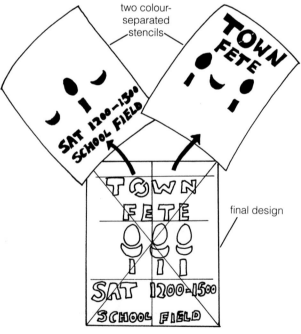

Colour-separated poster design

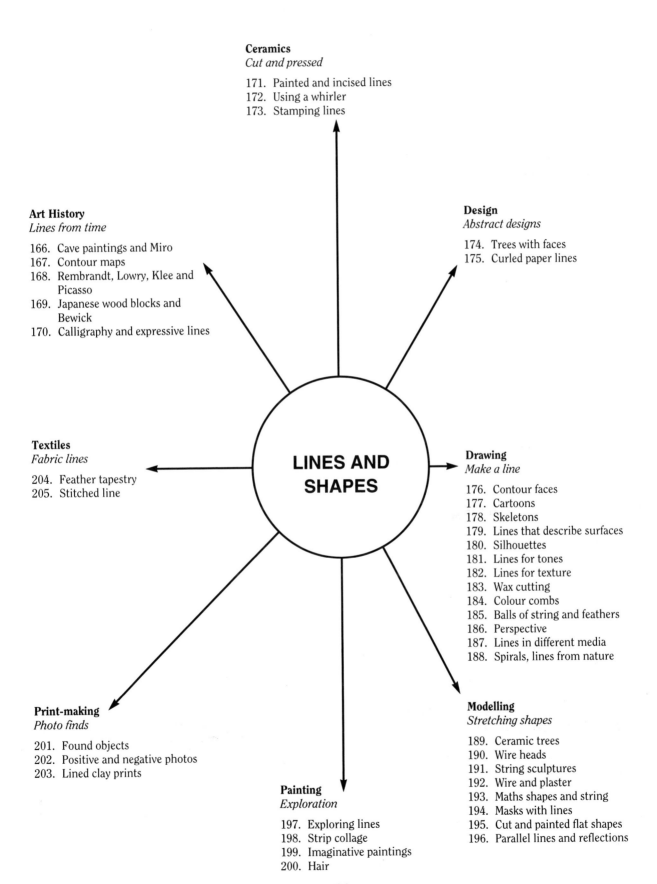

LINES AND SHAPES

Ceramics
Cut and pressed

171. Painted and incised lines
172. Using a whirler
173. Stamping lines

Art History
Lines from time

166. Cave paintings and Miro
167. Contour maps
168. Rembrandt, Lowry, Klee and Picasso
169. Japanese wood blocks and Bewick
170. Calligraphy and expressive lines

Design
Abstract designs

174. Trees with faces
175. Curled paper lines

Textiles
Fabric lines

204. Feather tapestry
205. Stitched line

LINES AND SHAPES

Drawing
Make a line

176. Contour faces
177. Cartoons
178. Skeletons
179. Lines that describe surfaces
180. Silhouettes
181. Lines for tones
182. Lines for texture
183. Wax cutting
184. Colour combs
185. Balls of string and feathers
186. Perspective
187. Lines in different media
188. Spirals, lines from nature

Print-making
Photo finds

201. Found objects
202. Positive and negative photos
203. Lined clay prints

Painting
Exploration

197. Exploring lines
198. Strip collage
199. Imaginative paintings
200. Hair

Modelling
Stretching shapes

189. Ceramic trees
190. Wire heads
191. String sculptures
192. Wire and plaster
193. Maths shapes and string
194. Masks with lines
195. Cut and painted flat shapes
196. Parallel lines and reflections

CROSS-CURRICULAR LINKS

Design and technology Strong structures based on reinforced strips

Drama and dance Skeleton costumes for dancing bones

Environmental studies Contour lines, latitude and longitude, lines in nature

History Of transport, railway lines, shipping and airlines

Language Poetry made in the shape of animals, lines of poetry going on a walk across the classroom wall

Mathematics Tessellations, string sculptures, simple two- and three-dimensional shapes, nets, tangrams

Music Made up on the stave, treble and bass clefs

Religious education The importance of certain shapes to spiritual values, mandalas, Islamic shapes and patterns based on pure mathematical ideas

Science Crystals, optic fibres, lines of light, holograms

ABOUT THIS TOPIC

This topic is strong in mathematics, geography, and design and technology as well as art.

Simply looking from your classroom windows will reveal a wide variety of lines and shapes enclosed by lines. The lines surrounding windows, along edge of building, stark and silhouetted branches and twigs of bare trees, fine lines of telephone and electricity supplies, vapour trails in the sky, variegated lines formed by continuous rows of tiles or slates all contribute to a strong network of structure. Surfaces of objects can be used for carefully controlled rubbings (positive and negative, white crayon on black paper). Blocks of card can be used for line prints and natural and made lines can be a useful way to introduce perspective.

Displays and resources

Use images or drawings and paintings that are essentially linear. Include drawings and designs by Rembrandt (etchings of landscapes), Holbein, Durer, Bewick, Japanese wood blocks and calligraphy, Van Gogh, Toulouse Lautrec, Miro, Klee, Matisse, Picasso, Lowry and Braque. Photographs of subjects with strong lines such as silhouetted electricity pylons, bare trees against the sky, Venetian blinds, stacked tubular chairs, high contrast images of hand or finger prints, are good, Also include in your display collections of such materials as spaghetti, corrugated card cut into strips, striped materials arranged so as to emphasise changes in the width of the lines, open weave items such as tennis rackets and loose wallhangings. Stretched string vests mounted on to black card and cut string patterns can be effective.

STARTING POINTS

- Geography, contour lines, lines of latitude and longitude
- Arrange for a visit by the police, discuss the way that finger and palm prints are formed by patterns of spiralling lines
- Handwriting, joined up writing, calligraphy
- Art history, the history of lines and shapes
- Lines around us.

LINES AND SHAPES ACTIVITIES

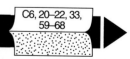
C6, 20–22, 33, 59–68

 ## Lines from time

Before you start

The expressive qualities of lines have been demonstrated since the cave artists drew hunters and bison with a few deft strokes of a brush. More recently, Japanese and Chinese calligraphy have shown us a really fluid use of lines. Old masters such as Rembrandt, Durer and Holbein made lines which elegantly described shapes, curves and even rounded forms. In the twentieth century, Picasso has brought a new freshness and power to linear drawings while Miro has picked up where cave artists left off with quirky, primitive, humorous drawings.

Artists' styles

Activity 166: Cave paintings and Miro

Put a slide show that includes pictures by Miro and some cave paintings that have been especially selected because of their linear qualities. Discuss the idea of making a humorous, abstract line drawing such as some of those by Miro. What kind of shapes can be drawn in a free, easy way? Get your children to do single line drawings of a horse, a bison, a lady carrying a bag, a man and dog going for a walk. (Colour can be used with care.) Compare these with the slides. Ask questions about using lines such as: 'What can a line do?' 'Is there anything that lines cannot do in drawings?' 'How can you make a line funny?'

You need
Slides of cave paintings and drawings by Miro, paper, felt tip pens, fine brushes, liquid paint.

Activity 167: Contour maps

Discuss how contour maps show changes to surface levels accurately. Features such as hills are often surrounded with concentric contour lines as they merge into different features. Give your children pieces of A3 white paper and a piece of card about 10 cms square. On the card ask your children to draw any shape they like and to cut it out. Using the cut out shape get your children to trace around it on to the paper. Do this five or six times so that the shape is repeated and spread out on the paper. Now your children should draw the contour lines around the shapes so that the paper is covered with a made up contour map. The quality of lines can be soft, hard, sharp or ragged. Spaces between lines can be coloured differently or the edges of the lines can be tinted. The object is to make the design as interesting as possible.

You need
Contour maps, A3 pieces of paper, felt tip pens, coloured pencils, wax crayons.

Contour lines

Drawing in the style of Picasso

Activity 168: Rembrandt, Lowry, Klee and Picasso

These artists used lines in very different ways. Show examples of their linear drawings or paintings. Rembrandt used very expressive lines in his etchings, carefully cut physical marks of great intensity. Lowry simplified complicated subjects; feet, for example, are often simple a wrapped-under line. Paul Klee, in his child-like way, still lived in a primitive world and managed to make very complicated yet naive pictures. He did so by varying the qualities of line and colour. Klee used a wide vocabulary of lines that include broad, tin, ragged, smooth and rough. Picasso, the true modern master, had a range of drawing techniques that excelled in every respect. Perhaps most interesting is his free, direct, apparently unrestrained style (see the illustration). Get your children to copy examples of the four artists' drawings and then to try out the different styles in their own compositions.

Paul Klee made up strange titles for his compositions. Get your children to work out some good imaginary titles for their drawings.

You need
Illustrations of drawings and etchings by Rembrandt, Lowry, Klee and Picasso, paper, felt tip pens, paints, fine brushes, pencils.

Activity 169: Japanese wood blocks and Bewick

Bewick used finely cut lines in wood to produce a range of tonal and textural qualities. Dense groups of lines produced dark and solid areas, whilst finely drawn and chiselled marks produced textures and highlights. Japanese wood block artists often used much more calligraphic and free flowing lines. **Copymaster 60** contains copies of Bewick's fine wood blocks, **Copymaster 61** contains an outline drawing based on a fine Japanese woodblock. Look at examples and discuss the different results that can be obtained from similar methods. Note that the Japanese design is composed of flat shapes which have a strong, linear feel while Bewick's work is composed of lines that produce areas of varied tones and textures. Get your children to imitate the two different styles using lino cutting as the method. Refer to the 'Print-making' section of this book for technical details. Make prints that are 15 cms by 10 cms and stick a finished copy on to the Copymasters as a record of the influence of other artists' work on your children's.

You need
Copymasters 60 and **61**, lino tiles, lino cutters, inks, rollers, inking plates, illustrations.

Activity 170: Calligraphy and expressive lines

Copymaster 62, contains a number of different calligraphic images and drawings that contain expressive lines. The abstract gestural marks somehow sum up the artists' feelings. Discuss how handwriting can be loose and flowing and talk about the kinds of lines that can be found in nature (such as curved, flowing, bent, straight and crooked lines). Get your children to use a large piece of paper (lined up if necessary), for free-flowing lines based on the alphabet and other forms studied from natural objects, or get them to invent calligraphic abstract marks based on animals, fish or flowers.

You need
Copymaster 62, large sheets of paper, brushes (medium sized finely pointed), liquid paint or inks.

 ## Cut and pressed

Activity 171: Painted and incised lines

Get your children to make ceramic vases or platters. Dip or paint them with coloured slip. As the slip dries, use sharp pointed sticks or opened out paper clips to engrave a pattern of lines. Extend the use of linear pattern on pottery by using a comb of wood as shown in the illustration. This can be used in a calligraphic way to

wooden comb

Using a comb

produce fine parallel lines. Look at the work of Bernard Leach and Japanese Potters. Following on from Activity 170 get your children to practise making elegant, flowing lines loosely based on natural forms such as fish, flowers, leaves or grass. When they have perfected a particular form let them choose a combination of colours for slip paintings or glazing biscuit pottery. Use the linear motif on the platter or vase.

You need
Platters or pots made by the children (green for slip and biscuit for glaze), coloured slips, paper, paints, brushes, glazes.

Activity 172: Using a whirler
Painting parallel lines of slip on a pot can be achieved by centring the pot on a whirler. Spin the pot to check that it is correctly placed, then use a brush loaded with slip and paint a firm line around the pot as it spins. Paint parallel lines using different colours as shown. Your children can experiment with a number of brushes joined together as shown.

You need
Whirler, pots, slips, brushes.

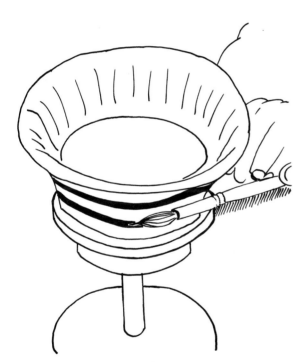

Using a whirler

Activity 173: Stamping lines
Collect together a range of materials that can be used to produce stamped lines in soft clay. These can include the edges of folded small pieces of card, linear gauzes (string vests) or corrugated card. Use the objects to impress patterns of lines over the surface of the pots or tiles. Pages 87–8 of the 'Ceramics' section of this book give information about making tiles and pots.

You need
Clay tiles or pots (still damp), items to press patterns.

Abstract designs

Activity 174: Trees with faces
Take your children to visit a park or wooded area where you know that there are some pollarded trees with interesting bark surfaces. Pollarded trees become deformed and often appear to contain head or face-like passages of bark, twigs and branches. Get them to make small (A5 size) sketches of these trees in their sketch books. The drawing should include one tree from a selected view point. (Use a frame for choosing the best view.) On return to class discuss the way that some trees, like the flames of a real fire, often seem to contain hidden or mysterious images. **Copymaster 63** contains a number of illusions and mysterious effects of lines and shapes. Ask your children to use fine brushes and black ink or combine these with black felt tip pens to do a linear design on Copymaster 63 based on their sketches. The designs can be planned out with soft pencils which can be erased after the ink has thoroughly dried. Get them to introduce a hidden face as part of their tree design. Encourage your children to vary the thickness of the lines. In planning the layout of their designs refer to the use of grids in helping to organise space.

You need
Sketches of trees, sketchbooks, paper, ink, fine brushes, pencils, felt tip pens, **Copymaster 63**.

Activity 175: Curled paper lines
Give each child a piece of black or dark coloured paper or card as a support for their collage. Using a variety of coloured papers (or only white), get your children to cut strips of varying lengths and about 2 to 15 cms wide.

Curled paper picture

Roll these tightly around different shaped formers (pencils, square and triangular sectioned wood). Open these various spirals as required and stick one edge firmly in place on the background. Compose the collage carefully, taking account of the different depths of the paper rolls, colours and sizes. Some spirals can be opened out a lot and encompass other elements in this abstract exercise. Alternatively, the spirals and curls could be glued together without a backing sheet. This could then be mounted against a window.

You need
Coloured backing card (needs to be fairly stout and about 50 × 30 cms), coloured paper strips, scissors, glue, brushes.

 # Make a line

Activity 176: Contour faces
Following on from Activity 167 you can discuss how a face can be thought of as contours of distance from the viewer. Get the children to work in pairs. Using a soft pencil and pieces of A3 drawing paper get your children to start by imagining the tips of noses as a conical hill. Using lines quite close together get them to map each other's faces with contour lines.

You need
Paper and pencils

Activity 177: Cartoons
Cartoons can combine genuine fun and amusement with technical ideas of real artistic value. **Copymaster 64** contains a number of simple exercises that help your children to draw cartoons. Encourage your children to use their sketchbooks to note how people and animals look. When they come to make cartoons emphasise a few rules. Keep shapes simple and start either with a stereotype head shape or a feature such as the nose.

Child's cartoons

Cartoons are very often simply composed of a few lines combined in a stylised way. Exaggerate features and keep them to a minimum. The 'Drawing' section (p 106) includes other information about cartoons.

You need
Copymaster 64, sketchbooks and tracing paper, pens, pencils.

Activity 178: Skeletons
If you can borrow some mounted specimens of animal or human skeletons get your children to make linear studies using white chalk or pastel on black sugar paper. Use a few pieces together for group work on a large scale. Alternatively children can use white wax crayons on white paper which is then washed over with black ink to reverse out a resist image.

You need
Black or white paper, white chalk, crayons or pastels, skeletons, inks, brushes.

Activity 179: Lines that describe surfaces
Before the lesson starts prepare a 35 mm slide in the following way. Use a fine waterproof (such as a Rapidograph or Rotring) pen or felt tip pen and draw a series of parallel equidistant lines on a piece of clear acetate as shown in the diagram. Make up a still life of white objects or objects painted white. In a darkened area of your room project the lines over the surface of the object. Set your children the task of drawing the lines that describe the surface of the objects. They should use charcoal pencils and concentrate on the lines rather than the objects.

You need
Prepared 35 mm slide, projector, large sheets of white, paper, charcoal pencils, charcoal, fixative (to be applied after drawings are finished).

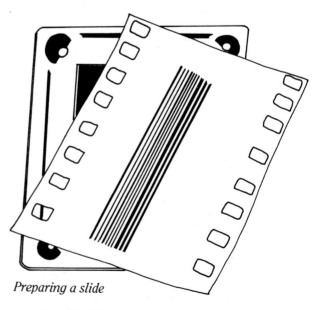

Preparing a slide

Activity 180: Silhouettes
A number of subjects can be used for linear analysis. These include skeleton leaves (projected on an overhead projector), electricity pylons or bare trees against a clear sky. Give your children fine felt tip pens to make

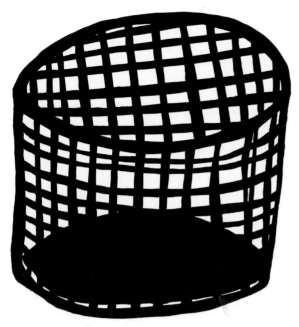

Child's drawing of a silhouetted subject

observational studies. Shapes can be cut out from contrasting shades of paper and mounted to produce strong silhouette images.

You need
Paper, felt tip pens, skeleton leaves, scissors, glues.

Activity 181: Lines for tones

Examine the way that Bewick produced changes in tone by the closeness and relative thickness of the lines that he used. Use **Copymaster 33** and ask your children to match the tonal values by using parallel lines of varying thickness and spacing. For very light tones your children will need to use very fine lines indeed. After this exercise give each child a piece of fruit or some other small, rounded object. After sketching the approximate shape and proportions get them to use a fine, black felt tip pen to approximate Bewick's style and use of parallel lines to render the subject in tones as shown in the illustration.

You need
Copymasters 33 and **60**, paper, pencils, fine felt tip pens, apples, oranges.

Child's drawing of an apple

Activity 182: Lines for texture

Using the same objects get your children to do a comparative study in which lines are used to show the textures of the surfaces rather than the tonal values.

You need
Paper, pencils, fine felt tip pens, apples, oranges.

Activity 183: Wax cutting

Give each child a piece of good quality, A5 size, white paper. First get them to cover the whole surface with thick areas of variously coloured crayons. The arrangement of the coloured areas will depend on the subject. Now cover this with a thick layer of black wax crayon. Using a sharp object, your children can engrave through the top layer of black crayon to reveal their chosen subject drawn in coloured lines contrasted against the black wax surface. This activity can be extended by combining it with collage techniques of cut paper and wax resist methods.

You need
A5 paper, wax crayons, sharp cutting point, scissors, glues, brushes, inks.

Child's wax cut image

Activity 184: Colour combs

Cut thick, chunky crayons with a series of 'V' shapes along one edge. This colour comb can be used to draw abstract patterns over large areas of coloured papers.

You need
Chunky crayons, craft knives

Activity 185: Balls of string and feathers

Set out a number of similar drawing displays. Place a white ball of string on black paper making sure some of the string is unwound and laid across the surface. Place some large lightly coloured feathers on other pieces of black paper. After choosing the subject for their drawings give your children white pastels and black paper to work on. The paper for the feather drawings should be about A4. For the string drawing it should be a little bigger. White lines of varying thickness will be the only way to draw the subjects.

You need
Feathers, string, black paper, white pastels.

Activity 186: Perspective
Copymaster 65, contains information about perspective. To help your children understand some of the principles behind perspective, set up the following demonstration. Set up a large sheet of clear perspex in a vertical plane. Place a set of geometric shapes on a table including a cube, cuboid, cone, sphere, pyramid and a metre rule. Lay out the display on gridded card. (Use **Copymaster 6** for making this up.) Place the perspex in front of the display and, using a felt tip pen, carefully draw the objects as you see them on the perspex. (You will need to maintain a fixed viewing position.) Trace the complete drawing on to a piece of tracing paper. Wipe out the drawing and reposition the perspex so that the view is from above. Trace the new drawing and discuss the results with your children. Give each child a copy of Copymaster 65. Get them to make their own drawings of the mathematical solids once you have discussed the ideas thoroughly. **Copymaster 66** contains information about making a perspective diorama which can be developed from this activity. Use **Copymaster 59** to make a viewing frame to help with this activity.

You need
Copymasters 6, **59**, **65** and **66**, mathematical solids, gridded card, felt tip pens, rulers, pencils.

Activity 187: Lines in different media
Give your children large sheets of white and grey paper plus a range of drawing materials. Ask them to make abstract arrangements of lines. The kinds of lines to include are: sharp thin lines, hard-edged thick lines, soft misty lines, wobbly regular lines, wobbly misty lines, straight, curved and elliptical lines. The task is to make an arrangement on the paper that is balanced, interesting and uses the whole surface of the paper.

You need
Paper (white and grey A2 size), charcoal, pencils, felt tip pens (various thicknesses), pens, inks, brushes, paints, graphite sticks.

Activity 188: Spirals, lines from nature
Use items from your display and sketches made on trips to find examples of different lines found in nature. In the preceding activity your children will have started to explore the variety of lines that can be made, now get them to use **Copymaster 67** to record types of lines and spirals found in nature. These lines will include bent, curved, broken, straight, curved and spiralling lines. After using Copymaster 67 get them to choose two or three special lines to draw on black or grey paper with white chalk. This combination of media will help realise the linear qualities of their subjects.

You need
Copymaster 67, paper (white and grey A2 size), charcoal, pencils, felt tip pens (various thicknesses), pens, inks, brushes, paints, graphite sticks.

 # Stretching shapes ▷

Activity 189: Ceramic trees
Give each child a lump of clay and a clay board. First get them to make a slab about 15 cms square and 1 cm thick. Roll out thick and thin ropes of clay. Using these ropes of clay get your children to make a relief model of a bare tree. The branches may be swaying in the wind while the trunk is solid and firm. Use edges of card to add linear patterns to the tree. Encourage your children to give spirit or feel to the different elements of their trees. The lines should be expressive. The finished plaques can be slip coloured, fired and glazed. If your children would like to wall-mount them then poke a couple of holes through the edges of the clay before drying and firing.

You need
Clay, clay boards, texture materials, slip.

Activity 190: Wire heads
Look at Miro's drawings, the open, see-through quality gives an impression of three dimensions. Give your children soft wire and pliers. Get them to make wire sculptures of their friends' heads. In doing this they will need to measure distance across and around parts of the head. They should use string and markers for this to measure distances. When the circumferences have been measured the wire can be cut and fixed with pliers. (Cut the wire using the cutters on the side of the pliers not between the jaws.) The open, see-through characteristic of this form of sculpture will be fascinating to your children. Compare their work with that of Miro.

You need:
Soft wire, pliers, string, felt tip markers.

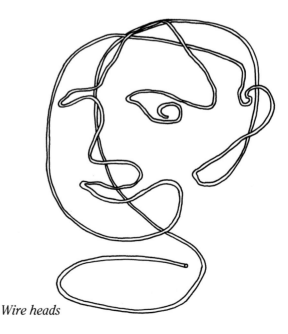
Wire heads

Activity 191: String sculptures

Children can work in pairs for this activity. Give each pair a large piece of black card and some thin white cord. Working either vertically or horizontally your children are to create a composition from pieces of string stuck to the black board. The general direction for each piece should be either vertical, horizontal or diagonal. Each piece can, however, have inflections or subtle movements from this strict direction. The string can be cut into various lengths, spaced a little apart or in some cases overlaid. Your children should consider the position of pieces carefully before gluing them in place.

You need
Black card, string, glue, scissors.

Activity 192: Wire and plaster

Show your children some examples of Giacometti's strange thin sculptures. Give them a theme such as the 'thin man' or the 'wiry dog', wire for an armature and Modroc, and scrim and plaster for the solid parts of their sculptures. Emphasise the thin linear qualities for this sculpture. Ask your children to consider the various views of the sculpture, will it be linear from one view and more substantial from another? See the 'Modelling' section (pages 111–12) for more information.

You need
Soft iron wire, metal gauzes, Modroc, scrim, plaster, mixing bowls, baseboards.

Activity 193: Maths shapes and string

Use **Copymasters 20–22** which contain a number of different mathematical patterns which can be used as the basis for string pictures. (These pictures, if they are to have value, should not be 'time filler' exercises.) The illustration shows how your children can knock nails in through the paper template which is then removed to

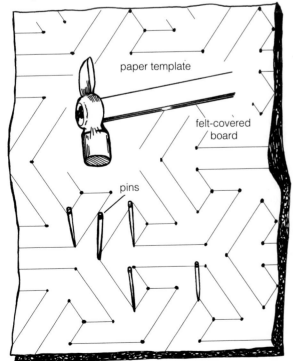

Hammering nails in to place

reveal the black felt backing. Discuss with them the best points on the shapes to choose for the positions of the nails. Against this black background your children can use brightly coloured metallic threads to form a strongly linear pattern that picks up some of the elements of the basic flat pattern. Your children can choose the colours and configurations of the string patterns. The coloured threads are simply tied neatly to the starting point and wound around nails as selected, finishing with another knot.

You need
Black felt baseboards (on chipboard), panel pins, **Copymasters 20–22**, coloured strings or threads.

Activity 194: Masks with lines

Make a simple face mask as outlined on pages 111 and 113 in the 'Modelling' section. Your children can decorate the masks using simple linear patterns of black and white (refer to Activity 184) or patterns that suggest contour lines.

You need
Face masks, black and white paint, brushes, pencils.

Activity 195: Cut and painted flat shapes

Children can work in pairs. Give your children pieces of corrugated card about 30 cms by 50 cms. Using one piece as the support, let them paint it any bright colour that they like. On other pieces of card let your children draw interesting shapes based on flowing, easy lines. Make the shapes irregular and have some large and others smaller. Cut out the shapes with a craft knife on a cutting mat. Use a mixture of Polyfiller® and fill the edges so the pieces look smooth and solid. Once the filler had dried, sand down to produce a good finish. Get your children to consider the shapes together and think about which colours would suit each one. Paint each shape according to the choices made. Use small pieces of card behind the pieces and glue on to the background and then on to succeeding new surfaces as shown in the diagram.

You need
Corrugated cardboard, paint, brushes, craft knives, cutting mats, glue, filler, sandpaper.

Activity 196: Parallel lines and reflections

This can be an individual or group activity. For individual work give each child a square of white painted corrugated card. Get them to draw parallel lines 3 or 4 mm apart with a felt tip pen. Fill in alternate gaps with a good black felt tip pen or paint carefully with a fine brush and Indian ink. Give each child a piece of reflective flexible mirror. They can cut strips and shapes from this piece. Let them make rings or other shapes that can be glued carefully on to the surface of the striped card. (Place some PVA in a dish and just dip the edge of the mirror into it.) Wall mount the resulting pieces of work. Discuss the results. Are the lines distorted? Where is the best viewing position?

You need
Squares of white card (or corrugated card), ink, brushes, rulers, felt tip pens, flexible mirror, glue, scissors.

Exploration

Activity 197: Exploring lines

Use a large piece of lining paper or a number of sheets of white paper and cover a wall of your room. In groups of four or five, let the children paint a series of lines that change their thickness and colour as they meander. Each group can continue as they please, changing or continuing a theme as they go. Let this activity be free from direction. Let each group discuss privately what subject or approach they will produce.

You need
Wall covered with white paper, brushes (of various thicknesses), paints, mixing trays.

Activity 198: Strip collage

Let each child bring in two illustrations from magazines that are the same size. For this example the size is assumed to be 20 cms square. Give your children a piece of card 20 cms by 40 cms long and another that is 20 cms square. Mark up the larger piece of card with lines that are 1 cm apart, as shown in the illustration. Carefully score and fold the card in concertina fashion. Flatten it out again. Cut the illustrations into 1 cm strips. Take care to keep the orientation and order of the strips correct. Stick alternate strips from each illustration in position on the concertina of card. When complete, fold the card up and stick the 'valleys' with glue on to the backing card. Viewed from the right side one picture will be seen, from the left the other picture can be viewed.

You need
Card, illustrations, craft knives, glues, brushes, cutting mats.

1. Cut same-sized pictures into strips.

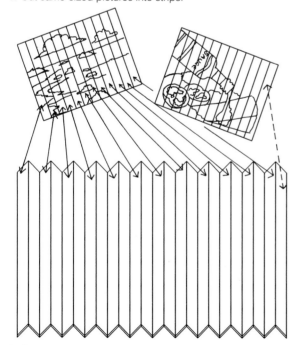

2. Glue alternate strips to concertina board support.

Making a strip collage

Activity 199: Imaginative paintings

There are many stripy or linear subjects that can stimulate your children's imaginations. Try these: a man in a striped suit, a tiger in a forest, parasols on a beach with bathing tents, reflections of reeds and boats in a river, a balloon festival.

You need
Paint, brushes, paper.

Activity 200: Hair

There are a number of ways of trying to paint hair. Your children can select three basic colours that are needed for a particular colour type. For example blonde may need a bright pasty white, a broken yellow and a Van Dyke brown. The shadows, mid-tones and highlights can all be rendered with these colours. First paint the main mass with a soft large brush, then indicate shadows and highlights with wrist movements using a finer brush to make parallel lines of colour. Another way would be to use a sponge. Dip the edge of the sponge in the mid-tone and with light pressure draw it over the paper surface to indicate the area of hair. With clean smaller pieces of sponge (cut with 'V' shapes if you choose) apply light coats of lines of shadow and then highlights. Allows the layers to dry between applications. The sponge painting can be refined by the subsequent use of brushes. Another way is to produce a series of masks or stencils, through which the various colours are stippled, padded or stroked.

You need
Paper, paints, brushes, pads of paints, sponge, scissors.

 # Photo finds

Activity 201: Found objects

Objects and materials that have strong linear structures or patterns can be used for imaginative prints. Individual items can be linked up with a roller or a pad of soft fabric or foam rubber loaded with ink or dye. Try to cover the ridges or prominent lines evenly with ink. Carefully press the objects against tinted paper or newsprint to take a print. Alternatively if you use an oil-based ink you can achieve remarkably fine results by inking up the surface and then rolling a gelatine roller over this wet surface. (You must take great care of gelatine rollers. Do not use water-based inks and only clean with turpentine.) This picks up an off-set image which can be printed on to a clean piece of paper. Suitable objects include palms of hands, netting, string, heavily grained wood, feathers and leaves.

You need
Oil- and/or water-based inks, lined objects or materials, ink plate, rollers, paper.

Activity 202: Positive and negative photos

Get your children to take a photograph of any subject that is highly contrasted. A face in strong sunlight, for example, will produce brilliant areas and dark, full shadows. Well-defined hair adds interest. Buy some small sheets of 'line' film from one of the discount photographic suppliers. Set up the usual trays of developer, stop bath, fixer and wash in the darkroom. Make a contact print from a chosen negative on to the line film by putting your enlarger out of focus and projecting light through the negative on to the film. Get your children to make a note of the enlarger settings, the height of the light source above the baseboard and the time for the exposure. (This line film can be handled safely in a red safety light as it is orthochromatic.) Process the film. A useful trick when developing is to view the film through the reverse: when you can see an image easily the line film is fully developed. Wash it immediately in the stop bath and then fix, wash and dry. Now use this high contrast positive and repeat the process to make a high contrast negative. Both the negative and positive can be used in the enlarger to produce prints on paper which are finely detailed line images. If you sandwich the negative and positive together (so that the emulsion sides are in contact), and slightly offset the images, then you can produce an even more interesting line image. This area of photography is full of opportunities for experiments. **Copymaster 68** contains a detailed illustrated account of this process.

You need
Ordinary negatives, high-contrast line film, developer, fixer and stop baths, an enlarger, darkroom, **Copymaster 68**.

Activity 203: Lined clay prints
Give your children small lumps of clay. Get them to bang clay on to a smooth surface so that they have a flat clay printing surface. Into this flat surface, press lined material such as corrugated card or materials that can be used to form lines. The printing blocks can be inked up with a pad of ink and printed.

You need
Clay, line pattern materials, inks, paper.

Fabric lines

Activity 204: Feather tapestry
Give each child a choice of dark felt squares as a background to the tapestry. Using the drawings that have already been made of feathers, your children can work out how to create the picture using sewing techniques and a variety of different cottons and threads. It is a good idea to sketch out the shape of the feather on to the felt with some dressmaker's chalk before using a needle. The various elements of the feather can also be marked along the quill and edges. Using simple stitches, first outline the quill. The fine, feathery elements will radiate from the quill from the base to the tip. Offer your children plenty of choice in the way they approach this and make sequins and other small scraps available for incorporating into their pictures. When the work is complete, stick the felt on to a piece of board and mount as part of the display.

You need
Feathers, felt squares, different cottons and threads, dressmaker's chalk, scissors, needles, backing board, glue.

Activity 205
Give your children a supply of wools, threads, and needles and a small piece of hessian. Get them to sew a system of spiralling lines starting from the centre of the hessian. As they progress, ask them to consider what their work suggests to them. Get them to complete the pieces using as much variation of line as possible in terms of colour, thickness and shape.

You need
Hessian, needles, threads, wools.

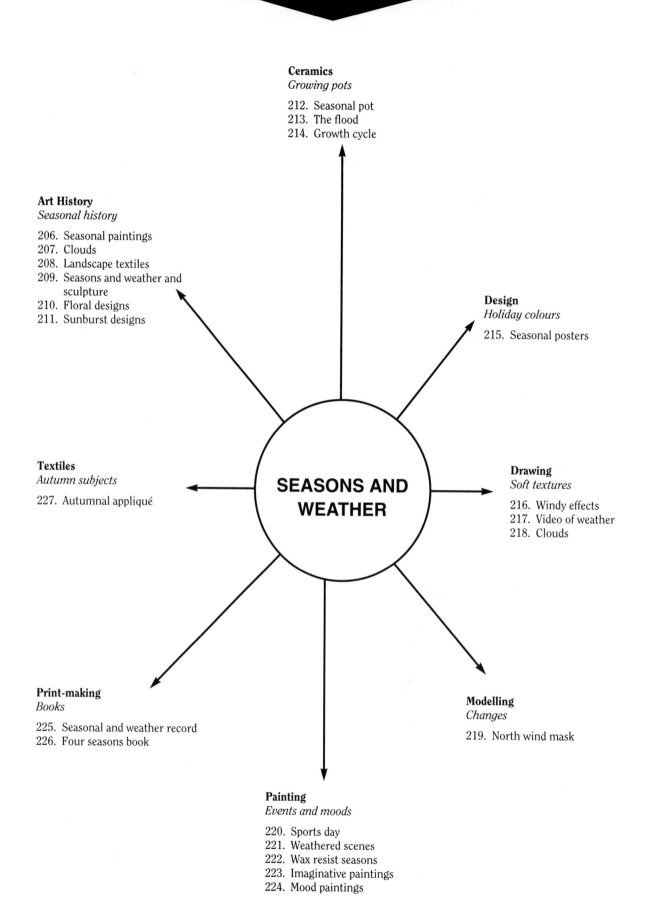

SEASONS AND WEATHER

Ceramics
Growing pots

212. Seasonal pot
213. The flood
214. Growth cycle

Art History
Seasonal history

206. Seasonal paintings
207. Clouds
208. Landscape textiles
209. Seasons and weather and sculpture
210. Floral designs
211. Sunburst designs

Design
Holiday colours

215. Seasonal posters

Textiles
Autumn subjects

227. Autumnal appliqué

SEASONS AND WEATHER

Drawing
Soft textures

216. Windy effects
217. Video of weather
218. Clouds

Print-making
Books

225. Seasonal and weather record
226. Four seasons book

Modelling
Changes

219. North wind mask

Painting
Events and moods

220. Sports day
221. Weathered scenes
222. Wax resist seasons
223. Imaginative paintings
224. Mood paintings

66

CROSS-CURRICULAR LINKS ▶

Design and technology Design and make weather testing devices and weather stations

Drama and dance Rain dance

Environmental studies The seasons, contrasting local and world weather, effect of rainfall, measuring the weather

History Effect of weather, how life has been changed and governed by the seasons

Mathematics Measuring tree rings, recording rainfall

Music Four Seasons by Vivaldi, 'Here comes the sun', Pastoral suite

RE The Flood

Science Effect of moon and sun, forecasting the weather, effect of hot and cold, effect of water and insulation

ABOUT THIS TOPIC ▶

Seasons and weather concern natural phenomena and can contain mini-topics such as growth and living things. All of these offer opportunities for science, mathematics, language and geographical activities. From the art point of view this topic contains many opportunities for personal expression where children are required to move beyond descriptive work. In order for your children to maximise their expressive potential it is essential that you offer a rich experience upon which to draw. Children's work will be full of feeling and meaning when the stimulus or source has relevance to them. Choose subjects that are suitable and encourage your children to be imaginative and inventive. The changing images of the seasons can be captured if your children have a range of flexible techniques. Children can be truly inventive only when they have some real relevant experience.

General points

Any season can be a point of departure. It makes sense, however, to start the cycle of life with spring and to give attention to the changes that occur throughout the year. You may spend a few weeks at the beginning of each term on this extended topic. Doing so will allow a sensible structure and real opportunities to review previous work and gain insights into changes that have occurred. There are many pieces of poetry that will conjure up vivid images, try some of these:

Weather
Address to a child during a boisterous winter evening
by Dorothy Wordsworth

What way does the wind come? What way does he go?
He rides over the water, and over the snow,
Through wood, and through vale; and o'er rocky
    height,
Which the goat cannot climb, takes his sounding
    flight;
He tosses about in every bare tree,
As, if you look up, you plainly may see;
But how he will come, and whither he goes,
There's never a scholar in England knows.
(extract)

Extract from *The wind in a frolic*
by William Howitt

The wind one morning sprung up from sleep,
Saying, 'Now for a frolic! now for a leap!
Now for a mad-cap, galloping chase!
I'll make a commotion in every place!'
So it swept with a bustle right through a great town,
Creaking the signs, and scattering down
Shutters; and whisking, and merciless squalls,
Old women's bonnets and gingerbread stalls.
There never was heard a much lustier shout,
As the apples and oranges trundled about;
And the urchins, that stand with their thievish eyes
For ever on watch, ran off each with a prize.

The wind
by Christina Rossetti

Who has seen the wind?
Neither I nor you;
But when the leaves hang trembling
The wind is passing through

Who has seen the wind?
Neither you nor I;
But when the trees bow down their heads
The wind is passing by.

Windy nights
by Robert Louis Stevenson

Whenever the moon and stars are set,
Whenever the wind is high,
All night long in the dark and wet,
A man goes riding by.
Late in the night when the fires are out,
Why does he gallop and gallop about?

Whenever the trees are crying aloud,
And ships are tossed at sea,
By, on the highway, low and loud,
By at the gallop goes he.
By at the gallop he goes, and then
By he comes back at the gallop again.

Rhymes and proverbs

Rain, rain, go away,
Come again another day.

A red sky in the morning,
Is a shepherd's warning.
A red sky at night,
Is a shepherd's delight.

Rain before seven,
Fine before eleven.

When the wind is in the east,
'Tis neither good for man nor beast;
When the wind is in the north,
The skilful fisher goes not forth;
When the wind is in the south,
It blows the bait in the fish's mouth;
When the wind is the west,
Then 'tis at the very best.

For every fog in March,
There'll be a frost in May,
A northern mist, brings
Fine weather from afar

Seasons
Buttercups and daisies
by Mary Howitt

Buttercups and daisies –
Oh, the pretty flowers,
Coming ere the springtime
To tell of sunny hours.
While the trees are leafless,
While the fields are bare,
Buttercups and daisies
Spring up here and there.
(extract)

The willow-man
by Juliana Ewing

There once was a Willow, and he was very old,
And all his leaves fell off from him, and left him in the
      cold;
But ere the rude winter could buffet him with snow,
There grew upon his hoary head a crop of mistletoe.
(extract)

Winter time
by Robert Louis Stevenson

Late lies the wintry sun a-bed;
A frosty, fiery sleepy-head;
Blinks but an hour or two; and then,
A blood-red orange, sets again.

Before the stars have left the skies,
At morning in the dark I rise;
And shivering in my nakedness,
By the cold candle, bathe and dress.

Close by the jolly fire I sit
To warm my frozen bones a bit;
Or with a reindeer-sled, explore
The colder countries round the door.

When to go out, my nurse doth wrap
Me in my comforter and cap,
The cold wind burns my face, and blows
Its frosty pepper up my nose.

Black are my steps on silver sod;
Thick blows my frosty breath abroad;
And tree and house, and hill and lake,
Are frosted like a wedding-cake.

Passages from Thomas Hardy that describe the perpetual cycle of sowing, reaping and ploughing will also invoke strong visual images for your children. Don't forget the biblical story of the flood and Noah's Ark.

Displays and resources
Include natural items; sets showing germination of cereals and beans; displays of spring, summer, autumn and winter produce such as flowers, cereals, apples and nuts. Posters of large flower heads, illustrations of artists' paintings and designs, photographs of cloud and weather conditions together with large blow-ups of verse and prose can be combined with colour combinations to produce a changing display.

STARTING POINTS ▶

- Weather observations, a visit by a weather forecaster
- Poems and stories
- Art history, focusing on either weather or the seasons
- Music including the *Pastoral Symphony, The Four Seasons,* and other music that contains stimulus to visual imagery

- Discussion about favourite times of the year
- Science, growth and decay
- Art activities based on the notion of change and decay, or growth and life.

SEASONS AND WEATHER ACTIVITIES

 ## Seasonal history ▷

Before you start

The list of artists and particular works that is given below has been sub-divided into seasons and weather. In a number of cases the galleries that house the works are given. This may help enable you to get slides or posters from those sources. Works that celebrate the seasons include:

Spring
Millet, Jean-Francois (1814–75) *Springtime*; Brown, Ford Madox (1821–93) *Pretty baa-lambs*, Birmingham, City Museum and Art Gallery.

Summer
Poussin, Nicolas (1594–1665) *Summer*, Louvre; Rousseau, Theodore (1812–1867) *A Summer Day*, Louvre; Velde, Adriaen van de (1636–72), *Summer*.

Autumn
Lambert, George (1700–65) *Hilly Landscape with a Cornfield*, 1733, Tate; Pissarro, Camille (1831–1903) *Les Toits Rouges* autumnal landscape with rooftops.

Winter
Breugel, Pieter (1530–69) *Winter, the Dark Day* Courbet, Gustave (1819–77) *Snow Scene*, (Ashmolean Museum, Oxford), Daubigny, Charles (1817–79) *Winter Landscape*; Leader, B. W., *February Fill Dyke*, (Birmingham, City Art Gallery).

General
Anon (C1415), *Occupation of the Months*; De Limbourg brothers (C1360–1416), *Les Tres Riches Heures du Duc de Berry*, scenes from the calendar.

Weather
Avercamp, Hendrick (1585–1634) *Skaters near a castle*, (National Gallery, London); Constable, John (1776–1837) *Weymouth Bay 1816*, (National Gallery, London), *Vale of Dedham 1828* (National Gallery of Scotland), also note particularly his cloud studies, Dufy, Raoul, (1877–1953) *The Paddock at Deauville*; Friedrich, Casper David (1774–1840) *Man Looking at Mountain with Rainbow*; Goyen, Jan van (1596–1656) *A Scene on the Ice* (National Gallery) plus many stormy seas; Monet, Claude (1840–1926) *Femme a l'Ombrelle*, Neer, Aert van de, (1603–77) *Frozen River, Evening*, (National Gallery London); Rousseau, Theodore (1812–67) *Under the Birches, Evening*; Ruisdael, Jacob van (1628–82) *Landscape with Trees in Wind*; Turner, Joseph Mallord William (1775–1851) *Dido Building Carthage* (1815 National Gallery, London), *Ulysses Deriding Polyphemus* (1829 National Gallery, London), *Buttermere 'Rainbow', After the Deluge* (The Tate); Van Gogh (1853–90) compare the following: *Cornfield with Cypress tree, Mountain Landscape Painted in May 1890, Landscape near Auvers of July 1890* and *The Ravine in December 1889*; Velde, Adriaen van de (1636–72), *Strong Breeze* (National Gallery, London);

Wouwerman, Philip (1619–68) *Snowy Day* examples of his work are in the National Gallery London.

Activity 206: Seasonal paintings

Select a range of diverse pictures from the list given above and put on a slide show. (Contact your local library service for help tracking down slides or contact some of the large, London galleries or the V&A.) Discuss how Pieter Breugel and others have depicted the seasonal changes in landscapes. Use terms such as background, foreground, balance, shade, hue, transparent, sketching. Include these terms in your display. Look at the way one artist such as Van Gogh painted the landscape at different times of the year. Compare his *Cornfield with Cypress Tree*, the *Mountain Landscape painted in May 1890*, *Landscape near Auvers of July 1890* and *The Ravine in December 1889*.

Activity 207: Clouds

The list above contains some wonderful Dutch masterpieces with dramatic, forceful and moody skies. Jacob van Ruisdael's *Landscape with Trees in Wind* is magnificent. He quite rightly described it as heroic. The mood of the storm and gloomy unrest of the trees is greatly enhanced by the fantastic sky which contains pale pinks and yellows breaking into the heavy grey-blue clouds. John Constable with his strongly English vision produced other memorable works. He is renowned for his close study of individual formations of clouds. Compare the way the Dutch masters and John Constable studied clouds. **Copymaster 69** contains an impression of a windy day. Get your children to make their own studies of a windswept landscape in the place provided. Use pen and ink or fine felt tip pens and washes.

You need
Copymaster 69, fine felt tip pens, pen and ink, brushes.

Child's drawing of clouds

Activity 208: Landscape textiles
Examine the way that embroiderers such as Verina Warren have tackled landscape images. (You will find many books on embroidery contain examples of her work.) Notice the clever way that she integrates traditional embroidery techniques with the careful use of paint and fabric pastels. This can lead to a further discussion of colour and seasons and subsequent practical activities. Combine simple appliqué methods in those areas of the landscape which are portrayed with flat areas of coloured felt with the use of pastels, paints or felt tip pens. Simple sewing techniques can also be integrated.

You need
Scraps, felt, felt tip pens, needles, cottons, pastels, paints, fine brushes, mixing dishes.

Activity 209: Seasons, weather and sculpture
Discuss how certain sculptures have been designed to be placed in the open air. For example the aeolian harp was designed to produce music solely through the action of the wind. More recently works by Henry Moore, Barbara Hepworth and others have been produced to be set in the landscape and to weather and change, thus becoming part of the landscape. Can your children design sculptures that will weather in interesting ways? What materials change in predictable ways?

Activity 210: Floral designs
Floral motifs and plants have long featured in the decorative arts. **Copymasters 70–73** contain floral and plant designs by William Morris. Discuss with your children which colour schemes could be used with these designs. Choose one for each season. Let them choose which design to use for each season and finish them carefully with their chosen colours.

You need
Copymasters 70–73, paints, fine brushes, mixing palettes.

Activity 211: Sunburst designs
Copymaster 74 contains a number of designs that are based on aspects of the weather or seasons. Exponents of Art Nouveau and Art Deco often used sunburst effects as part of their designs. Get your children to make a design for a radio or door based upon a design from the weather or seasons.

You need
Copymaster 74, paints, illustrations of Art Deco and Art Nouveau designs.

 # Growing pots

Activity 212: Seasonal pot
Discuss with your children images that typify the seasons. Get them to make simple sketches and designs for all the seasons. Try to ensure that they make a number of different options and then choose the ones that they prefer. Give each child a lump of clay with which to make a pot. Divide the surface into four

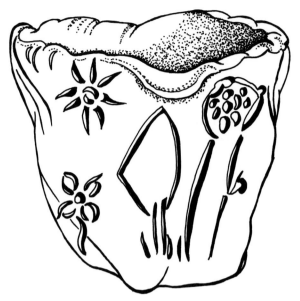

Pot with images in relief

separate sections. (It does not have to be like the segments of an orange; it can be divided very freely to suit their designs for the seasons.) Collect objects with textured surfaces, e.g., bark, nail brushes. Use these to help decorate their season designs on the surface of the container. Use coloured slips and/or glaze to colour each section appropriately.

You need
Clay, materials to texture the surface, slips, glazes, brushes, suitable surfaces on which to work, modelling tools.

Activity 213: The flood
One of the most celebrated stories that involves the weather is that of Noah and the flood. Read this to your children. Get them to make notes of what they consider to be most interesting. Give your children sufficient clay to make a tile of approximately 20 cms by 10 cms by

Child's image of the flood

1 cm thick. Pierce two holes at both top corners (for wall mounting). Get your children to produce a relief panel depicting an episode from the story. Colour using slip or glaze. If you are going to use glaze then refer to page 89 in the 'Ceramics' section.

You need
Clay, rolling pins, 1 cm section wood, sketches to help with the design, materials to texture the surface, slips, glazes, brushes, suitable surfaces on which to work, modelling tools.

Activity 214: Growth cycle
Discuss ideas that are linked with the cycle of growth and look at objects and specimens that exemplify certain of these stages. Include words and phrases such as: growth, bursting seed, mellow fruitfulness, decay, and sleep in your display. Give your children clay and ask them to make a container or pot that represents one of the words. Dry, fire and glaze the pots.

You need
Clay, materials to texture the surface, slips, glazes, brushes, suitable surfaces on which to work, modelling tools.

 Holiday colours ▷

Activity 215: Seasonal posters
Posters for seasonal holidays such as skiing and sun-seeking call for different combinations of colours and typefaces. Set your children the task of producing holiday posters or posters advertising the 'Wind in the willows' or 'The sun and the wind'. Use **Copymasters 32** and **58** to help organise space for posters.

You need
Copymasters 32 and **58**, A3 paper, pencils, erasers, paint, brushes, felt tip pens.

 Soft textures ▷

Activity 216: Windy effects
Memories of real or dreamed events can be revived by reading poems or passages from stories. After a period of windy weather read and talk about the imagery of storms. Look at pictures as well, particularly the work by Ruisdael mentioned in the above list. (Refer to **Copymaster 69**.) Give your children some tinted sugar paper, some textured and some smooth plus a range of media that includes pastels, inks and paints. Get them to make pastel or felt tip drawings of imaginary windy days or drawings based on their dreams.

You need
Various types of papers, pastels, brushes, water, felt tip pens, **Copymaster 69**.

Windy day

Activity 217: Video of weather
For presentation at a school assembly your children can produce a video showing various aspects of weather or the seasons. To do this well will require substantial planning and editing. (Make sure you keep the master tapes or vital images could be lost.) Producing a video on the seasons will require a script and a production plan and will be a long term project.

You need
Video equipment.

Activity 218: Clouds
This is to follow on from Activity 207 in which your children compared the way the Dutch masters and John Constable studied clouds. Collect and sort illustrations of skies and clouds. Using small pieces of pastel paper get your children to make studies of clouds using pastels.

You need
Illustrations of clouds, pastels, pastel paper.

 Changes ▷

Activity 219: North wind mask
Let your children search for suitable illustrations that will help them to make the mask. Make up the papier mâché (as described on page 111) with the addition of a small quantity of PVA which will toughen the finished mask. The box can, in fact, produce four masks. Draw over the corners of the box. Cut the corner mask shapes from the box. Work out where the eyes, nose and mouth should be and cut holes. Ensure that the mouth is round and large enough to let the north wind blow. The north wind should have full balloon-like cheeks so, when your children start to work with the papier mâché

Seasonal mask

to build up the features, it is worth pointing this out. Let the mask dry out thoroughly when the features are completely modelled. When the mask is dry reinstate the holes and pierce two holes from which to attach an elastic thread. Get your children to try them on for size and a comfortable fit. The north wind's hair can be modelled partly with papier mâché and partly with wool, string or raffia. Finally paint the masks using PVA-based paints.

You need
Papier mâché, plastic bucket, PVA adhesive, a cardboard carton (large), felt tip marker, scissors, paints, paintbrushes, mixing trays, water, wool and string for flowing hair, craft knife and cutting mat.

 ## Events and moods ▷

Activity 220: Sports day
Events throughout the year can be used as a stimulus for group work. One such event, sports day, can be recalled as a starting point for group collage.

You need
Scrap materials, illustrations from magazines, paint, brushes, backing paper and boards, glue, scissors.

Activity 221: Weathered scenes
On a trip around your school you will find evidence of weathering and decay at different times of the year. Your children can make studies of scarred and gnarled surfaces, flaking and rusted paint. Initially they may make studies in their sketchbooks using pencil or charcoal. Later they will need to mix colours sensitively and use a subtle range of broken colours for this work. Another similar activity would be to paint similar scenes during spring (at sunset) or during winter (during rain and storm). Discuss with your children their use of

Weathered surfaces

specific colours. Ask them to describe when and why they would use an orange-red such as vermilion rather than a blue-red such as crimson.

You need
Paper, paints, mixing palettes, brushes, pencils, charcoal.

Activity 222: Wax resist seasons
Give each child a piece of good white paper about 60 cms long by 30 cms high. Using a white wax crayon get them to make a pattern of triangles and other geometric shapes over the whole surface. The pattern needs to be quite dense but should not cover all the surface area. Using a variety of coloured inks let your

children build up a colour design that shows a passage from spring through to winter from left to right across the paper. The colours should be used imaginatively, picking out forms and shapes which are reminiscent of natural forms and the colours generally will move from cool to warm and back to cool. It may be useful to look at some of Klee's work while this activity is being undertaken.

You need
Paper 60 cms × 30 cms, inks, white wax crayons, waterproof inks (all colours), brushes, illustrations of Klee's work.

Activity 223: Imaginative paintings
Snow scenes always evoke romantic and moody images. If it has snowed recently and your children have a chance to study the landscape do not miss the chance of showing some work by acclaimed artists and giving your children a chance to do their own direct or imaginative paintings. Give your children sheets of grey or black sugar paper, powder or PVA colours and a range of brushes. First let them sketch the scene including houses, trees, roads, footpaths and people using charcoal. White powder paint is especially good for snow as it is bulky and helps cover the paper surface well. Use it with a range of PVA colours. Point out to your children that just as there are bright and striking areas to tackle there will also be dark and sombre colours. Colour mixing and trials are really important here. The dark paper will help sort out the 'mid-tones'.

Snowy scene

Activity 224: Mood paintings
Playing passages of music from 'Here comes the sun', 'The four seasons' or 'Night on a bare mountain' can be used as a starting point for imaginative paintings. Give your children a choice of papers, large tinted or white

sheets. Encourage the use of a variety of techniques including wash, dry, scumbled, dripped, run and splattered paint. Use a variety of tools to apply the paint: sponges, rags, fingers, rollers and brushes. Try marbling and monotype prints as part of a composite approach.

You need
Music, sketchbooks, large sheets of paper, paints, inks, brushes, pencils, sponges, rags.

Books

Activity 225: Seasonal and weather record
Use colour photography to record the seasonal weather changes. Take the pictures from the same position at different times of the year. Make a class montage from the results to create a sense of space.

You need
Cameras, film, colour print, glue, backing boards.

Activity 226: Four seasons book
Make a class 'Four seasons book'. Keep records of cross-curricular activities and as a frontispiece for each season get your children to produce lino prints in one colour chosen to suit the season, or in black.

You need
A2 paper folded and stitched to make the class book, lino blocks, lino cutters, inks, rollers, rags and protective clothing.

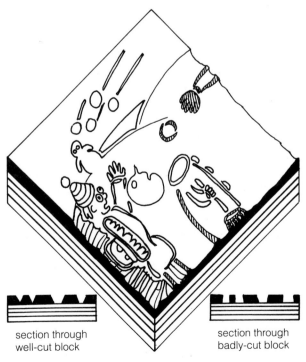

section through well-cut block

section through badly-cut block

Block for seasonal print

Autumn subjects ▷

Activity 227: Autumnal appliqué

Give each child a piece of paper about 20 cms square. Get them to make some sketches of autumnal subjects such as leaves, hibernating animals, horse chestnuts or smoking bonfires. Get these worked up into simple designs by tracing and omitting too much detail and adding colour. Give the class a chance to select the fabrics from your scraps bag. They need to be very careful in choosing colours and textures. Each child will need a piece of old sheet or felt as a backing piece. This will need to be 20 cms square. Using their designs get the children to cut out shapes from fabrics and to assemble and stitch them as small appliqué panels. Get them to sign and date the pieces using needle and thread. Join all the panels together to make a wallhanging.

You need
Fabric scraps, tracing paper, 20 cms squares of paper and backing fabric, glue, scissors, needles and threads.

ART HISTORY

A postage stamp, Picasso's *Guernica*, Walt Disney's *Fantasia*, a performance of *Les Trois Gymnopedies*, Eric Clapton's 'Lela', La Duomo in Florence, a reading of *James and the Giant Peach* by Roald Dahl and a sprint by Linford Christie can all be works of art. There are different wonders which are not works of art, these include natural landscapes, effects of natural light, waterfalls and rainbows. This simple difference is worth picking up and discussing with your children whenever possible.

Children's practical art skills develop better if they have knowledge and understanding about other people's art. This is true whether those other people are ancient Egyptians, Aztecs or contemporary fashion designers. Looking at all the kinds of things that artists have made is a vital part of art education. As children grow you need to use a firm structure for building knowledge and understanding about art. This structure needs to be systematic and provide an overview.

You are advised to link knowledge and understanding with relevant practical activities. A good way to do this is to criticise art and to make art products similar by following similar processes. Pupils need to recognise the importance of what they *know*, as well as what they do. You will have to use an increasing number of technical, subject-specific, terms. These words and phrases are best taught as part of practical work in progress but there is no reason why you should not review a whole range of terms as part of a thorough series of discussions.

The National Curriculum requires that your children look at art from early, Renaissance and later periods and art of influential artists. In doing this you must set the wider context otherwise your children may only learn about a collection of haphazard details. Your children are required to understand and appreciate art in varied genres and styles from a variety of cultures, Western and non-Western. You need to be able to include art from North and South American Indians (Aztecs and Incas), Islam, India, Japan, China and Asia.

Moving through Key Stage 2 and on to Key Stage 3
As children develop from infant to junior and beyond, they become more aware of adult art. As they do so it is important that they become aware of buildings and the various forms of design as well as painting and sculpture. Try to work in an atmosphere of enquiry and experiment. Greater maturity brings with it stronger personal ideas and tastes. While you explore with your children the art of other cultures and periods don't forget to consider the art all around you in the school, home and local environment.

Building on the work at Key Stage 1 your children will apply their knowledge of other artists' work increasingly to their own work. Surround your children with images from art of different periods and schools. Draw upon these as support for practical work. Your children will now be able to discuss how artists have depicted specific subjects, compare the work of Michelangelo and Epstein for example, take note of the different ways nature is represented by different artists and talk about how subjects are illustrated in Assyrian, Greek or Egyptian wall designs.

Briefly, you need to provide your children with three elements of knowledge and understanding:

1. The ability to identify different kinds of art and their purposes
Images, visual signs, and symbols play an important part in our lives. Your children need to develop their visual literacy and an awareness of what counts as art. They need to look at art from different cultures, pottery, weaving, fashion, architecture, posters, paintings, prints, sculptures, TV advertisements and film and portraits. Your children will need to discuss the content and meaning of works, using technical terms to explain the moods and compositional features.

2. Knowledge of different periods, cultures and traditions in art, and the work of influential artists
To achieve this it is suggested that you approach the task by reference to the simplified historical perspective given below. This locates artists and schools within larger periods. These periods are 'Ancient/Classical, Medieval, Renaissance, post-Renaissance, nineteenth century and the twentieth century. Children will need to be able to identify and compare some of the methods and materials that artists use. The kinds of classroom activities might include: the examination of an 'unknown' work (what is its purpose and meaning? how was it produced?), looking at the historical influences on work (such as *Guernica* and the attacks on the Spanish town, or Lowry's dismal view of industrialised life), discussion of styles and movements in art.

3. The ability to make imaginative use in their own work of a developing knowledge of the work of other artists
This can be done by visiting galleries, or arranging for artists to visit your school, teaching children to make connections and reach conclusions about other artists' work, carefully relating practical and theoretical aspects of art.

Your children are likely to be eager to compare their work with that of adults and generally look further

A child's self portrait and their version of Rembrandt

beyond themselves than they did as infants. If you have set your children the task of producing self portraits that show strong feelings it makes sense to show examples of work by influential artists working in the same way. Try to make the visual resources that you provide to support and extend the stages of your children's development.

Displays and resources

Slide shows can be excellent as a warm-up to a series of practical activities or as a conclusion when comparisons and discussions can take place. Remember that relevant visual resources will have a direct impact on the quality of your children's work. An exhibition which is changed regularly is a vital ingredient in any primary classroom. A list of slides or colour reproductions sent in to your school museum or library service may produce just the stimulus that your class needs. Be specific but include alternatives, librarians always try to help. You need to ensure that books, posters, works of art and natural and made objects are displayed in a relevant, logical and purposeful way. You may find that your Regional Arts Association can arrange for an artist to visit your school or even take up residence for a period of time. Understanding and knowledge can be developed if your children are involved in group projects that lead to the production of presentations to the school (audio-visual), books on specific themes, displays or celebrations based on art that they have seen and discussed.

Art history and skill areas

It is most important not to miss the pleasure of seeing, discussing and thinking about the work of others without some practical outcome being sought. Works of art should be enjoyed for their own sake. However visits to art galleries can be made more valuable when linked to subsequent practical activities. This chapter of the book contains a skeletal historical framework, biographical details and what I hope to be a little yeast of enthusiasm to encourage your interest. **Copymasters 104a** and **b**, a double page spread, contain a simplified time-line which includes all important periods, schools, style and influential artists. In the later, practical skill sections suggestions are included which link art history activities with practical skills.

An historical perspective of art

It is impossible and unnecessary to cover the whole of art history with junior children. Information is included here about the various periods of art history that are necessary for you to cover Key Stage 2 requirements. Links to various cultures and periods are also suggested. Besides this, specific works by significant artists are described in some detail.

ANCIENT EGYPTIAN ART

The art of ancient Egypt spanned the period from 3300 BC until Egypt was conquered by Alexander the Great in 332 BC. Much of the art was dedicated to the afterlife. Realistic everyday and ceremonial scenes, painted with water-based paints, were used to decorate the walls of tombs. Realistic portraits of the deceased were often painted onto wooden coffin lids using wax encaustic techniques. Architecture was massive and built to most exacting standards of accuracy and fine finish. Natural plant and animal forms were stylised and integrated into designs of astonishing power. The meanings of symbols were highly developed and a vital element not just of art but for society as a whole.

Statues for the dead were a very important form of art. Massive scale and realism were hallmarks of their sculpture. The many relief sculptures and carvings were often painted or decorated with resinous colours. Binders for colours included fruit juices, milk and gums.

Links

The flattened images such as 'Amenophosis making an offering to the Sun' (**Copymaster 75**) can be compared with the stylised paintings of El Greco, hieroglyphs and signs and symbols and Topic 1.

THE ART OF GREECE

C76
–8

Western art owes more to influences from ancient Greece than anything else. From the Romans through the Renaissance and even today we seem able to learn new things from the Classical ideals. A number of distinct periods of Greek art are worth considering as each has its own value and will interest your children in different ways.

Neolithic period (3500–2500 BC)
The art of this period is mainly of hand-made pottery, monochrome with decorations in relief or engraved lines. Some vases are painted and adorned with linear or spiral motifs in various colours: dark red, yellow, black and white. There also exist figurines in terra cotta or stone and small, realistic feminine idols.

Cycladic art (2500–1900 BC)
This period of art is contemporary with that of the Minoan Empire in Crete. Cycladic sculpture (from islands in Aegean sea) herald the very dawn of Greek art. Most remarkable are the primitively symbolic 'idols' in marble, objects with obvious magical purposes. Typical are the grave sculptures found in Keros. The beautiful little pieces often combine straight and curved lines with surprising skill. Artists wrought marble in ways to bring out its purity and beauty. The largest pieces measure about 152 cms in height while many are very small. Typical subjects include musicians and female nudes. They are carved in such a way that they are very impressive in terms of simplicity, smoothness and style.

Links
The most primitive sculptures have strange shapes resembling a violin. Your children may be able to make useful cross-cultural links by focusing on similarities of shape such as this. Look at Eskimo and Mexican work.

Also, further useful connections can be drawn with African masks and modern paintings by Picasso, Miro and Modigliani and sculptures by Henry Moore, Marini and Brancusi.

Mycenae art (1600–1100 BC)
A warrior race, the Mycenaeans, took over from the Minoans. The art of Mycenae is similar to that of the Vikings and in some ways to that of the Egyptians. The Mycenae were very concerned about the afterlife and much of their art is in the form of gold funerary masks and jewellery. Royal tombs contained fine mortuary gold masks, and many precious objects, masterpieces of jewellery and ivory sculptures. **Copymaster 76** shows the designs used as funerary gold jewellery based on octopi and other natural forms.

Links
Viking, Aztec and Art Nouveau jewellery.

Geometric style (1050–700 BC)
The Mycenae civilisation was destroyed by invading Dorians from the North. Greece went into a period of darkness that lasted for three hundred years (similar in some ways to the middle ages in Europe). However, during this period of artistic inactivity one unique element arose, pottery. Originally simple geometric designs on pots were made at the beginning of the bronze age. These developed, with great vigour, until the new geometric style of ceramics was fully realised between 900–700 BC. The most striking feature of this pottery decoration was its orderliness and precision. **Copymaster 77** contains a detailed image of a typical Geometric amphorae design. Areas were clearly marked

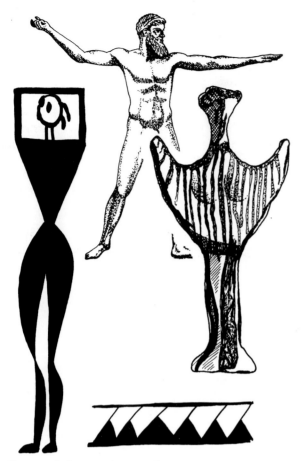

Geometric human form and sculpture

out with a logical and harmonious plan. The different elements were held together in a unified way while retaining their own clearly defined character. Vases, amphorae and craters (of all sizes) were masterpieces of technical perfection, pure shapes were richly decorated. It is worth pointing out to your children that these magnificent ceramics are a major art form and that they existed at a time when sculpture, painting and architecture did not exist in a significant way. Also, in the representation of simple, stylised human beings these ceramics held the seed which was to develop into that great form of art of Classical times figurative monumental sculpture.

Links
Medieval illuminated abstract patterns, Islamic fretwork and patterns, Apache baskets and Pueblo painted pottery, mazes, Lowry's stick figures, carpet designs, printed circuit boards, spirals, finger prints, Klee, Miro.

Archaic art (700–490 BC)
At this time the Greeks began to produce monumental sculptures. The earliest stone temples also date from this period. Very often statues of young men (often larger than life and painted) were set up in the temple precincts. These nude statues set in train a whole new genre which has continued ever since. These archaic figures were made according to a strict plan very much in accord with their Egyptians predecessors and they can look rather stiff and awkward to our eyes. Two forms of archaic sculpture are important, the Doric (like the early order of architecture) and the Ionian. The Doric sculptures were massive, and built according to a system. The Ionian were softer with careful handling of surfaces with finely worked lines that drew the eyes upwards. These two types united to produce the Classical style found in the Parthenon.

Links
Sculpture of Egyptians, Medieval religious sculptures, early Mexican sculptures.

The Classical style (480–350 BC)
The Classical period is noted for major achievements in sculpture and architecture which have continued their influence until today. The earlier, rather rigid, figure sculptures were replaced by those which were much more natural. This naturalness was enhanced by an ability to place the main weight on one leg of a figure (contrapposto). This ability gave artists the opportunity to make much more lifelike and complex interlocking sculptures. Harmonious proportions emphasised the ideal form while faces and the position of arms and hands did contain expressive characteristics. The development of the Classical style reached its high point in the Parthenon. Artists managed to express in sculpture heroic human qualities while still referring to godlike images. The work of Praxiteles (particularly Aphrodite) exemplifies the fineness of form combined with profound ideas that have so much influenced the whole of western art. Architecture achieved a new majestic place where proportion, style and technical expertise in the use of materials have provided a bench mark for succeeding periods. **Copymaster 78** contains a detailed illustration of the three main orders: Doric, Corinthian and Ionic.

Links
Sculptures of Donatello, Michelangelo, Rodin, Henry Moore, paintings of Raphael, Michelangelo, David.

Hellenistic style (340–30 BC)
Over this period Greek culture was spread throughout all the lands bordering the Mediterranean. Sculptors gave more attention to moods, feelings, passions and dynamic qualities rather than simple realism. The most imposing work of this period is portraiture. The enduring vision of the Greeks was the union of mortals with gods.

ROMAN ART

Greece's first conquerors, the Romans (145 BC to AD 395) pillaged and devastated all the great sanctuaries and cities of Greece. The Romans took with them all the vast quantity of bronze and marble statues that existed in Greece. The spirit of Greek art, however, did not die, in fact it conquered Rome. Generally speaking, Roman art was merely a pale imitation of what had come before. Notable exceptions are the superb mosaics, wall paintings and engineering feats such as aqueducts and viaducts. Wall paintings developed from flat style to a point where perspective and illusions of space were carefully constructed and full of architectural details. A Roman style of portrait and relief sculpture existed, they were highly realistic and personal. The idea that the Romans were led by divine rulers gave rise to a somewhat idealised vision in the way emperors were portrayed. Relief sculptures (such as Trajan's column) were full of narrative details, rather like a strip cartoon. Many centuries after the plunder of Greece, copies of Greek sculptures were discovered by the great artists of the Italian Renaissance who brought about a rebirth of Classical ideals. Greek and Roman ideas were spread across the world, not only through Europe but also to America and Asia.

MEDIEVAL ART

C79 –81

After the decline of the Roman empire Europe experienced a series of period that include Byzantine, Romanesque, and Gothic until the Renaissance asserted itself.

Byzantine art (330–AD 1450)
This is the art of the Christian Empire that took over from the Romans in the east of the Mediterranean. This style of art and architecture survived until the seventeenth century in Russia and the Balkan countries. The art is mainly religious, churches being decorated with carvings, mosaics and frescoes. The subject matter was regulated by the church with a strict limitation on the way the human figure was shown and the use of plants and geometric motifs was highly developed in response to church dogma. Icons painted with simple tempera techniques were also heavily controlled in terms of style and layout. The Byzantine style of architecture brings together Oriental, Roman and Greek styles. Classical purity of form is replaced by a rich surface embellishment. Byzantine art continued until the fall of Constantinople to the Turks in the mid-fifteenth century. **Copymaster 79** contains a typical composition for an icon. Discuss with your children what kind of colours to use before they complete the picture. Gold paint will be needed.

Links
Islamic, Viking, Roman and Greek abstract patterns.

Romanesque art (750–AD 1220)
This period of art was again mainly linked to religious functions. The wide geographical area covered by the Romanesque influence led to considerable variations in style. The illuminated manuscripts are full of complex geometric forms that show Byzantine and eastern influences. While mosaic and fresco paintings were common, probably the most important development was the re-emergence of monumental stone sculpture either as architectural features on in the form of large figures found in the niches of religious buildings. Typical features of Romanesque buildings are the rounded arches and heavy piers and the introduction of the ribbed, groined vault. **Copymaster 80** contains significant architectural and pattern details from this period.

Gothic (1150–1450)
Architecture of this period, particularly cathedrals, featured pointed arches, cross ribbed vaults and flying buttresses. This combination allowed the use of thin stone walls and gave a vertical feeling to the space which was symbolic of man's desire to be close to heaven. The construction techniques allowed stained glass work to be developed to a high standard. In painting, religious imagery was dominant. The Sienese school, including Simone Martini (1284–1344) were influenced by Gothic ideals from France. Martini used linear, rhythmic compositions, his most celebrated work being the Annunciation (1333, Uffizi Florence). Besides Martini, Giotto made important advances in painting. Known as the father of modern painting, Giotto added a sense of space and solidity to his pictures, the like of which had not been seen before. Because Martini is cited in the National Curriculum document and it is often difficult to find examples of his work, I have included a simplified drawing of one of his works as **Copymaster 81**. Your children can discuss his style and propose and use colours for completing the drawing.

Gothic styles and script

The International Gothic style included carefully observed details, fine modelling and the use of light in a poetic way. Other artists of the period include Hans Holbein the Elder (1465–1524), and Grunewald (1475–1528) whose detailed and emotionally painful images of Christ in his Isenheim Altarpiece is a positive counter blast to the Renaissance. Hieronymus Bosch (1452–1516) was a master of a disturbing form of fantasy, the nightmare images of the Middle Ages gave much to the development of the Surrealist imagery of the twentieth century. Choose images to show your children very carefully as they can be disturbing.

The illustrations on page 79 show typical English styles of Gothic architecture, early English, decorated, and perpendicular. Another important development in art was calligraphy which was practised mainly in monasteries. Gothic script has thick down-strokes and thin up-strokes as shown in the illustration.

Links
Expressionism and Surrealism of the twentieth century, music and the rather macabre Gothic stories of the nineteenth century.

RENAISSANCE ART

Many people say that European painting began in Florence and Sienna at the start of the fourteenth century. This period is typified by notions of rebirth of Classical ideals. Rebirth does not mean of course that there was no art in the Middle Ages, rather that there was a growing humanism and a tendency away from the Gothic religious imagery.

Early Renaissance (AD 1400–1500)
This period includes a uneasy coexistence between humankind and God, of religious and humanist ideas. Renaissance ideas spread slowly throughout Europe. The focal point was Italy where linear perspective was invented by the architect Filippo Brunelleschi (1375–1446) and developed by a number of painters including Ucello (1396–1475) and Piero della Francesca (1420–92). Again in Italy, Leonardo da Vinci first used the method of dark and light (chiaroscuro) and developed oil painting as a new technique, while Raphael (1483–1520) and Titian defined the laws of Classical art. Another famous artist, Sandro Botticelli (1445–1520) from Florence, had a highly individual style which was strongly linear. His flowing and sweet images of women did much to inspire the Pre-Raphaelites of nineteenth century England. Other important 'rebirths' included secular portraits which had not been painted since Roman times and landscape painting as a new genre. Classical ideals also were brought to the fore in sculpture with Donatello and the massive works of Michelangelo.

Elsewhere in Europe Gothic imagery was sustained for longer. In the Low Countries Jan van Eyck (1385–1441) and Pieter Breugel (1530–69) were very important Renaissance painters.

Jan Van Eyck (1385–1441)
Arnolfini Wedding Portrait is the earliest surviving interior scene painted in oil on a panel. This jewel-like work full of symbolism and interesting imagery is well worth studying with your children. The handling of atmosphere, light and the feeling of space is quite remarkable. The composition, drawing on the tradition of illuminated manuscripts, is a masterpiece which unites Renaissance ideals with a medieval perspective. This work started a period of three hundred years of importance for the art of the Lowlands.

Breugel (1530–1569)
Breugel had a strong individual style which he used to describe all that he observed in the country life of Belgium. He was a witty realist. Look at the painting of the *Blind Leading the Blind* and read your children the passage from St Matthew 'If the blind lead the blind, both shall fall into the ditch'. The painting is direct and brutally frank. The conditions of the group of six figures are poignant. The leader falls while the others, not knowing their fate, are about to roll together in a heap. Their clothes show the owners' obvious poverty while details of the tranquil stream, foliage and the church in the background are totally convincing. Breugel, a great landscape painter, stood out against the Italian influences of Flemish art.

Albrecht Durer (1471–1528)
Durer brought the Renaissance to Germany. He travelled widely and made a number of visits to Venice. He met Giovanni Bellini and was heavily influenced by Leonardo and Mantegna.

High Renaissance (AD 1500–1527)
Includes works by Michelangelo, Raphael and Leonardo.

Michelangelo (1475–1564)
Michelangelo produced paintings and sculptures which are compositions made up of volumes and surfaces depicting the futility of human strength struggling against the power of God. His massive sculpture of David (five metres high) owed much to the Greek statues that he had seen in Rome. His major work, *The Last Judgement*, in the Sistine chapel is typified by violence as the massive Christ strikes down mankind. At the same time that Michelangelo was working, the architect, Bramante, brought back the proportions of antiquity to buildings, re-establishing classical orders and designs.

Leonardo da Vinci (1452–1519)
He experimented with colours as part of his huge scientific interest. He used a variety of binders in his development of oil painting. His unfortunate use of bitumen and fugitive colours have had awful results on his paintings as they have deteriorated badly. Leornardo, a man with universal interests, tried to deal with the psychological innermost feelings of his

subjects. The most obvious example of this is the Mona Lisa.

Raphael (1483–1520)
He produced a visual definition of harmony and balance. He is known for his use of simple, pure oval face shapes that typify his Madonnas and which were taken from classical sculptures. Raphael's portraits are calm and full of composure.

This short period of time was overwhelmed by the power of the three Italian masters who brought into full focus the Classical ideals of purity, harmony and balance together with the technical virtuosity to match nature. All truly Renaissance artists sought to give their own versions of man's place within the universe. (Remember that at this time Europe was in tumult because of new scientific discoveries and religious controversy that also shattered much of the mythology of the Gothic world.) As this period passed, many artists from Amsterdam to Madrid, unable to match the power and vision of Michelangelo, Raphael and Leonardo, followed an easier path into the distorted world of Mannerism.

Links
Perspective, viewers, making and using oil paints, shapes and faces, proportion of the figure.

POST-RENAISSANCE ▶

Mannerism (AD 1530–1600)
This style was founded in Italy and was a reaction to the Classicism of the Renaissance. The style spread all over Europe. El Greco (1541–1614) typifies the style in which emotional forces and elongation of the figures were combined with distorted perspective to produce highly subjective images. Other artists include Tintoretto (1518–1594), Parmigianino (1503–1540) and the sculptor, Cellini (1500–1571).

Baroque (1600–1750)
Sometimes rather a theatrical style that dominated European art and architecture. This dramatic form found its most perfect exponent in Bernini (1598–1680) who combined architecture and sculpture with a clever use of light and space to give an emotional immediacy to his work (particularly the *Ecstasy of St Theresa*). Painters of this period include:

Caravaggio (1573–1610)
A lively character often involved in fights and scandals. His use of contemporary costumes and sharply projected realism were progressive and radical. He worked directly on to canvas from his models rather than from sketches or studies. He arranged the lighting of his subjects (very often from a single strong source from the upper right hand side) to accentuate strong tonal contrasts. His use of light and dark, chiaroscuro, influenced Rubens and Rembrandt in a profound way.

Links
Take contrasty photographs with one light source, contrast Caravaggio's work with that of the soft and atmospheric Impressionists (refer to the chapter on Colour and light).

Peter Paul Rubens (1577–1640)
Rubens was a most energetic and prolific artist. He travelled widely and was influenced by all styles except Gothic. He studied from life and nature. His paintings of women combined Italian ideals within his own unique style. He imported Baroque art into northern Europe. Rubens' method of working has been recorded. Apparently he would sit and think for a long period then with great passion and speed, paint with a powerful driving impulse.

Links
Look at the work of Rubens and Renoir in their paintings of women. Rubens' *The Three Graces* can be compared with Renoir's *Judgement of Paris*. Both have Classical backgrounds, both contain soft and realistic styles based on observational work from life. Other links can be found in prehistoric, Cycladic, Classical and Romantic images of women.

Frans Hals (1580–1666)
A contemporary of Rembrandt whose work is extremely lively. Your children will find his work very accessible, his portraits can be compared with art from all periods.

Links
Portraits of all kinds, ancient Egyptian, Coptic, photographs, posters, stamps.

Rembrandt (1606–69)
While many Dutch artists kept clear of religious subjects, Rembrandt often sought inspiration from the bible. He was most impressed by the theatrical lighting used by Caravaggio which he adapted in his dramatic religious works. Probably of more interest to your children will be his amazing visual autobiography of sixty self portraits that describe his whole adult life. Rembrandt's preoccupation with human feelings makes him uniquely approachable. His life was full of huge changes in fortune but he remained strong and steadfast in developing his own personal visual style. You may find that the thickly applied paint of his later work provides a good link with Van Gogh and modern abstract art techniques.

Links
Get your children to collect family photographs and make two or three portraits of family members in youth, middle and old age; Van Gogh.

Pieter de Hooch (1629–84)
A perfect example of his art is *The Courtyard of a House in Delft* (National Gallery London). The wonderful light

81

is typical of de Hooch's and Vermeer's art. The happy domestic scene of apparent naturalness is, in fact, a carefully controlled and executed abstract composition of shapes and lines. Your children can emulate this scene from their own sketches of home life.

Other artists to consider include Vermeer (1632–75), Van Dyke (1599–1641), Claude Lorrain (1600–82) and Velasquez (1599–1660).

The Dutch school includes landscape painting with its main exponents being Ruisdael (1628–82), Van Goyen (1596–1656) and Rembrandt. Whilst poetic, the paintings are also realistic and have had a huge influence on the development of nineteenth century landscape painting and subsequently on Impressionism.

Links
Topics on 'The sea', 'Colour and light' and 'Food and farming'.

NINETEENTH CENTURY ART

C70 –73

Neoclassical
Classical influences were revived by artists such as Jacques Louis David (1748–1825) and Ingres (1780–1867). Romanticism (an important nineteenth century movement) followed as a reaction to Neo-classicism.

Romanticism
Goya (1746–1828) changed his approach from Neo-classicist to Romantic. Other important Romanticists are Gericault (1791–1824) and Delacroix (1798–1863). These were followed by the dignified realism of Millet (1814–75) and the rough images of human life by Courbet (1819–77) (an artist of striking realism who rebelled against both Romantic and Classical ideals) and the quiet pastorals of Theodore Rousseau (1812–67). These in turn (according to some sources), with the influences of Turner and Constable, led to the development of Impressionism, the ultimate attempt at naturalism.

Impressionism
The chief exponents of Impressionism include Auguste Renoir (1841–1919), Claude Monet (1840–1926), Alfred Sisley (1839–99), Edgar Degas (1834–1917), and Georges Seurat (1859–91).

In sculpture Auguste Rodin (1840–1917) is easily the most important nineteenth century sculptor. Notable in his wide range of work are *The Thinker*, *The Kiss* and the *Balzac* monument. He brought a new directness and fluidity to figures that Henry Moore extended into the twentieth century.

Links
The topics on 'Colour and light', 'Food and farming', look at Monet's early paintings which were academic and strongly tonal (although some people link him with the Impressionists).

Expressionism
This modern school was started by Van Gogh (1853–90). His search for a way of expressing feelings and visual effects through heightened colours and distorted shapes and lines found its roots with Grunewald (c. 1480–1528). Van Gogh (who really defies categorisation) through his use of strong colours, thick expressive strokes and a simple direct composition brought a new freshness and moved away from the Impressionist interest in fleeting moments to a highly personal vision. He led the way for many major twentieth century artists. His unique contribution will be memorable for all children.

Links
Mood paintings and the chapter on 'Colour and light'.

English art
In England landscape was a very important genre with different kinds of exponents: John Crome (1768–1821), whose main influence was the Dutch school (Hobbema); John Constable (1776–1837) and JMW Turner (1775–1821), while making their own unique images both contributed to the development of Impressionism; whilst Samuel Palmer (1805–81) made small, intense visionary landscapes. The Pre-Raphaelites looked back to a mythical time in a languid, somewhat chocolate-box way. Another Victorian artist, John (mad) Martin (1789–1854), was a highly melodramatic painter. His massive and spectacular historical scenes are 'over the top' by today's standards. One of his most memorable paintings is *The Plains of Heaven*. Compare his excessive theatrical style with the religious works of Rembrandt. The work of William Morris (1834–96) (**Copymasters 70–73**) in the decorative arts is most important.

TWENTIETH CENTURY ART

The artists and schools of the twentieth century are so varied that the ones you need to cover are given alphabetically below.

Abstract art
Greek writers (Plato) first described abstract art. The beauty of lines, shapes and surfaces was preferred to all

others, as these were considered to be pure, unchanging and natural. Leonardo used stains on walls as starting points for landscape compositions. (Try this with your children and link it to blot paintings.) For religious reasons the art of Islam is devoid of human forms and has raised pattern-making and geometric designs to a high spiritual art form. In a similar way much of medieval art was dominated by the importance of abstract patterns. Since Impressionism and the development of photography some western artists have raised abstract art to a 'fine art'. Cubism was the father of modern, western abstract art. Important abstract artists include Braque, Picasso, Kandinsky, Klee, Miro, Mondrian followed by the Abstract Expressionists such as Jackson Pollock. Optical abstract art exponents include Vasarely and Bridget Riley.

Bauhaus

This school of design and architecture employed some important teachers such as Klee and Kandinsky. If you look around and see modern blocks of flats and offices then you and your children are seeing the results of (often misinterpreted) Bauhaus ideas about architecture.

Links

Look at high rise blocks, paintings of Mondrian, songs like 'Little boxes'.

Bonnard, Pierre (1867–1947)

An individualist amongst the Impressionists. He was strongly influenced by Japanese prints (their flat decorative compositions). He painted intimate, quiet, brilliant interiors.

Links

Vermeer, de Hooch and contrasts with Rembrandt and Caravaggio.

Brancusi, Constanin (1876–1957)

A sculptor who specialised in simple smooth abstract shapes. He was a friend of Modigliani.

Links

Paintings of Modigliani and Eskimo and Cycladic sculptures.

Braque, Georges (1882–1962)

Building on the work of Cezanne, he worked with Picasso to develop the new artistic style of Cubism. This is simply the showing of a number of views of a subject (often a figure or still life) simultaneously in a painted or collaged composition. His later vigorous still lives are wonderful. Cubism is the forerunner of all modern abstract art.

Calder, Alexander (1898–1976)

The inventor of mobiles, his paintings and sculptures were strongly influenced by Miro.

Links

Making mobiles, paintings by Miro, and the cut out paper collages of Matisse.

Cezanne, Paul (1839–1906)

The first modern artist who rightly belongs in the twentieth century. His aim was to replace

Impressionism with a more substantial art. He sought to paint pictures (mainly landscapes) which relied on strong structural forms and a sculptural use of colour that dispensed with traditional perspective.

Dali, Salvador (1904–1989)

Best known as a Surrealist, Dali started as a Cubist. His sometimes vulgar and excessive images are full of improbable associations of realistic painted objects. Melting watches, beans and distorted figures are mixed in ways that defy analysis.

Links

Dreams, memories and the paintings of Archimboldi, Magritte and Miro.

Giacommetti, Alberto (1901–1966)

A sculptor with particularly interesting final style. Having spent some time as a Surrealist he returned to realistic thin, single figures. He often built up the sculptures from plaster on a wire armature and netting.

Links

Early figurines from Greece, the elongated relief figures from ancient Egypt and the stick figures of Lowry.

Jahns, Jasper (1930–)

A pop artist who uses collage, paint, transferred images, plastics and metal casts. His bronze beer cans can be emulated by Junior children using plaster and clay.

Kandinsky, Vasily (1866–1944)

Using calligraphic and expressive lines, Kandinsky is the founder of pure abstract painting.

Links

Klee, Miro and the free expressive painting of Jackson Pollock.

Klee, Paul (1879–1940)

A lyrical, free fantastic artist. Memorable for his 'taking a line for a walk'. He was a close friend of Kandinsky.

Kollwitz, Kathe (1867–1945)

Famous for her series of 'Mother and child' works. Her work is full of personal passion as she recalled the death of her son and grandson in two world wars.

Links

The family, Van Gogh, Rembrandt's drawings, war images.

Lichtenstein, Roy (1923–)

A leading US Pop artist who uses cartoon images blown up to a large scale. He has experimented with take offs of Picasso portraits and features everyday consumer products in his paintings. The Tate Gallery has a number of works including 'Whaam' a painting of an attacking aircraft.

Links

Advertising, images of Americana, dot pictures (Pointillism and newspaper pictures magnified).

Matisse, Henri (1869–1954)

His wild use of colour (he was a Fauve 'wild animal') was followed by a period in which he was influenced by the patterns and colours of Near Eastern art. In his final years he produced some elegant cut paper collages.

Miro, Juan (1893–1983)
The leading Spanish Surrealist. His work became more abstract as he matured, although his shapes always had specific meanings 'it is always a sign of something ... a man ... a bird or something else.'

Links
Prehistoric cave paintings, Geometric style pottery, North American signs and symbols, ancient Egyptian hieroglyphs.

Modigliani, Amedeo (1884–1920)
His paintings are fluid and somewhat Mannerist in style. He was influenced by African sculpture and Picasso and echoes Botticelli's images of women.

Links
Botticelli, Cycladic, African and Eskimo sculptures.

Mondrian, Piet (1871–1944)
His work moved from fairly realistic landscape paintings through a series of semi-abstract tree studies to a full geometric abstract art that combines rectangular designs complemented by a strong sense of colour.

Links
Islamic patterns, colour shape exercises, **Copymasters 20–22, 42–3**.

Moore, Henry (1898–1986)
Probably the major sculptor of the twentieth century, thought of by some as the modern day Michelangelo. His sculptures are characterised by their size, smoothness and open shapes. He produced a remarkable series of drawings of people sheltering in the tube stations during World War II.

Links
Prehistoric monuments such as Stonehenge, pre-Classical sculptures, Egyptian sculpture, sculpture of the Mayan civilisation and Michelangelo.

Op Art
An abstract form of art that aims at producing visual effects by combing and overlaying patterns. Main artists are Vasarely and Bridget Riley.

Picasso, Pablo (1881–1973)
The pre-eminent artist of the twentieth century. He led movements and was involved in most major developments. He has painted a wide variety of subjects with different palettes and in a wide variety of styles. The major influences on his work are African art, Cezanne and Gothic imagery, the drawings of Ingres and Classical ideals. When discussing his work with your children, *Guernica* really must be included. The background of the Spanish Civil War that stimulated Picasso's great statement about the awfulness and beastliness of conflict can provide a focal point from which your children can analyse the way he painted the picture. Consider the semi-abstract and distorted images, the position of the parts and how the work was received by people.

Pollock, Jackson (1912–1956)
An action painter who dripped, splashed and spread paint onto canvases. He said that he wanted to express his feelings directly rather than to illustrate them. Ask your children what the difference is between expressing and illustrating.

Links
Drip, splatter and finger painting.

Pop Art
A style of art that uses the world of advertising and glamour as its main subject area. Starting in the 1950s in the UK, and developed further in the USA in the 1960s. Some key figures include Paolozzi, Hockney, Warhol, Lichtenstein and the sculptor Oldenberg (who specialised in large soft sculptures).

Links
History of advertising, films, cartoon characters.

GLOSSARY OF TERMS

Abstract Art
Aesthetic appreciation of formal aspects such as line, colour rather than representational quality of work. Not a modern concept, examples are found throughout art history.

Action painting
Form of Abstract expressionism often associated with Jackson Pollock. Similar to drip painting techniques used by young children.

Aegean Art
Twenty-fifth–twelfth centuries BC Greece, mainland and islands. Try to get images of Cycladic sculptures as these are very elegant and simple in form and interesting to juniors.

Arts and crafts movement
Movement in England starting approximately 1865. Ruskin and William Morris were central to this reaction against the growing industrialisation of crafts. They wished to make a return to more individual craftworks of high quality and reasonable prices.

Black-figured pottery
Like the red-figured pottery, this is ancient Greek. Featuring either black or red decorations on red or black backgrounds. This can be a good point of departure for pupils when designing their own pots.

Book of Hours
Richly illuminated books of prayers. Excellent for linking with decorative alphabets and handwriting patterns.

Cruciform
Cross-shaped as in the floor layout of churches, use the shape drawn on a baseboard as a starting point for models of churches.

Dyes
Soluble colours used for colouring fabrics.

Earth colours
Paints made from earths such as red oxide, early forms of colours that can be made up using pestle and mortar in class.

Expressionism
Best known exponent is Van Gogh, his work stresses the intensity of feelings that are shown through a personal use of colour, shape and textures. Other artists include: Kokoschka, Munch, Rouault and Soutine. Introducing painting activities for pupils by discussing particular feelings such as anger, fear, happiness can be very effective.

Fast colours
Colours that do not fade. You can easily set up some simple experiments by selecting a number of colours, painting them on sheets of paper, covering half of each sample then placing all the samples in strong sunshine for a few weeks. Afterwards uncover the protected part of the samples and compare with the unprotected elements.

Fauves
Group of expressionist artists including Matisse, Derain, Dufy, Marquet and Rouault, active from early twentieth century.

Fresco
Mural painted directly onto fresh lime plaster. As children pass through Key Stage 2 they can try painting onto small plaster animals with watered-down PVA paints, building up colours slowly by overpainting.

Geometric patterns
Hellenic art (870–700 BC) and Islamic art are full of rich decorative geometric patterns. Use the Copymasters to build appreciation of tessellation and making abstract designs.

Greek art
Hellenic art

Greek pottery
Vital for understanding life in ancient Greece and for appreciating fine shapes and design.

Icons
Painted orthodox religious images usually on wood panels.

Illumination
The art of decorating manuscripts, often with large decorated leading letters of text. Try to introduce decorative alphabets in class or individual books.

Impressionism
Form of art that paid special attention to using pure colours to paint images (often painted outdoors) that celebrated light and atmosphere, Monet, Renoir, Pissaro, Sisley and Degas. Many of these were impressed by the work of Constable and Turner.

Objective art
Art that is the antithesis of abstract art. It includes cave paintings and all works that rely on representing subjects.

Op art
1960s Art that uses patterns and colours to produce optical effects, Vasarely and Bridget Riley are the main exponents. **Copymaster 97** contains a simple pattern that can be used to introduce making simple optical designs.

Pattern
For children it means either a plan for a painting or model, or the motif from which a repeated image can be made by painting, printing or rubbing.

Pigment
Fine colour powder without any extender, binder or medium. Usually defined by association with the source, such as earth colours. You can try to mix small quantities of real pigment with different binders such as egg white, linseed oil, PVA or even hot wax.

Prehistoric art
Most notable are the cave paintings of Lascaux in France and those of Altimara in Spain. The extreme magical importance of this art, to control elements of nature, can be compared with the more simple observations of nature which make up much of art.

Primitive art
The art of Africa and other groups of people from non-westernised cultures. Typical art objects are masks, carvings and other religious objects from metal, wood, clay or textiles.

Proportion
The relationship of parts to each other and to the whole. Pupils can trace around each other, making the size of heads, eyes, arms, then measure and compare to see how many heads make a body for example.

Realism
Realistic representation of people, animals and scenes without distortion.

Style
A particular way of grouping work together, either by time, place or artistic characteristics that cross between time and place, for example, impressionist, realist, futurist or Flemish.

Surrealism
Art that is linked to dreams and the subconscious mind.

CERAMICS

The majority of contemporary industrial pottery is considered to be hopelessly bad in both form and decoration. Banality, pretentiousness and crudity in colour are the hallmarks of most domestic pottery. Bring examples of good craft pottery into school and also some examples of the gross designs that pass themselves off as pottery. Discuss with your children what makes good and bad design. Refer to ancient forms from Greece, Japan and China and examine the limitations of hand-produced ware. Go to museums or arrange to make a trip to a local potter's workshop. Look at the rich vein of English pottery. See the medieval pitchers and platters which have such simple dignified forms. They have a kind of 'honesty'. What does this kind of honesty mean? The range of beauty found in primitive pottery of Africa, Greece, North and South America often found its source in the hands of women who worked without wheels and with the simplest of tools. Look at the differences between hand built and wheel thrown ware (refer to Activity 113 for this).

Look at the cost of simple, good craft pots, plates and cups and saucers, compare these with those commercial items that can be bought in shops. Which would bring a little beauty into everyday life? Can a more beautiful environment change the lives of people? Ask your children about these ideas.

Pottery can give your children the chance to build an appreciation of aesthetic qualities and manual and technical skills. The basic skills in this section are general to many activities using clay but they are related directly to making, drying and decorating functional ceramic items such as pots and tiles.

Materials and equipment
Purchase either buff or red plastic clay. If you can get and use local clay so much the better. You should remember that any clay that you dig needs to be tested for shrinkage (any more than 10% is no good and you will need to add grog). Also, home-prepared clay needs to be weathered before use (see Leach, B., *The Potters Book* published by Faber and Faber, for details on this). You will also need buckets for glazes, a variety of sieves for straining the glazes and slips, bowls, jugs, sponges, modelling tools, sieves and sieving brushes, brushes, fabric for making slabs on, damp cloths (for covering partly finished work made from white or fine clay), wood for the frames, scrap materials with which work may be imprinted, glue. Plastic bins and polythene bags for storing clay and partly completed work, blunt knives and glazes and slips, hacksaw blades and rubber and metal 'kidneys' are very useful for working leather-hard clay.

Storage of clay
Keep your clay in a cool damp, frost-free place. Ideally keep it in plastic bags inside a plastic dustbin. Another approach recommended by Leach is to mix up enough plaster of Paris to form a 4 cm covering of the bottom of the bin, allow the plaster to set. Then put a couple of pieces of battening underneath a wooden base (see diagram) in the bottom of the bin. You can then keep the atmosphere damp inside the bin by pouring small amounts of water over the plaster. The clay will remain damp (without getting mushy) by being kept on the wooden plinth.

If your children are using white clay then you may need to store work that is underway by covering it with

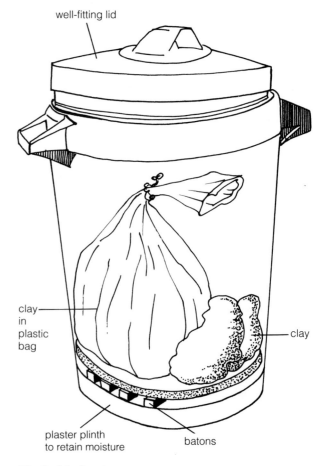

Plastic bin for storage

86

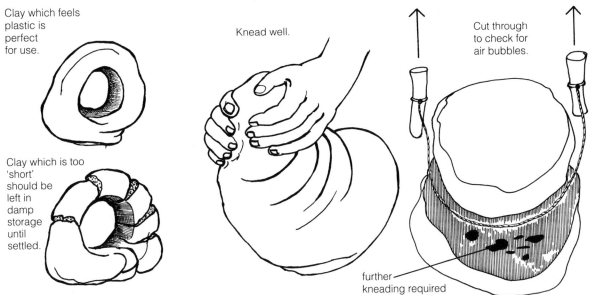

Clay which feels plastic is perfect for use.

Knead well.

Cut through to check for air bubbles.

Clay which is too 'short' should be left in damp storage until settled.

further kneading required

Testing plasticity, wedging and kneading

damp cloths. Clay must be in good condition before it can be worked. For general use it needs to be plastic and evenly textured. To check its condition roll out a thin rope or coil. Wrap this around a finger, if the surface is smooth it is ready to use, if the surface is cracked then the clay is 'short' and needs to be left for a while to settle. To check whether or not the clay is free from air bubbles use a wire and cut through the clay. If there are air bubbles you will need to wedge and knead it until there are none left.

Managing clay work

Clay has the advantage of being cheap, versatile and great fun. Some teachers believe that it is inherently messy. It does not need to be any more messy than paint. Proper preparation and storage are, of course, vital. Ideally you need a small separate room or corner where water can be used and cleared up easily. The floor covering should be vinyl tiles. Do not work near carpeted areas. You will need stout work tables covered with hessian, canvas or cotton duck, wooden boards or newsprint. Do not allow your children to work on

plastic surfaces as these tend to produce a lot of flaked and dusty clay. Remember that silica, present in clay and glazes, is a health hazard so the over-riding health aim is to work in a dust-free environment. Ceramics should be worked with abrasives when leather-hard and not when thoroughly dried or fired. Take note of the technical information that accompanies products. Use damp cloths to wipe up dry clay or glazes. Access to a kiln is vital to complete clay processes. When using plaster do not pour excess down the drain! Use a siphon tube in the waste hole to stop rubbish going down the drain. When using coloured slips for decoration they must be used before the biscuit firing. Glazes are applied after the biscuit firing.

Activity 228: Thumb or pinch pots

Pinching is the most basic of all clay processes. A small ball of clay is hollowed by pinching to form a pot.

Activity 229: Making a coiled pot

Pots and hollow forms can be constructed with thin ropes or coils of clay. The ridges can be smoothed out. Get the children to knead a couple of handfuls of clay.

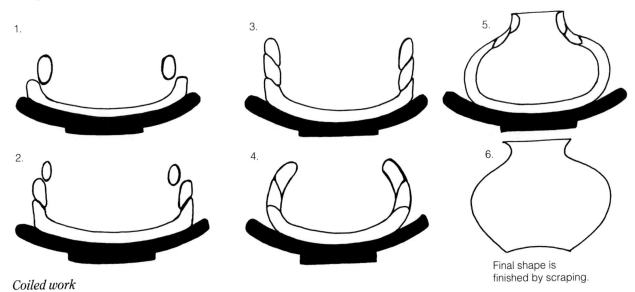

1.

2.

3.

4.

5.

6.

Final shape is finished by scraping.

Coiled work

Form into a ball and roll it out on a flat damp surface to form a stumpy cylinder. Cut a piece and roll that out with both hands into a long cylinder about 1 cm diameter. Care needs to be taken to make the 'ropes' or coils of clay smooth and without ridges. Make several coils of clay. Now coil up one roll to form a circular base of a pot about 10 cms diameter. Get the children to flatten and smooth the coils to make a solid mass. Take another rope of clay and coil it around the edge of the base, round and up, pressing each ring firmly on to the one below to press out any air cavities which might explode in firing. Level off the top, and use finger tips to smooth the inside and outside of the pot. The pot can be decorated by means of incised lines, coloured slip, glaze or if the pot is not going to be fired then ordinary water-based paints can be used on the dry pot.

Activity 230: Making slabs and tiles

Making decorated tiles is described in the same topic in Activity 27. Alternatively your children can make and use slabs in the following way. Square or rectangular shapes can be built up by using flat slabs of clay about 1 cm thick. The slabs are easily and quickly made between two pieces of wood (laths) 1 cm thick about 15 cms apart on a piece of canvas. Beat or roll the clay in to the hollow, filling it completely. Scrape off superfluous clay with a straight edge, then use a rolling pin to flatten the top surface. (Lift the clay occasionally to release it for further rolling.) When the clay is about 1 cm thick it is ready for use. You may wish to nail the laths in place. Alternatively roll the clay out directly on canvas without wooden guides.

Activity 231: Joining slabs

Your children can make pots, containers or sculptures by joining slabs and combining them with slices of extruded clay shapes and textured finishes. To make a simple container draw the five sides as a net (remember the thickness of the clay in calculating the sides). Transfer the outline of this simple net on to the clay. Mark the surface with a tool to mark the outlines. Then cut almost all the way through the clay to the board. A blunt butter knife is suitable for this. Let the slab dry

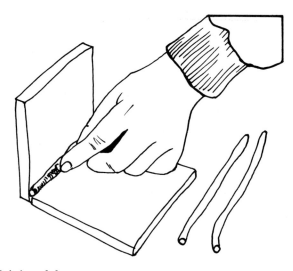

Joining slabs

out a little to toughen up. To assemble the parts, roughen the edges to be joined and prepare a thin rope of clay. Apply a thick slip to the edges to be fixed. Hold one side against the base and work a piece of the clay rope firmly into the angle between the two parts. Press the edges well together, complete the other sides in the same way. If your children use an old wet toothbrush to roughen up the edges to be joined, a slurry is formed and really helps ensure a good joint. This technique can be used with all kinds of slab work; making imaginary buildings, sculptures and decorated boxes.

Activity 232: Making mould-formed platters

Refer to Activity 117 for details of this process.

Activity 233: Decorating surfaces

Surfaces can be decorated in many ways. One of the easiest is to mark, incise and texture the surface. Discuss how textures can affect the look of ceramics with your children. Make an interesting display of visual textures and crayon rubbings from surfaces. Now you can show how clay can be used to 'take rubbings'. Roll out thick slabs of clay (or use damp slab pots), press, scratch and mark the surface all over, or press ready-textured objects into the clay. Beads, bark, hands, baskets or rough fabrics will make good impressions.

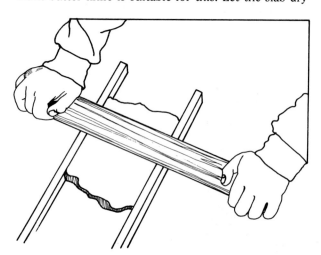

Rolling clay and making tiles

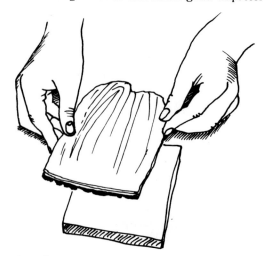

Pressing clay

Small samples of each textured surface can be cut and glazed to make pendants or a library of textures with notes about how and when they were made. Get your children to discuss how they have made their textures.

The following activities deal with decorative methods: Activity 80: Agate ware tiles; Activity 81: Slip decoration with paper stencils; Activity 116: Slip decoration; Activity 171: Painted and incised lines; Activity 172: Using a whirler; Activity 173: Stamping lines.

Activity 234: Drying work prior to firing

All ceramics should be dried carefully and slowly before they are fired. If you hurry the process claywork can crack. A cupboard over a radiator is useful or a long period in a warm room. The stage when clay can still be trimmed and finished is called 'leather hard'. This means that the clay has dried and shrunk but still retains its original wet colour. Breakages will occur if your children keep poking their work around while it is drying. Often it is quicker to make repairs after firing. Clay that has been dried is called greenware. Inspect the work before firing. Is it thoroughly dry? (If not, it may explode!) Hollow forms need to have a hole pierced in them to allow hot air to escape.

Activity 235: Biscuit firing and loading the kiln

Firing is a very exciting time. After a piece of claywork has been thoroughly dried, it is fired at 1000 or 1100 degrees centigrade. This is called biscuit firing. Besides making the piece hard and resilient it also shrinks it by about 8 per cent. Pack the kiln carefully with a full load. Later, glazing earthenware should be undertaken at about 1080 degrees centigrade. Make yourself familiar with kiln features and the manufacturers instructions before firing your children's work.

Activity 236: Slip decorating and glazing

Work that is not going to be fired can be coloured by using water-based paints and then varnished if required. Coloured slips can be painted on to leather hard clay. Glazing is a coating of glass applied to porous ceramics that is in the 'biscuit' state. Then it is fired again until it fuses into the surface. Glazing is by far the most exciting time, but it may also be the most disappointing. To carry out good glazing your children must have an idea of the finished colours, so carry out test firings on a small piece of fired clay beforehand. The glazes need to be creamy for ease of painting. When firing you should raise the temperature of the kiln quite slowly and after firing cool it down slowly to avoid cracking the glaze.

Activity 237: Line work decorating with slips

The application of painted or poured slip is an interesting and very old method of decorating ceramics. It is very similar to icing a cake. For older children an icing bag full of slip will complete this simile. Make up a creamy slip from clay and water. You may need to sieve this to ensure that it is lump free. Different colours can be added to quantities of the basic slip. Slips should be applied as soon as possible after the piece has been made and is just firm enough to handle. Dampen the surface with a sponge before painting the slip onto the piece.

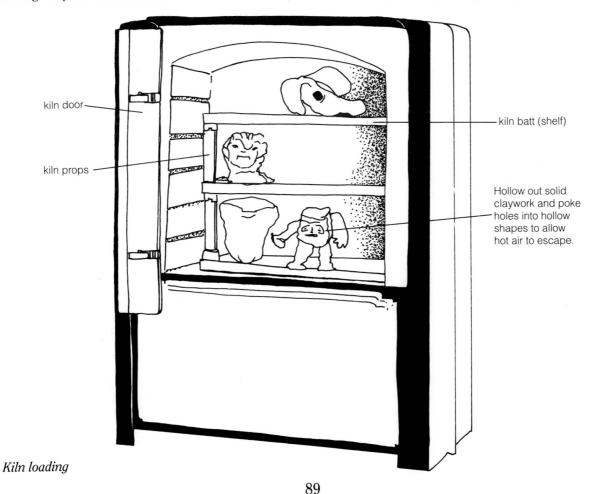

kiln door

kiln props

kiln batt (shelf)

Hollow out solid claywork and poke holes into hollow shapes to allow hot air to escape.

Kiln loading

GLOSSARY OF TERMS

Bat
A plaster, wood or fireclay slab on which pottery is formed and dried. Fireclay bats may be placed in a kiln, plaster bats help absorb excess water.

Biscuit
Fired but not glazed ceramics, also called Bisque.

Bisque fire
The first firing.

Body stain
Colour mixed into the body of the clay, i.e. not a slip covering or glaze. Body stain can, however, be used to make up slips.

Brushwork
Fluid and calligraphic painted patterns can be very attractive. You could extend the work of handwriting patterns to decorating ceramics with considered abstract shapes.

Ceramic colours
Powdered metallic oxides used for glazes, pale when unglazed full colour after firing.

Clay
Available in a number of colours, called plastic when ready to use.

Coil
Method of forming pottery and forms by building up a series of 'ropes' of clay. Smoothed and finished by hand.

Combed decoration
Different coloured slips are applied in bands and then feathered to produce an attractive finish.

Earthenware
Opaque ceramics fired at about 1100 degrees centigrade.

Firing
Process of exposing work to intense heat usually in a kiln. The heat permanently changes the chemical composition and physical nature of the fired substance be it clay or glaze.

Glaze
A thin coating that is fused to ceramics by firing in kiln. It is applied by dipping, spraying or painting. The most common glaze is a transparent one. Take care when making up glaze, it can be a health hazard. Add powder to water after having being sieved through fine mesh. Stir mixed glaze while using so as to ensure a consistent thickness. Pottery is glazed ware.

Glost firing
The second firing, done to vitrify the glaze to biscuit ware. Biscuit ware needs to be porous enough to absorb glaze.

Greenware
Ceramics that have been formed, allowed to dry but have not been fired.

Grog
Ground up, previously fired ceramics, roughly powdered brick or pottery that is added to plastic clay to thicken it and to reduce shrinkage.

Hardening on
Process in which ceramics are heated to 320°C to burn off organic materials present in underglaze decorations. It is used to prevent blistering.

Kiln
A furnace for firing ceramics. Heat inside is measured by pyrometric cones observed through a peephole.

Kneading
After storage, wedged clay requires kneading prior to use to make it more pliable and of consistent texture.

Leather hard
Clay that has dried to the limit of shrinkage while still retaining its wet colouring, can be trimmed and finished in this state.

Lustreware
Ceramics decorated with metallic irridescent glazes.

Mould
Hollow container that is used in casting. The shape of the mould is imparted to a substance such as plaster when it hardens.

Pinched
Method of shaping clay by pinching walls or parts with fingers.

Plastic
Pliable clay.

Press
Method of texturing surface of clay by pressing objects into the plastic surface of the clay.

Pyrometric cones
Clay cones used to determine the temperature of a kiln that does not have a temperature gauge (pyrometer which operates above the range of mercury thermometers).

Scratch and sgraffito
Originally used by Italian potters in the sixteenth century. A coloured body was dipped or painted with white slip, allowed to firm and then engraved through the slip to reveal the design on the coloured base.

Settle
Maturing of clay as it becomes plastic, takes two to eight weeks.

Slab method
Method of making pots or sculptures. Rolled and cut slabs of clay may be bent into various shapes and joined to other slabs by slip or 'ropes' of clay pressed home into joints.

Slip and slip decoration
Creamy liquid mix of clay and water, coloured and used

90

for decorative finish. Slips have a tendency to settle and often form lumps. Shake and sieve slips before use. If a piece is dipped in slip the resulting surface is delightful to work on, being smooth and silky. Use **Copymaster 46**.

Slip casting
Slip poured into a mould made from absorbent plaster and rolled around to cover the whole surface will rapidly dry out. Pour out any excess then when dry add further coats of slip to thicken the wall. When dry the slip cast will shrink away from the mould and produce a perfect smooth cast.

Stencil
Paper stencils can be pressed against the dry clay surface and colour brushed or dabbed over them. Positive (or negative) paper patterns can be stuck to a damp surface which is then dipped into slip, when dry the paper is removed. Leaves can be used for this. It is advisable to keep stencils simple.

Wedge
Thumping clay on a solid base until all air and lumps are removed.

91

DESIGN

ART, DESIGN AND TECHNOLOGY

C8, 32, 50, 55–6, 58

Design is integral to both art and technology. Think of it as a planning or hypothesising stage; the stage when how a thing is going to be made or how it will look is first considered.

In this brief skills section techniques are given which will help to develop your children's abilities to think ahead and to consider the implications of what they wish to do before committing time and resources to the task.

By bringing good quality pieces of craft work, posters or well-designed objects into your school you can help your children to pose questions which will enhance their critical awareness and improve their own practical work. Design can be an important aspect of print-making, ceramics, painting and modelling. A number of processes are used including:

These processes are often most clearly associated with product and graphic design. When your children are involved in design they may well also be concerned with:

- Observing and studying existing products
- Surveys of likes and dislikes
- Criticism. Asking questions such as: Is this poster a success? Can you read it? Do the colours suit the subject?
- Identifying needs or problems
- Imagining solutions to problems
- Finding resources
- Checking the suitability of materials
- Choosing materials and tools
- Drawing

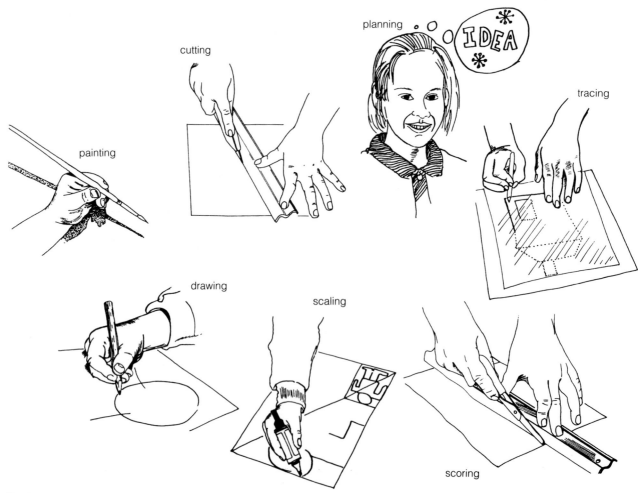

Design processes

- Scaling
- Visualising
- Thinking in 3D, moving from 2D to 3D
- Making
- Thinking about structures
- Making economical use of materials and time
- Changing qualities of materials through manipulation and processes
- Graphic design and packaging
- Testing and evaluation.

Before you start

The activities given below (and those in the Topics section) should be introduced in such a way as to ensure that your children do things that have value and purpose. Do not involve them in pointless or staged design activities. Relate designs closely to the materials which are available for making the products. Wherever possible insist that your children select the materials they will use in advance and specify (approximately) sizes and colours for the finished work.

Materials and equipment

Paints, pencils, rulers, paper, squared and other gridded papers and card (various different grids for scaling and planning are included in the Copymasters), erasers, brushes, palettes and mixing trays, felt tip pens, scissors, illustrations.

Organising space

Probably one of the most important concepts common to all design activities is the appropriate and aesthetic use of space. One of the most common mistakes when designing a poster is to fill in all the white space with images and text, encourage your children to think of open areas positively rather than as empty spaces. Many of the copymasters contain a number of ways to organise flat areas of space. Illustrated below are the Golden Mean and an oriental method which continue to affect profoundly the way pages in magazines are laid out and the proportions of buildings.

Activity 238: Using grids

Nearly all printed matter has an underlying structure, an invisible grid of planning lines. Give your children a variety of newspapers, magazines, labels, packages and ask them to find the grid lines, mark them with felt tip pens, measure the widths. Are there any common factors? What about the sizes of pages? The simplest form of layout is the one column grid. The simplest of

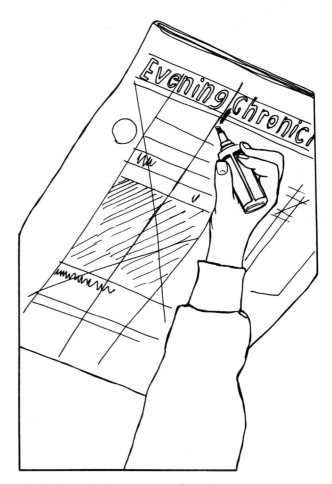

Analysing grids in newspaper layout

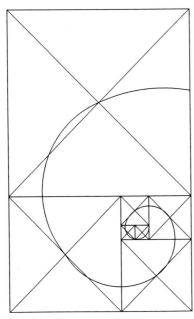

Construction for Golden Mean

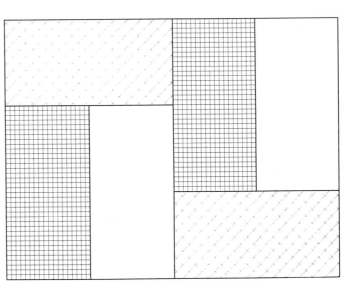

Oriental system for organising space

these has an equal margin all around as shown in the diagram. For facing pages it may be necessary to have a wider margin on the centre folds. Give your children three or four pieces of A4 paper. Ask them to design single column grids that give the impression of luxury, informality or being businesslike. Discuss the placing of headings, pictures and body text.

Activity 239: Newspaper page

Move on from the preceding activity by discussing news stories, local or national with your children. Get them to collect newspaper photographs. Using word processors and Paintbrush® or Draw® type computer graphics get them to produce mock-up sheets for their own newspapers. Use **Copymasters 8**, **32**, **50**, **55–6** and **58** to help with this activity.

Activity 240: Pasting up

Preparing artwork requires a clean and tidy approach. To produce a poster or newsletter will often require several items to be brought together and stuck in place. First, get your children to rough out their designs to scale using felt tip pens or pencils. It can be helpful for your children to use the grid system that will be used for the finished artwork for their roughing out as well. Use **Copymaster 8** to scale up drawings and **Copymaster 50** to help with cropping. Use word processors to produce text and then glue the elements in place on the finished grid.

The Topics section of this book contains a comprehensive range of design activities. For convenience these are listed below.

Architecture
Activity 9: Ancient computing; Activity 10: Large-scale tomb; Activity 31: House for a hot climate.

Fashion
Activity 49: Penguin and bird stencils; Activity 50: Sea sports and beach wear.

Packaging
Activity 119: Healthy food.

Posters and promotional material
Activity 82: Firework poster; Activity 155: Layout and enlarging grids; Activity 156: Typefaces; Activity 157: Promotional posters; Activity 158: Designer video; Activity 215: Seasonal posters.

Other products
Activity 29: Masks for *The chicken*; Activity 30: Plaster relief based on the Parthenon; Activity 51: Design a safer snorkel; Activity 120: Design a crockery set; Activity 121: Design a theatre set; Activity 122: Kitchen fabrics and tiles; Activity 124: Hand seed drill; Activity 174: Trees with faces; Activity 175: Curled paper lines.

GLOSSARY OF TERMS

Colour scheme
The use of dominant colours in a carefully orchestrated whole to give an overall unified impression.

Dry mounting
Method of mounting work by sandwiching a dry laminate between the work and mount and then heating it to melt the laminate and fixing the work in place.

Mat cutting (mounting)
Cutting window mounts for improved display of work.

Portfolio
Large folder for keeping work in good condition.

Template
Useful pattern device for repeating standard motifs or shapes, like a stencil.

DRAWING

INTRODUCTION ▶

When introducing drawing activities the first thing to remember is that everyone can draw and that you can help develop your pupils' skills. At Key Stage 2 children will normally have developed far beyond their first earnest scribbling as infants. At that time drawing was the most immediate way of expressing themselves. Now they have aural and written forms of language skills which will tend to take the edge off the need to make images. At the same time they are now more aware of 'adult art' and may be discouraged by what they feel is their lack of competence in copying the styles of adult art. At this transitional stage you need to be sensitive and flexible in your approach. You can set tasks that will increase your pupils' technical abilities and you should encourage your children's own expressive work while maintaining a questioning and positively critical attitude. As they grow, they will be able to draw, using perspective and adding greater detail through careful modelling. As children become more aware of adult work, they will tackle more difficult problems. Careful development of skills will build their confidence in their ability to succeed. Children will not improve their performance by being left to their own devices. Nor will they develop confidence in their own powers if they are crushed by insensitive comments.

ART HISTORY AND DRAWING ▶

If you wish to link your children's practical activities with the work of other artists it can be very helpful to look at specific elements of the visual language such as line, texture or tone. You can of course take a process or subject based approach by looking at portraits, landscape, plants, architecture and cartoons or the use of techniques or materials.

Elements of visual language and drawing
Line
Compare medieval manuscripts, drawings by Miro and Klee, designs by William Morris, Japanese graphics (or pen drawings by Hokusai) and the way line has been used by cartoonists such as Fougasse, Scarfe and Searle.

Shape
Raphael's oval faces, Mondrian's rectangular designs, Matisse's cut paper shapes.

Tone
Look at the way tone is produced in newspaper images, some through coarse grids of dots sometimes through line images similar to Bewick's work. Seurat, Rembrandt, Holbein and the photographs of Ansel Adams all use tone for different purposes.

Texture
The flicking scratching marks of some of Van Gogh's drawings give marvellous impressions of texture as do drawings by the Japanese master Hiroshige and the carefully studied drawings of Albrecht Durer.

Pattern
Geometric, Islamic, and patterns found in medieval manuscripts. Spirals appear in nature and can be compared with those drawn on Cycladic vases and Anglo-Irish work such as the *Book of Durrow*.

Perspective and space
Find examples of perspective from high, low and angled positions such as those found in the drawings of Hiroshige, Le Corbusier, Escher, Michelangelo and de Chirico.

Form
Rembrandt's wash drawings, Leonardo, Raphael, Moore. Other links with art history can be made. For example your children can discuss your school and the immediate environment and make drawings of what they see. They can choose their favourite drawings, write about them and compare their reasons for liking them in discussion with their classmates. They can search for shapes, lines and marks in drawings and see if they can sort them into types or sets and then consider whether some artists use certain shapes more than others. Your children can try to use some of the techniques of other artists in their own work. Get them to try copying Raphael's method of using red chalk on a coloured paper or Ingres's fine pencil technique for example.

95

TECHNIQUES AND PROCESSES ▶

The rest of the activities in this section are mainly technical, showing how to draw in different ways. The exercises, as in the other practical skills sections, must not be set in isolation. Please ensure that your children are given opportunities for drawing without such constraints. Also make sure that a balance of classroom activities and individual creative work is maintained. The activities are organised in such a way that skills are developed in a natural way from marks and lines, then flat shapes through to fully rounded and perspective drawings. The elements of this growth include, dots, marks, lines, open and closed shapes, tone, textures (produced with a range of materials and tools), perspective and head and figure drawing. Observation, memory and imagination can all be helped and stimulated through such exercises.

Materials and equipment
Pencil, felt tips and crayons are all suitable materials for recording observations. Be careful not to allow the wax crayon unbridled freedom. It can be responsible for destroying sensitive and fine pencil drawings by obliteration. Crayons can be used to good effect, for example when black wax crayons are drawn on a coloured ground. For precise and accurate work your children will need to use pencils (sharp ones, please), pen and ink or felt tip pens instead of crayons. Provide the right materials for the job in hand. You will need:

brushes, cartridge paper, chalk, charcoal, coloured pencils, wax crayons, compass, Conté crayons, erasers, felt tip pens and markers, paint, pantograph, pastels, pastel paper, pens, pencils, rulers, tracing paper, brushes.

You will also need a collection of resources of all kinds. These could include, shells, baskets, old boots, scraps of metal, bark, marble, pebbles, small toys (soft and hard), natural and made materials, fabric scraps (some with patterns), drapes, teasels, thistle heads, plants and flowers.

Before you start
The exercises in this section are intended to help your children to draw using a number of approaches. In doing so they should see and understand relationships between parts and the whole. Any subject, whether it is imaginative, observational or based on memory should be conceived as an integrated whole, rather than a lot of bits stuck together. The exercises cover basic building blocks and you should get your children to use thinking, seeing, observing, touching and handling as ways of feeding their drawings. Tell your children that their drawings will be better if they think about what they are going to draw before picking up a brush, pencil or felt tip pen. Try to imagine the drawing on the paper before starting.

MARKS AND LINES ▶

Activity 241: Rubbings and sketches of textures
One of the suggestions of the National Curriculum is that children should take rubbings samples and use these rubbings as a background to pictures. The most usual way that children introduce themselves to rubbing is by rubbing wax crayons over the surface of thin paper laid on top of a coin. Set the task of producing a gallery of rubbings that will match words: smooth, rough, grainy, ribbed, patterned and random. There are a number of ways of extending this simple technique to produce different marks and lines. These include rubbings from doilies, metal plates and from cut and assembled pieces of card. All sorts of objects, natural and made, can be used to good effect. Try bark, leaves, cut pieces of corrugated card and bits and pieces of string, rope and metal grilles. Make a collection of rubbings from different surfaces, cut out small sections and fix to backing paper as a permanent record. If your children use coloured paper then they will need to use a light wax crayon for the rubbing. Now get your children to make sketches of the original subjects using pencils, charcoal or felt tip pens as they see fit. Arrange and fix the small rubbings and drawings alongside each other on a large piece of sugar paper added to your class display.

If you make a visit to a local church your children may be able to make brass rubbings and rubbings of

other surfaces. Rubbings and drawings of knights can be used as resources from which your children can make authentic and original craft work upon their return to school.

You need
Textured objects, papers, coloured wax crayons, pencils, charcoal, felt tip pens, glue, scissors.

Activity 242: Visual equivalents
Get your children to choose four objects from your resources box. Allow them a variety of materials such as crayons, charcoal, pen, pencils (different grades), coloured paper, erasers and white paper (textured and smooth). Ask them to consider what qualities their objects possess and to write down two or three words for each including reference to colours, shine and textural qualities for example. Get them to draw four rectangles on a piece of paper. Now get them to produce areas of paper marked, coloured and scratched to produce a visual equivalent of the qualities they see or feel in their chosen subjects. It is important that they concentrate on the particular features that seem most important. When they have made their equivalents cut them out and stick them in place and label, date and name the sheets.

You need
A suitable choice of materials and objects, papers, coloured wax crayons, pencils, charcoal, felt tip pens, glue, scissors, brushes, paints, coloured pencils, erasers.

Activity 243: Marks and feelings
Discuss with your children the kind of feelings that they experience. Include: anger, love, hate, coldness, warmth, fear, happiness, anticipation, excitement, boredom, laziness. Give them a range of drawing materials and a variety of different papers to work on. The paper (A3) should include black, grey, blues, reds, yellow and rough and smooth white. Get them to produce abstract marks and composite marks to express two or three chosen feelings. For each feeling they will need a separate piece of paper.

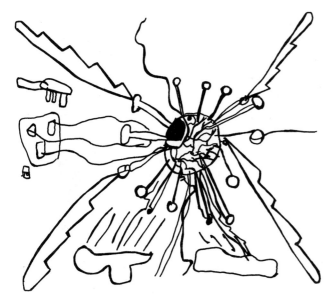

Child's abstract feeling drawing

Look at the drawings of Leonardo (*The Deluge*) when tackling this activity. The drawings by Leonardo were not simply drawings of water splashing and whirling about. They were drawn around AD 1500 and it seems that every 500 or 1000 years everyone becomes worried about the end of the world. Leonardo's drawings were serious abstract statements about the end of the world.

You need
A3 white paper, coloured wax crayons, pencils, charcoal, felt tip pens, brushes, paints, coloured pencils, erasers.

Activity 244: Foliage
On a fine day take your children outside to make studies of foliage. First go close (within a metre) to a tree or shrub and get your children to use a viewer to select a small cluster of leaves and branches (as shown in the diagram). Let them use black felt tip pens, fine brushes with liquid black paint (plus water for thinning) or pencils to make their drawings. Let them work for 15 minutes or so. Now move away from the shrub to a distance of about three metres. Get them to repeat the exercise. Talk about how they can show the less clearly defined parts, what are they going to have to leave out, whether they can find equivalents for the variously lit twigs, branches and leaves. Finally move away to a distance of more than ten metres. Still using the viewer and making drawings of the same size make one final drawing. What new problems are faced? Some elements will be reduced to single varied black lines. The details in the shadows will be more difficult to render. Take the drawings back to school and discuss further the use of marks as equivalents for the visual world.

You need
Sketchbooks, papers, pencils, felt tip pens, brushes, paints, erasers, viewers.

LINES

Activity 245: Exercises for fingers, wrist and arm
As infants your children may well have followed a number of exercises to loosen their hand mobility and in producing finger strokes, wrist and whole arm lines.

Small details and shading is best done through finger strokes. Your children will need to hold pencils or other drawing materials in exactly the same way as writing.

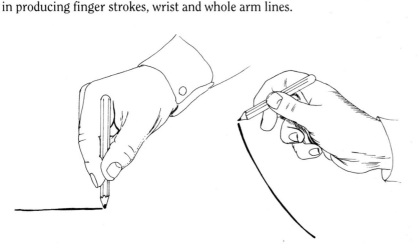

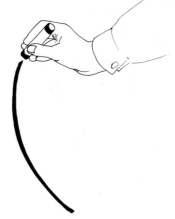

Finger strokes   *Wrist strokes*   *Full arm strokes*

Using a pencil or pen with wrist strokes (up or down) will allow your children to produce smooth, large scale, graceful lines or curves to be drawn. Get the children to try loose free lines away and towards their bodies.

Full arm strokes are necessary for larger scale work. Give your children a supply of some large sheets of newsprint. These can be either on a table or easel. (Young children find it easier to work on a flat horizontal surface than an easel.) Get them to experience freedom and control in using full arm strokes with crayons, pastels, large marker pens or brush and paint.

Activity 246: Abstract line compositions
Do two exercises. Give your children two pieces of paper, one A4 then another about A2. On the smaller piece ask your children to use charcoal pencils or charcoal to divide the paper into rectangular sections similar to Mondrian's compositions. The lines must be straight, of varied thickness and drawn without rulers. If a line is intended to have a sharp edge than it must be clean and crisp. On the second piece of paper get your children to make as many types of lines as possible. Vary the size, thickness and direction of the lines, using finger strokes, wrist and arm strokes. It is important that your children consider the relationships of the lines to each other and the paper itself in making a composition.

Activity 247: Handwriting patterns
Juniors can develop handwriting patterns as a basis of composing abstract forms. On a large piece of newsprint get your children to draw with charcoal some large repeated letters. The curves of large letters will tie in with attempts to produce flowing linear drawings of natural forms. Increase the size of letters until the letters are 20–25 cms high.

Hand writing patterns

Get your children to use brushes and liquid paint or ink as well. When using paint emphasise the need to maintain good even line thickness and smoothness. Your children will find that they can draw large, sweeping graceful curves with loops and down strokes. Get them to produce patterns of linked letters across a sheet of newsprint. Open and closed areas can be coloured according to each child's preferences. Differently shaped letters may lend themselves to certain colours rather than others. Children can become selective in their use of colour and the way they organise space.

Activity 248: Sketchbook lines
Discuss the kinds of lines that can be seen in the natural and made world: straight, twisted, bent, hard, soft, curved, rhythmic, thick, thin broken and strong. Get your children to make a list. Make a trip along a canal or river bank and ask your children to find as many examples of lines as possible and to record them accurately in their sketchbooks. Look at the reflections, the way that reeds bend and break. Find examples and draw how lines grow and join together to form more complicated forms. Ask the children to measure and map the key features working from the centre to the circumference. Use pencil first, and a soft rubber to correct mistakes. Later use a fine felt tip to finish the drawings. Do not shade the drawings.

You need
Sketchbooks, pencils, felt tip pens, erasers.

Child's lines from nature

Activity 249: Lines from crayon and chalk
During the trip along the river bank get your children to make line drawings of ripples and reflections using coloured pencils. When you return to class the reflected lines can be used as the basis for chalk and crayon transfer work.

Start with a small picture. However when experiments have been completed, your pupils may well find that pictures of reflections in canals, the sea, lakes or simply in mirrors can be worked to a fairly large scale using a similar approach and materials.

Activity 250: Different materials, the same subject

Give each child a copy of **Copymaster 83** which contains two frames for comparative drawings of the same subject produced by using different materials. Arrange an outdoor visit and provide each child with two type of media such as hard and soft pencils, felt tip pens and black paint, brushes with water. Choose an interesting subject with foreground, midground and background. Vary the media throughout the class and set everyone the task of making two studies of the same subject. When the work is complete you will have a collection of varied drawings to discuss upon return to school. Mount and display examples of the drawings.

Activity 251: Colour combs

Ask your pupils to produce designs which use only curves of a series of parallel coloured lines. Spirals, circles and curves are often found in nature (pools, ripples, hills and dales) and in made objects such as wheels and helter-skelters. If you are running a topic on wheels, curves, spirals or some similar title then you can extend the design element of your work by using colour combs. Wax crayons can be modified and used in a sweeping motion to produce a series of parallel lines. Notch the side of chunky wax crayons to produce combs. This type of technique can be extended by buying some of the new and unusual 'stripies' from NES Arnold. These multicoloured crayons give a calligraphic feel to drawings and can be used to give star-burst effects.

Activity 252: Colour cutting lines

Another well-known wax crayon line technique is colour cutting. Many subjects are suitable for this technique, from brilliant coloured birds to the sky at night. When introducing this technique it is sensible to keep to a small scale. Get your pupils to cover a piece of card with a rainbow of wax crayons. These colours must then be covered entirely with a thick coat of black or darkly coloured crayon. When this is complete your children can use a sharp point to make their designs. The technique of scratching through to reveal the brilliant colours below can be varied and different tools used to achieve different effects. It is necessary of course

to take care when using cutting tools. (This sgriffito technique was originally used to describe the cutting through of one layer of plaster to another of a different colour thereby producing a design. It can now be applied to cutting through one layer of wax to reveal a design on the different coloured layer below.)

Activity 253: Continuous lines

Ask your children to select objects from your resource collections. Each child will need a piece of A3 white paper and a free flowing pen with black ink for preference. Before starting to draw ask your children to look at and think about their subjects. What sort of shapes are they looking at? What pressure should they use when making the lines? Now set the task of making a drawing using one single continuous line. The children should only look at the object, not their drawings. They must not remove the pen from the paper nor look at the paper while drawing. They should concentrate on feeling their way across the paper as they map their subject. Subjects that contain considerable detail such as small baskets, cross-sections of cabbages or a vase of flowers can all be tackled. This exercise should not be hurried. These drawings can be coloured. This exercise should help develop your children's spatial awareness.

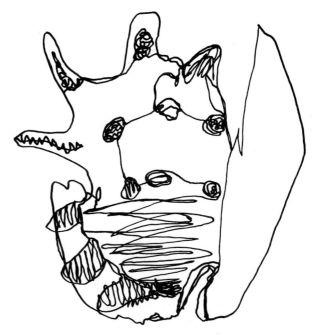

Continuous line drawings

SHAPES AND FORMS

Lines that are closed produce shapes, shapes that have substance become forms. Classroom activities linked to these phases are inherently progressive, developing two- and three-dimensional spatial awareness.

Activity 254: Drawing flat shapes

Your children will find it helpful when trying to plot shapes accurately to use some aids. Get your children to choose an object that they find interesting, a shell, fir cone, toy, a small log with plenty of surface detail and a few attached twigs. Place the objects on the table in front of each child. Give each child a piece of A3 cartridge paper, pencils, rulers, felt tip pens and erasers. Ask your children to look at their subjects, trying to assess where the central point is located. Once they have decided, you can demonstrate the following method in front of the class. Draw a vertical line and intersect it with one which is exactly horizontal. The point at which the lines cross is to be the central point of the children's subjects. The illustration shows clearly how useful this is. Your children will find it much easier to locate the outline of the subjects and subsequently to place all the elements. Now get your children to start with a simple outline. Use dots to map the extreme points and the important features, working from the centre towards the circumference, indicating the important internal and external boundaries. The four quarters will help to plot and check. Once the outline is dotted use lines (light ones to start with), to define the enclosed shapes more clearly.

Do not try to make the drawing appear solid. Resist the temptation to smudge shadows, keep the drawing clean and linear instead.

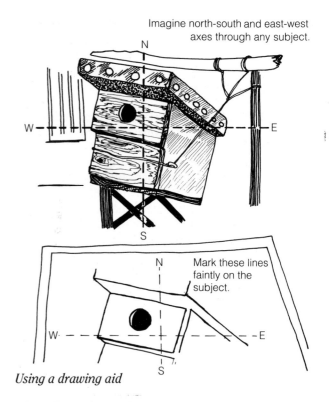

Imagine north-south and east-west axes through any subject.

Mark these lines faintly on the subject.

Using a drawing aid

OUTLINES

Give each child a fine brush (size 3 or 4) and ink and a small freshly cut branch with leaves. Talk about how the plant grows: the leaf has grown from its stem through its veins to the tip. With flowing arm, wrist and finger strokes get your children to draw calligraphic images of the plants on a piece of A3 sugar paper. This will require concentration and sensitivity.

Activity 255: Outline and contour drawing
This activity is similar to the continuous line exercise except that your children should concentrate on the outline or shape of their subject. Working in pairs get them to try silhouettes of their friends.

Activity 256: Copy outline drawing and trace to modify
This skill is described in Activity 32: Gods in the chapter on 'Ancient Greece and Rome'.

Activity 257: Use computer draw/paint package
This activity can be found as Activity 9 in the chapter on 'Ancient Egypt'.

Child's computer drawing

TONE AND SOLIDS

C33

Activity 258: Making and using tone
Tones are different shades of grey and black. Tonal values from white to deep black can be made in a number of ways. **Copymaster 33** contains a grid that includes a series of tones. Get your children to make equivalent tones to those shown on the grid. They should use hard, medium and soft pencils, charcoal pencils, felt tip pens, pen and ink and paint thinned down into washes of different tonal values. When using paint two approaches should be used; the first involves adding water to a basic black, the other involves blending quantities of white with black to make a full range of tones. Techniques should be varied also, using dots, marks, hatching and cross-hatching when using pen and ink. Solid tone from 4B and HB pencils and washes of different densities when using brushes and

100

Tone drawing of pebble

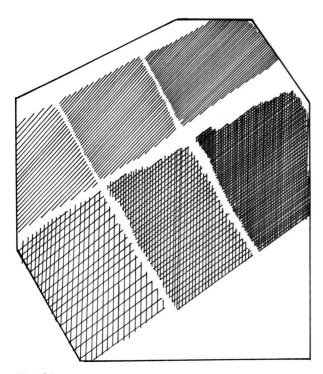

Hatching

paint. Each square of the Copymaster is to be completed.

Activity 259: Contrast

Set up a group of objects on a table, include bottles, baskets, bits of machinery, shells and vegetables. Light this still-life subject from one side. This will have the effect of producing a strongly modelled and heavily shadowed subject for drawing. Set your children the task of drawing the subject using simple areas of tone, avoid putting in details. Pencils, ink or washes of thin paint can be used. When using pencil encourage the use of erasers to cut away areas of tone to produce light areas and highlights. Now light the subject from two sides and get your children to do another drawing with more attention to detail.

Activity 260: Tones of contours

Let your children select one pebble each from your resources box. Try to make sure that the pebbles all contain some light and darkly toned areas with some variation in pattern while at the same time being smooth. Place the pebbles on a white piece of paper and light them from the side. First discuss with your children the range of tones that they can see including the shadows below the pebble on the paper and the highlights. Give each child a tone/colour viewer. This is a small square of grey card (5 cms × 5 cms) with a hole punched in the centre (use a hole-punch). This simple device will be very useful for many activities. Get your children to look through the hole at the pebble, shadows and highlights. (Hold the card close to the surface of the object.) They will find that some of the lighter areas appear to be lighter than the white paper on which they will draw. This in itself may be something of a revelation. How are they going to cope? Ask for suggestions. This is in fact a problem which has plagued artists throughout history. One answer is to use the

white paper for the brightest parts of the picture and to modify all other tones accordingly. Now look at the darkest parts. What kind of materials can match that blackness? If your children are going to use pencils then they will only be able to reach a certain dark grey but not a black. This will require another compromise in the drawn range of tones. I suggest that they use pen and India ink after the initial pencil work. In this way the tonal range will be much greater.

Now for the drawing. Give each child a piece of A5 white smooth drawing paper. First get them to plot the outline using fine dots of pencil. Also get them to plot the shaded areas on the paper taking note of the density and depth of the shadows and comparing by using the viewer. Make the drawing no less than 12 cms by 8 cms. Carefully build up the tones across the whole picture. When using a hard pencil it will be much easier to produce light tones. Always use a sharply pointed pencil to maximise control. If the surface of the drawing looks rough use an eraser and then work over again to bring the surface up to an even tone. For many drawings your children will need to be able to apply a particular tone to a precise place, therefore it is useless to let them simply smudge a rough area and think it is all right. If your children wish they can use fine pen marks to add to the tonal range, but remember they will need a very fine nib and to make light tones will require the use of very fine widely spaced marks or lines.

If your children can produce pebbles with a truly round feeling then they will be able to draw anything.

Activity 261: Dots and tonal values

The pebble exercise above can be approached by using fine felt tip pen dots to render the tones and produce a rounded form. If you show your children newspaper photographs they will see that the darkness or lightness of an object is shown by the size and number of black dots and corresponding white areas. Every dot should have its own shape. Try to be careful with every mark that they put on paper. (If you are undertaking the exercises yourself choose subjects that include round solid objects set with the light from one side.)

101

Viewpoints and reflections

You will find a number of good drawing activities in the topics section including some to do with textures and shadows, fabrics and drapes. The National Curriculum suggests that your children draw bird's eye views around the school (AT1a). Take them around the playground get them to look up, down, through and across familiar objects and views. Ask them to make three or four drawings from different viewpoints. The National Curriculum also recommends that your children make drawings from the reflective surfaces that they find around the school.

SPACE AND PERSPECTIVE

C50, 59, 65, 84

There are obvious difficulties when drawing in three dimensions on a two-dimensional piece of paper. This brief introduction suggests simple ways of exploring and to some extent overcoming the problems. **Copymasters 65** and **84** contain diagrams which explain graphically the following terms and suggest a few activities.

Picture plane

Our eyes normally rove around the visual world, producing many continuous images from two points of view (i.e. our eyes!). Try to imagine that each and every one of us is at the centre of a sphere of vision (like being inside an onion, each layer of skin holding parts of our perceived world at specific distances from us). Here is the first problem and compromise. The drawings and pictures we make, to be truly accurate should be made on small sections of spheres not on flat bits of paper. By making drawings on flat surfaces we are bound to distort the way we see and portray things.

Look at the diagram and you will see that the piece of paper represents a plane (picture plane) onto which we attempt to show accurately what we see. Many artists such as Durer used frames to help represent an accurate picture. Make up a frame as shown and let your children work on squared paper to produce drawings. **Copymaster 59** contains a design for a viewing frame.

Horizon and eye level

For perspective work it is essential to establish a horizontal horizon line. The horizon line is drawn on the picture plane at eye level (obviously as you move your head's position so does the horizon line move).

Centre of vision

The diagram shows the viewer's eye as it looks directly at a series of railway sleepers and the way these may be shown on a picture plane. As they go into the distance the apparent length of the sleepers decreases towards nothing. The second drawing shows what it looks like from the viewer's point of view with the centre of vision shown absolutely in the middle of the drawing.

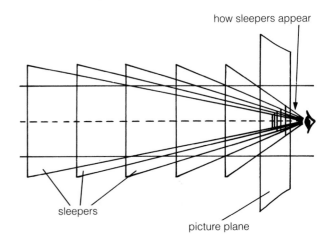

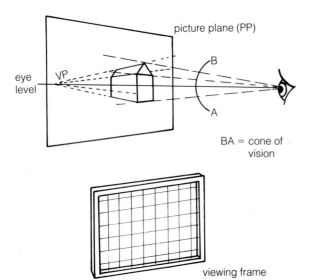

viewing frame

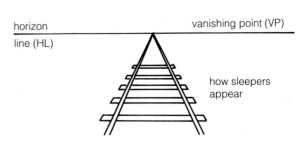

View of railway sleepers

Vanishing points (left and right)

Vanishing points are always exactly as high as your eyes are. They will always be on a horizontal line, the horizon, and they move just as you move. If you sit the horizon comes down too, if go up high then the horizon is raised too (if you stand on the top of a cliff you can see much more of the sea than if you are on the beach). All the lines below your eye level vanish upwards to a point on the horizon, those above vanish downwards to a point on the horizon. Lines that are exactly on the level of your eye will be drawn exactly horizontally. Parallel lines don't meet. But, as shown below, the fact that they appear to is vital for perspective drawing.

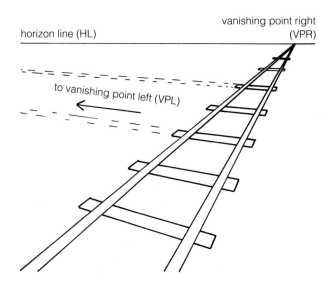

Railways lines disappearing to right

The next diagram shows what happens when the railway lines disappear off to the right of the viewer rather than directly in front. The railway lines go into the distance and at the VPR (Vanishing Point Right) they seem to disappear on the horizon line (HL).

Look at the diagram and you will see that a simple building can be shown by using two vanishing points where the two sides converge.

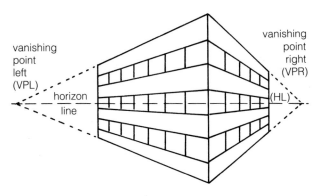

Perspective building

Verticals

Remember that verticals should always be shown as vertical whereas horizontals (unless on the eye level) radiate towards vanishing points at different degrees of the diagonal.

Showing scale by using eye levels

The three diagrams below give some idea of how the scale of an object can be shown by the position of the horizon. Get your children to try to distort and change the appearance of things by adopting unusual or extreme viewpoints and horizon lines.

Perspective is a very demanding area and should be introduced as a way of showing the world. It should be remembered that it provides a theoretical view of the world and does not conform exactly to how we actually see the world.

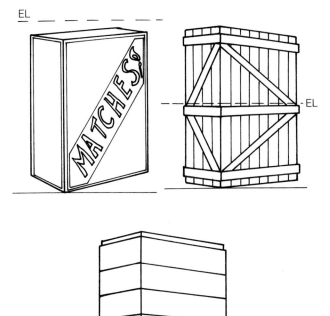

Three different views to show scale

Activity 262: Measuring

For observational, scale and perspective drawings your children will need to take some measurements of what they see around them. In the above activities the use of Durer's frame was suggested. This can be an ideal way of accurately measuring and drawing architectural or figure subjects (when drawing figures it helps to overcome problems of fore-shortening). Your children can also start to use vertically and horizontally held pencils (or thumbs) to measure and select in a standard artist's way.

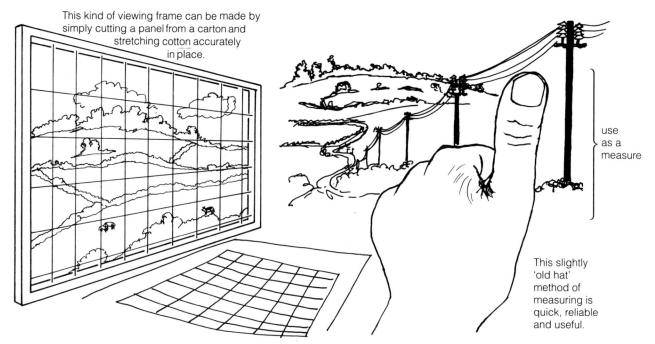

This kind of viewing frame can be made by simply cutting a panel from a carton and stretching cotton accurately in place.

use as a measure

This slightly 'old hat' method of measuring is quick, reliable and useful.

Durer's frame and finger measuring

Activity 263: Using window or viewfinder

Many kinds of compositional problems can be tackled by using **Copymaster 50** as a cropping aid. Frames and viewers can be used to select elements from existing flat images such as illustrations in books or magazines, or for close and careful examination of colours in isolation from surrounding colours. Free-standing frames can be used to select a view of the real world from which to work. Doing this can help enormously to give your pupils an understanding of perspective.

This class activity can be useful in building perceptual skills. Get all the children to set up free-standing frames at 1 m from themselves and 1 m from the subject (still life or figure). Now set them the task of making a representational study of what can be seen through the frame. When the first drawing is complete move the frame so that it is only 50 cms from the same subject while now it is 1.5 m from the pupil. Using the same materials and paper of the same size set the task of reproducing the view through the frame so that the finished study is exactly the same size as the first effort. Compare and discuss the results. Use **Copymaster 59** for this activity.

Activity 264: A perspective model

Copymaster 66 includes a diagram of how to construct a perspective model. The model divides the visual field into foreground, midground and background. Pupils should select an interesting image from a collection of magazine illustrations. The illustrations should include elements that clearly fall into the three categories mentioned. Trace the illustration and nominate each element so that it is either foreground, midground or background. Copy the elements on to thin card and cut out each as a silhouette and copy the colours and designs from the original as carefully as possible. Make up small simple free-standing dioramas of the same size as the original illustration with the various elements physically arranged in the correct position. View the dioramas. Which ones are the most effective as 3D models?

Activity 265: Experiment with three dimensions

Copymaster 85 contains an improbable drawing. Get your children to use tone and colour to make it even more confusing. Ask them to try to make up their own odd, world drawings.

FIGURES AND FACES

C64, 86

Before you start

Drawing figures and faces is wrongly thought to be difficult. Your class has an abundant supply of models and all you need to do is to try to encourage your children's confidence. Before going on to the activities it may be useful for you to have some general information about the proportions of head and body. The human body includes the following main parts: the head, neck, trunk (the chest and abdomen or belly), the upper extremities including shoulders, arms, forearms and hands, the lower extremities including the hips, thighs, legs and feet (including the ankles).

In general terms the proportions are (in head-lengths):

Adults

The average body is seven heads tall (the Greeks considered small heads to be a sign of beauty so their proportions were often eight heads), shoulders at the widest point about two heads, from the centre of the chest to the tip of the middle finger is about half the height of the body.

The body proportions of adult women are such that the trunk is large in proportion to the lower limbs. Whereas an adult man's trunk is relatively smaller in relation to the lower limbs.

Children

Up to one year old the height is about three and a half to four heads, five years five heads tall, nine years about six heads, 15 years about six and a half heads and thereafter seven heads tall. **Copymaster 86** on figure proportions can be a useful resource.

Activity 266: Proportion survey

Use **Copymaster 86** to explain the approximate proportions of the human body at maturity and get the children to check this against their own observations. Put large sheets of lining paper on the floor and trace the outlines of children and adults, then measure the parts and compare them. Finally make a chart of survey results.

Activity 267: Drawing from a model

Get your children to work in groups of five or six, each taking turns as a model. Although they will feel a bit embarrassed at first try to explain how they can help each other a lot by being still and not messing about. Set each model in a good light about four or five metres from the artists. Cartridge paper (A3) and soft pencils or charcoal are the best for your children's first drawings. Get your children to hold their pencils between first and second fingers and thumbs so that they can use supple wrist and arm strokes to experiment with the general shapes.

Explain by demonstration that the whole figure can be seen to fall within a rectangle (see diagram below). Get your children to work out what shape of rectangle they need for the drawings from their point of view. Outline a rectangle lightly so that it nearly fills the paper. (This should ensure that all the figure can be fitted on to the paper.) Roughly place a central point on the paper which coincides with the centre of the body. Draw a light dotted north-south and east-west axis through this central point. Mark the extremities of the head, soles and shoulders or legs. Measuring with a pencil at arm's length, get your children to find the greatest widths and mark them with light strokes. Take a line for a walk down the centre of the body, from the top of the head, through the throat, chest, abdomen and the base of the pelvis. Look for symmetry and balance. Follow the line through the legs until the 'walking lines' end up at the right and left heels. Check the placing of the important parts and features. Now your children can follow this approach to the smaller details of the face, arms, hands, legs and feet. Finally, consider the clothes, and dressing the figure. Do not let your children get into messy smudges and fiddly details, keep to the structures and main shapes.

Imagining a rectangle around subjects can help spatial awareness.

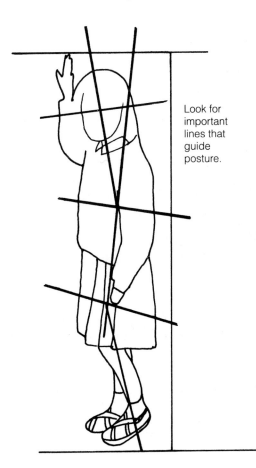

Look for important lines that guide posture.

Figures in rectangle and on axis

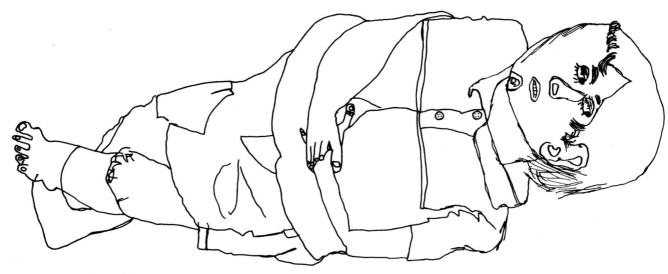

Drawing of model lying on the ground

Follow this with other exercises. Include timed sketches made from the model. Give your children ten, five, two and one minutes to make drawings of different poses using pencils on A4 paper. Also do front, back and side views. In these cases try to give an impression of roundness by varying the tonal qualities of the pencil. Try views of models lying on the ground, sitting and kneeling. It is unlikely that you will have easels but if you do, give your children the chance to stand and draw at an easel. It makes a lot of difference.

Activity 268: Figures, faces and art history
Look at the way Byzantine artists, El Greco, Rubens, Michelangelo and Raphael have drawn the human body and faces. Let your children do drawings in the manner of selected artists.

Activity 269: Expressions and imagination
Get your children to work in pairs with the object of making drawings which represent feelings and expressions. Get your children to notice the changes that occur with different expressions. Look at smiling, for example. Smiling makes the face broader, and makes the upper lips and corners of the mouth draw upwards and sideways, which in turn makes a furrow under the eyes, the groove below the nose becomes shallower and broader and the forehead is usually unchanged.

Laughing, crying, looking sad, frightened, content can all be observed and drawn.

Activity 270: Large scale portraits
Get your children to make large scale portraits in charcoal to depict a character described in a story.

Activity 271: Faces and figures cartoons
Encourage your children to draw cartoons with pencils and felt tip pens. Besides copying their favourite characters from *The Beano* discuss with them how to develop their own style. **Copymaster 64** shows how concentrating first on one feature, such as the nose, can help develop an individual style. Get them to make six or seven versions of the same basic face and then change them by adding long hair for a girl, a helmet for a policeman, a silly hat for a silly person, a dog collar for the vicar, and a turban for the sikh. Details need to be careful but very simply stated.

Activity 272: Fixing
Pencil, pastel and charcoal drawings will need to be fixed. Using a fixative will prevent pencil, pastel and charcoal drawings from being smudged. It is best for you to use an atomiser with fixative for this purpose. Coat with two or three fine sprays, allowing the work to dry between coats.

GLOSSARY OF TERMS

Bird's eye view
Overhead view of a subject.

Calligraphy
Handwriting art, undertaken with lettering pen or fine brush.

Camera obscura
Optical device that projects an image on to a surface which can then be traced accurately. (Used by many artists.)

Carbon pencils
Fine, drawing pencil made from carbon rather than graphite for final drawings.

Cartoon
A full sized preparatory drawing.

Cartridge paper
Inexpensive, good quality drawing paper.

Charcoal
Soft black crayon usually made from willow. Drawings must be fixed to resist smudges.

Conté crayons
High quality French pastels.

Contour drawing
Drawing made when artist fixes eyes on subject and draws without looking at the drawing, nor removing pencil from paper.

Crayons
General term for stick drawing material.

Cross hatching
Pattern of drawn lines that form a net, the closer the lines the darker the tone.

Cross section
Drawing of section through object.

Enlarging
Making a picture larger without altering the scale of the elements in it.

Felt tip pens and markers
Nylon and felt tipped drawing tools.

Horizon line
A real or imaginary line in a picture; the basis for relating other elements in the picture together through perspective.

Lay figure
A small articulated figure, useful for approximating human poses.

Life drawing
A drawing of the human figure from a model.

Line drawing
A drawing in which forms and shapes are shown entirely by use of lines.

Outline drawing
A drawing of an object in which only the outline is shown with an even line. No tone, texture or internal aspects are shown.

Pantograph
A mechanism for copying, reducing or enlarging drawings.

Pastel
A coloured crayon composed of pigment and water-based binder.

Pastel paper
Special, textured paper designed to hold pastel firmly to its surface.

Pencils
Use to refer to small pointed brush, now covers large range of coloured, carbon, flat, charcoal and graphite pencils. Often on a scale from 6H through HB to 6B, H being hard, B being black or soft.

Perspective
A way to represent a view of a three-dimensional scene accurately in two dimensions.

Render
Accurate way of drawing.

Scale
Relationship between drawn items and the original, i.e. 1:50.

Scraperboard
Type of scratch board.

Shading
Merging of one tone into another.

Sketch
A preliminary drawing sometimes done quickly.

Stump
Tightly rolled paper used to blend or smudge pencil or charcoal to give a smooth finish.

Tone
The lightness or darkness of colour or monotone.

Vanishing point
Imaginary point where parallel lines converge on the horizon.

Worm's eye view
A picture produced from a low level point of view.

MODELLING

INTRODUCTION

The National Curriculum requires that children experience working at different scales and using a variety of materials to produce work in two and three dimensions. It is important that your children work in 3D on a regular basis. The value of such work lies in the development of concepts such as form, scale and space; using materials, processes and tools while developing an awareness of the different characteristics of a variety of materials. Modelling materials should not be restricted to clay and wood; make a wide range available including card, junk and textiles.

Mask-making provides numerous opportunities for modelling in 3D. When children model they create forms, building up or changing the shape of materials. Plasticine, clay, card, junk and papier mâché are all used in modelling masks. These materials can be rolled, cut, squeezed, pushed and pulled. Other techniques used in the making of masks include carving (plastic cartons) and construction.

Construction processes include measuring, cutting, fixing and finishing various kinds of materials. It is essential that you create a safe environment for modelling. Pay particular attention to the use of craft knives and use a cutting mat and safety rule to keep fingers safe.

Modelling skills cross the boundaries between art and design and technology. Working as artists rather than technologists children will emphasise their own personal responses to materials and express personal ideas and feelings. Since there is such a wide range of modelling activities in the topics section, this skills section offers additional technical guidance only. Three-dimensional work is divided here into the processes of construction, modelling and sculpture. Under each of these headings the relevant cross-reference to Topic activities are included.

Materials and equipment

Three-dimensional activities should not be limited to traditional materials such as clay, stone, metal and wood. Children should also experience using plastics, wood, paper, card, found objects, textiles, malleable materials such as clay and plasticine, and construction kits. You will need various types of card including squared (photocopy **Copymaster 6** onto card – check the photocopier manual first), cardboard (from packaging such as Tri-wall) paper, glues, scissors, craft knives, cutting board, safety steel rulers, balsa wood, dowelling, small craft saws or junior hacksaws, junk of all kinds, guillotine, clay, plasticine, baseboards for clay work (1 cm chipboard pieces approx 45 cms × 35 cms), pencils, paints, brushes, glazes, slips, rolling pins, rags, clothes and sponges, papier mâché, foils. Protective smocks or old shirts for children.

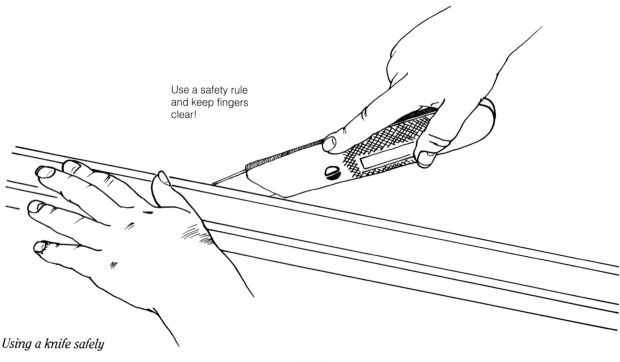

Use a safety rule and keep fingers clear!

Using a knife safely

HISTORY OF MODELLING AND SCULPTURE ▶

The way that different civilisations and cultures have made sculptures and constructions has aesthetic and technical aspects. As an example you can trace the way that the human figure has been represented since prehistoric times. You can consider the simple stick-like figures shown in the magical dance of hunting scenes of cave paintings. Try to understand what the drawing tells us about how people were depicted then and, of course, about the artist as well. Remember to consider the social context in which sculptures have been made. Still considering the human figure, move on and examine the simple fertility sculptures of Wilendorf, the simple figurines of Cycladic art and the changing urges to make more perfect sculptures of human beings. The perfection of form and harmonious

balance achieved in the figures of Classical Greece tells us much about the cultures' values. Their central concern being the celebration of the human and divine in perfect physical form. The Christian era has been marked by violent changes in attitudes to the representation of figures. In the Renaissance the importance of human feelings was re-examined and the human figure approached in a new way, existing on its own without the usual religious contexts. This modern tendency has resulted in the powerful human portrayals of Rodin and Henry Moore. The way figures have been portrayed is, of course, linked to the shapes, lines and scale of work. You can discuss the way animals and other subjects have been portrayed and the development of abstract sculptures.

CONSTRUCTION ▶

The following activities can be found in the topics section: Activity 13: Model the great pyramid; Activity 37: House model; Activity 63: Paper bag puppet of a mermaid; Activity 89: Moving lights; Activity 90: Colour sculpture; Activity 132: Packaging for food; Activity 133: Working model of mouth; Activity 160: Model town; Activity 161: Packing souvenirs; Activity 193: Maths shapes and string; Activity 194: Masks with lines; Activity 195: Cut and painted flat shapes; Activity 196: Parallel lines and reflections; Activity 219: North wind mask. In addition to these activities you will find information about joining clay together in the section on Ceramics (see page 88).

In this section we are concerned with card, paper and scrap materials. Paper and card construction usually involves cutting, creasing, folding and fixing pieces together with glues, tapes or fasteners. An important part of learning to work with sheet material such as card, is investigating the many ways in which it can be folded, shaped and formed to give it increased strength and rigidity. Probably the quickest and simplest way to stiffen a sheet of card is to use strips of card folded at right angles and stuck on to the sheet. **Copymasters 87** and **88** contain substantial help and guidance for construction with cardboard. **Copymasters 89–92** contain a number of nets for solids. They need to be enlarged on to card using a suitable photocopier. Get your children to work out the tabs.

Containers, boxes and solids can all be constructed from card. Care should be taken when cutting, scoring and gluing. Cut and form sections as shown to strengthen the sides of the solids. Use corner pieces and balsa wood to strengthen corners. Collect examples of different, small folded card packs, such a sweet containers. Get your children to open them out carefully to discover the nets. Get them to design simple nets and make up solids. Use Polydron® to help plan nets. As an extension to this get your children to design and decorate the surface of a cuboid before making it up into packaging for soft fruit or other products or gifts for parents.

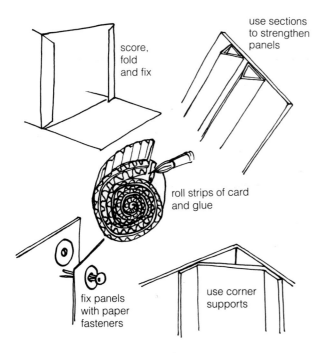

score, fold and fix

use sections to strengthen panels

roll strips of card and glue

fix panels with paper fasteners

use corner supports

Methods of working with card

Activity 273: Fixing wheels and axles
See **Copymaster 87**. Wheels can be attached in a variety of ways to cardboard vehicles and mechanisms. Mark the position of the axle accurately on the side of the vehicle and punch holes with a hole puncher. If the card is thin, use an additional card washer made from card to reinforce the hole. (See diagrams overleaf.)

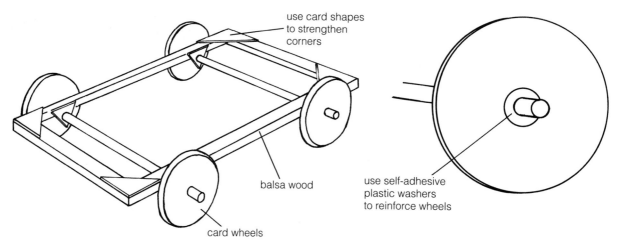

use card shapes
to strengthen
corners

use self-adhesive
plastic washers
to reinforce wheels

balsa wood

card wheels

Fixing wheels

Activity 274: Pop ups
Children may need to make pop ups for greeting cards or presents. There are a number of ways of making pop ups in which horizontal and vertical surfaces can form backgrounds, where horizontal surfaces can stand parallel to the card and v-folds which are very often used for greeting cards.

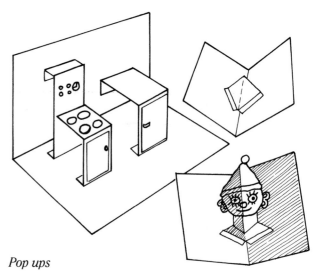

Activity 275: Making complex geometric shapes
Use **Copymasters 89–92.** Children can make up numbers of the solids which can then be used as building blocks for all kinds of more complex constructions. Parallel planes can be coloured the same.

Pop ups

MODELLING ▶

The following activities can be found in the topics section: Activity 6: Archaeology game; Activity 14: Animal sculptures; Activity 34: Cycladic figurines; Activity 35: Aristophanes' masks; Activity 36: Oil lamp; Activity 61: Diving mermaid; Activity 62: Tidal wave, whirlpool or skimming stones; Activity 129: Model meal; Activity 130: Funny food; Activity 131: Scale changes; Activity 189: Ceramic trees; Activity 191: String sculptures; Activity 192: Wire and plaster; Activity 194: Masks with lines; Activity 219: North wind mask.

Modelling involves making forms by manipulating materials. Children can convey feelings, observations and ideas through using solid and sheet materials such as junk, paper, card and balsa wood and soft materials such as clay, plasticine, and papier mâché. Modelling can include the skills of designing, cutting, folding, fixing, colouring, sawing, pinching and rolling. Modelling offers a bridge between working with flat shapes and solid forms. Modelling with clay develops children's physical perceptions in an immediate way that requires few tools. Squeezing, pinching, rolling and coiling are typical ways of making forms.

Children should be encouraged to undertake observational and expressive or story telling modelling. Children should discuss and handle natural and man-made objects before modelling them. Ask questions such as: 'How big is it? What is it for? and How is it made?' Look closely at details of insects, buildings, fruit, shells, bottles and pieces of machinery. Clay can be used to describe an event or a memory such as a birthday party or a role play which children can base their models or characters on, or a cartoon can be made in a series of tiles. Modelling can also be used in a factual way to support other areas of the curriculum. Children could, for example, model sections through volcanoes or features from history like castles.

General points
Clay can be used by very young children to build animals and all kinds of forms without any special tools. As children progress they will need tools to cut slits, to scoop out and to texture the surface of clay. Properly used clay is no more messy than paint or papier mâché. It is best to provide an absorbent surface. Avoid polythene or a vinyl covered table. Hessian, card,

wooden boards or thick hardboard are the best. Make sure that if you are going to fire models that you hollow them out to minimise the risk of the pieces shattering. Guidance on storing, colouring, drying and firing clay is given in the section on Ceramics.

Modelling methods such as slabwork, pinchwork, coilwork and carving cheese-hard clay can be found in the Ceramics section of this book.

SCULPTURE

Like modelling, sculpture can include the processes of moulding, assembling, modelling and casting, and in addition, the activity of carving into solid blocks. It often involves the decoration of surfaces of sculpted forms with textures, glazes and stains. Carving can take place into materials such as wax, wood, plaster and soap. It is a process which needs special attention and sound advanced planning.

Papier mâché is a useful modelling and sculpting material which is cheap and shows how waste materials can be transformed into strong and light products. The recipe below can be used in most activities that call for papier mâché.

Activity 276: Making papier mâché

Ingredients

1 complete newspaper
4 tablespoons of whiting
4 tablespoons of Gloy® or white paper paste
2 tablespoons of either raw or boiled linseed oil
4 tablespoons of white flour
4 drops of wintergreen or oil of cloves
This makes 4.5 litres of papier mâché.

Method

1. Tear the newspaper sheets into small pieces, approximately 2 cms square. Place the pieces into a bucket and cover with water, soak overnight.
2. Boil the mash for approximately 20 minutes having added 2.25 litres of water. Mash the mixture to a pulp.
3. Place this pulp into a strainer to remove surplus water.
4. The pulp should now be a soft, wet consistency.
5. Add the whiting, glue and linseed oil to the pulp. Stir the mixture thoroughly then add the flour and oil of cloves. The mixture is ready to use once it has been thoroughly stirred.

The quantities specified can be varied considerably. More glue makes a stronger finished product; more whiting make a whiter, denser mâché. If the mixture is too watery just add more flour until it is a pliable stiffish consistency.

The glue and the paste bind the mixture. Do not use cellulose paste that includes antifungal agents and do not use PVA. The whiting acts as a filler and colouring agent and adds to the density of the mix. Linseed oil is an 'extender' and adds pliability, strengthening the finished product. Oil of wintergreen or cloves acts as a preservative and prevents the mixture from going off.

Activity 277: Making a papier mâché mask

An old cardboard box can be used with papier mâché to produce four different masks. First, draw mask shapes over the corners of the cardboard box. The masks need to be long enough to cover the children's faces. Cut out the basic shapes and then the eyes, nose and mouth. make sure that the holes are big enough to see and speak through. Apply a coat of PVA to the basic mask shapes. Let it dry and then your children can build up the features of the masks with papier mâché in whichever way they like. When dry, the masks can be painted and finished with string, feathers or other scrap materials. Fix the mask with elastic, so that it is comfortable when worn.

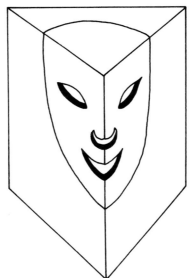
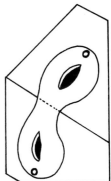

Cut either whole face masks or eye masks from box corners.

Making masks from box corners

Activity 278: Mixing plaster

To prepare the plaster, take a plastic bowl and fill it about one third full with water. Make sure your hands are dry and then gently sprinkle the plaster into the water. When the plaster forms a mound with the top sticking out of the water, you are ready to start mixing. Put your hand below the surface of the water and gently stir the plaster. You will feel when all of the powder plaster has been absorbed without lumps and is the right consistency to use. Pour the plaster into the moulds for the blocks, casts or tiles that you have previously prepared. Adding a little washing up liquid to the water, will tend to delay the hardening of the plaster. Your children can learn a lot by observing the heat that is given off as the plaster turns from liquid to solid.

Use scrim to reduce the quantity of plaster necessary. Scrim is an open weave fabric which is embedded in the liquid plaster and greatly strengthens plaster when cured.

Activity 279: Simple plaster casting
This supplements the information given in Activity 64: Casts from fishbones. Use a mould (as described in Activity 278) to contain the object to be cast and the plaster. Use a small piece of clay to make a relief model of a face or an animal and place on the base of the mould. Make sure that it is below the level of the top edge of the mould. Mix and pour plaster over the clay model until it reaches the top edge of the mould. Let the plaster 'go off'. When the plaster is solid, remove the mould and turn the plaster upside down. Remove the clay from the plaster. When all the clay has been removed, wash out the plaster. To make a cast, let the plaster dry out thoroughly, paint the surface well with two or three coats of washing up liquid. Mix up a small quantity of plaster and pour into the plaster mould. When dry, the plaster cast should come out easily, providing there are no undercuts.

Activity 280: Carving plaster blocks or tiles
Young children, can be introduced to carving by working in relief on plaster tiles. Before children can carve plaster, you will need to mix and form plaster blocks or tiles. The tiles should be about 15 cms square by 2 cms thick. To make the moulds, use hardboard as a base and sections of wood the right size and shape for the plaster block you want. Before using the mould, paint the inside with liquid detergent or soft soap as a release agent. If you have added washing-up liquid to the plaster, it will be easier to cut. First, get the children to do a drawing on paper the same size as the plaster tile. Trace this on to the dry plaster, discuss which areas of the plaster should be cut into, to make the design stand out. Paint the areas to be cut out and then start to carve into the plaster until the image is complete. When finished, the surface of the plaster that is uncut, can be painted to show the design more clearly.

Activity 281: Repoussé work
Copper or pewter metal sheets have been used to produce pictures for many years. These metal sheets are hammered with different punches on the reverse surface against a soft, yielding pad or former. Sometimes, when only a shallow design is required, a piece of metal sheet can be hammered against a soft wood such as pine. Repoussé may be introduced to young children by using thin metal foils over a shaped former and simply pressing the foil into the indentations. (Such as the carved tile from Activity 280.) When complete carefully remove the foil and mount on to a card support.

Activity 282: Making mobiles
Mobiles can include all kinds of objects or elements. You can use objects found on the beach and scrap materials of all kinds. Odd shaped objects will need to be securely tied with strong cord before hanging. Other items can include shapes from cut out cardboard, motifs made from multi-coloured Mirriboard, light or transparent appliqués made from cellophane or acetate stretched across frames of twisted cane. To make frames simply take thin cane, cut out a length of 60 cms and bend it to form a circle. Overlap the ends and strap them together with cotton and PVA glue. Such frames can be placed on to sheets of acetate or tissue paper traced and the backing shape cut out and stuck to the frame with glue. Once the backing has been cut, additional pieces of paper can be cut and stuck in place. For older children the canes can be used as a support for embroidered designs for mobiles.

Once the designs on the elements have been finished you will need to hang all the elements so that they balance and can move freely. The main hanging support can be made from cane, dowelling or wire. Whatever you use, the successful hanging of the mobile will depend on a trial and error approach. Use invisible thread (such as fishing line) to support the individual elements. Hanging the whole mobile is worked out by balancing out the different weights of each element against the distances from the fulcrum points on the supporting bars or canes. The diagram below gives a simplified view of a standard arrangement. If your children wish to suspend heavier items then the strength of supports and threads will, of course, have to be suitable.

No undercuts make mould casting easier.

Undercuts make casting impossible.

Undercuts

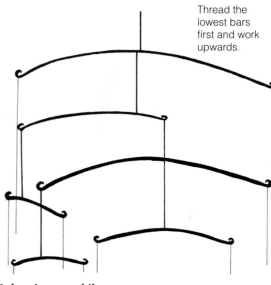
Thread the lowest bars first and work upwards.

Balancing a mobile

Activity 283: Flat card masks

Use **Copymaster 26** which contains a diagram of position and proportions of a standard face. Sheets of card (cut from large cardboard boxes) can make all kinds of masks which can be supported on rods or dowelling and held in front of your pupils' heads for dramatic presentations.

Making puppets extends the 3D work of mask making, generally on a smaller scale. You should try to relate two and three dimensions positively. One way to do this is to work on flat puppets (shadow puppets) and gradually make increasingly rounded puppets. Working from flat patterns to solids also will reinforce spatial concepts and introduce mathematical concepts. **Copymaster 93** includes patterns for finger and glove puppets.

Activity 284: Making shadow puppets

Patterns for shadow puppets can be derived from many sources. A collection of puppets from other cultures will stimulate an interest in how other people have brought their own characteristics to puppet-making and how the technology of puppet-making differs the world over. Some commonly available puppets are: Chinese string and finger puppets, Balinese shadow puppets, Golek puppets, Grebon puppets, Menak Islamic puppets, Yokthe Pwe string puppets and puppets from Hindu epics.

The flatness of Balinese puppets made from hide is part of their charm. This two dimensional quality is counterbalanced by the intricacies of the fretworked patterns. The silhouetted patterns have a depth and richness all of their own.

This activity can be extended to a more general study of silhouettes, from famous Swiss designs to the Victorian craft of miniature portrait profiles cut as silhouettes. Pupils will have to consider how certain elements are crucial to the success of silhouettes and to ensure that these essential characteristics are not lost in the simplifying process of reducing the three dimensions to two.

Activity 285: Making a shadow puppet theatre

Making a shadow puppet theatre can be great fun. It is a good idea to make up a theatre that combines a light source as part of a fixed unit rather than have problematic loose free-standing light sources.

Make a frame, as shown in the diagram below, which combines a rectangular structure (over which a mesh is stretched) and an open box that contains and directs the light from a fixed fluorescent tube. The exact size of the construction will depend on the size of the tube and its fittings, nevertheless it will need to have a screen about 60 cms high by 120 cms long. The light fittings are secured on the insides of the box. Notice that the design of the box includes a small shield that directs the light on to the screen and not into the eyes of the puppet operators. Paint the inside of the light box area with white paint to maximise the amount of light which will hit the screen. It is essential that you have the electrical components and wiring checked by a qualified electrician as part of your school's regular servicing programme – and before using the theatre with your children. By making a ready-lit unit like this you will reduce the chance of accidents and ensure that light is spread evenly over the surface of the screen.

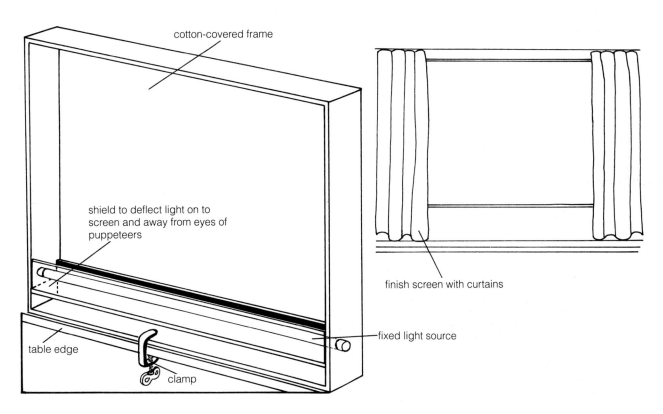

Making a shadow puppet theatre

GLOSSARY OF TERMS

Acetate Transparent coloured plastic, useful for projecting coloured lights and for mobiles.

Artcor Laminated foam board, light, strong with card surface ideal for quick clean model making and for mobile elements.

Armature Skeletal support for sculptures made from plaster, clay or papier mâché.

Balsa wood Useful and light traditional material, needs to be glued or pinned.

Bas relief Type of relief work

Callipers Wooden or metal device with movable jaws for measuring across three-dimensional shapes (such as the width of someone's head).

Card There are various types including pulpboard, folding boxboard (used in cartons for sweets and chocolates), manila, straw-board and corrugated.

Casting To produce (reproduce) an object by using a mould and casting material such as plaster of Paris.

Corriflute Corrugated plastic – expensive with rather limited uses.

Corrugated card There are various thicknesses, the Tri-wall type is particularly strong. Cartons can be cut into panels and used for many purposes.

Diorama A representation of a scene in three-dimensions often on a small scale. Clever use of perspective and painting can give realistic impressions when viewed from the right position.

Folding boxboard Surfaced thin card used for containers such as chocolate boxes, toothpaste packets. A very useful product which can easily be cut and scored with scissors.

Glues For general use PVA is excellent either diluted or neat. Be wary of hot glue guns and solvent-based adhesives.

Manila (or pasteboard) Easily cut and folded coloured thin card, often in four sheet thickness.

Maquette Sketch version of sculpture (in clay) often on a smaller scale than the finished piece.

Modelling tools Tools for shaping clay or plaster, made from boxwood, open wire ended. Some are pointed, serrated or rounded.

Papier mâchê Excellent modelling or moulding material made from torn paper and binder (recipe included see page 111).

Parting compound Material, such as soft soap, used to ensure that cast separates from mould.

Patina The finish on bronze sculptures that results from natural ageing or weathering, the removal of patina is mistaken and can destroy much of the character of fine pieces.

Plaster of Paris White powder which when mixed with water, is used for casting. When plaster 'goes off' it becomes hot and hardens, the speed at which plaster goes off can be changed by adding liquid detergent or PVA.

Pulpboard Often used for mounting purposes, often six sheets thick and needs to be cut with craft knife or guillotine.

Relief Shallow modelling or sculpture, for example, a head on coins is an extremely fine form of relief work.

Replica An exact copy as opposed to a mere reproduction, often made by the original artist.

Repoussé Method of decorating thin sheets of metal by hammering the back of the piece, infants can use thin metal foils such as embossing foil from NES Arnold.

Scrim Open fabric used with plaster to build strong lightweight moulds or casts.

Strawboard Stout board used for folios and bookcovers. Needs to be cut with craft knife. Does not fold but panels are useful strengtheners.

114

PAINTING

INTRODUCTION

As children pass through Key Stage 2 they combine an ability to move between visual worlds which are highly imaginative and those which are realistic. Painting has a number of important functions including creative and therapeutic aspects. All children love to use paint and they should be given help and encouragement. Drawing and painting often merge in children's work. Painting unites their own personal style with greater technical and manual skill in a unique way. Paint, as a medium, is potentially colourful and bold. It can give children an expressive vocabulary that is extended beyond that of pencils, crayons and felt tip pens. Painting is a flexible and vital medium. It can be quick, expressionist and violent or soft, slow, deliberate and delicate. Your children will be able to sustain their efforts over longer periods of time and will be able to tackle all kinds of ideas, feelings and images. Painting also provides a vital

uninhibited route to dealing with personal and social issues. Junior children can collect ideas in notebooks or sketchbooks for use in paintings. The positive move from one material to another to suit the purpose is a hallmark of growing maturity and progression. Painting often involves work on a larger scale than drawing and you should ensure that your pupils are involved in groupwork such as creating large murals.

Make sure that good materials and tools are available so that your pupils will develop their manual skills quickly. They will come to recognise the need to select the right tools and materials for specific tasks.

Comics, TV, videos and advertising will become increasingly important as sources of imagery to your children. By providing opportunities to become familiar with the work of influential painters you will help extend your children's visual language.

HISTORY OF PAINTING

C104

As with drawing it is probably easiest and best to link practical activities to formal elements such as colour, shape, texture or form. Alternatively you can look at the various genres such as landscape, still life and portraiture. Taking these approaches will allow for comparison while avoiding the pitfalls of merely touching upon individual artists in isolation.

Line
Look at the linear qualities of Simone Martini, Japanese silk painting and calligraphy, Hartung, Nicholson, Klee, Miro and the linear aspects of work by Pollock, Warhol and Lichtenstein.

Colour
Compare the way colour was used by Titian, Claude, Turner and Van Gogh. Compare impressionist and expressionist use of colour (include Grunewald in the expressionist group). Look at the way Pop artists and the later 'hard edge' painters used commercial colours. Examine the way colours have been produced since neolithic times. Make a display of colour names and raw materials.

Shape
Compare El Greco's use of shape (Spanish Mannerism) for example in his *Burial of Count Orgaz* with Ruben's (Flemish Baroque) *Assumption*. Look at the different

types of abstract shapes, for example those of Kandinsky, Klee, Leger, Mondrian, Robert Delauney (Runners 1926), and the collages of Rauschenberg (1925), John Heartfield and Kurt Schwitters (1887–1948).

Pattern and abstract forms
Painted geometric ceramics, Byzantine works, Cezanne, Kandinsky (*Looking into the Past*, 1924), Picasso (cubist), Bridget Riley, Vasarely, Mondrian, Miro, Albers, Rothko, Pollock, Debuffet (*Glass of Water*, 1966).

Textures
Look at the way Rembrandt used heavy impasto technique to express textures in a very physical way. Contrast this with Durer's and Holbein's techniques and that of Gainsborough.

Space and perspective
Examine how space and depth have been portrayed since the flat painted images of Egypt, the linear qualities of Byzantine works, the distortions of El Greco, the monumental spatial effects of Michelangelo. Look at the new structure of Giotto's pictures, the perspective of Mantegna and Leonardo and the interiors of Saenredam, de Hooch and Vermeer. Examine the way space has been shown in landscapes.

Tone and light
Caravaggio, Rembrandt and Wright of Derby; the use of chiaroscuro.

Landscape
Rubens, Ruisdael, Rembrandt, Clause, Poussin, Turner, Constable, Corot, the Impressionists, Cezanne and early works by Mondrian.

Still life
Willem Kalf, Braque, Picasso, Cezanne, Morandi (bottles and plates).

Figures
Painted sarcophagi from Egypt, Martini, Icons, Giotto, Michelangelo, Rubens, Cezanne, Renoir, Picasso. Compare the way that Titian and Manet painted women.

Portraits
Encaustic Egyptian, Holbein, Reynolds, Hals, Rembrandt, Picasso, Van Gogh, Cezanne and Modigliani.

Looking at art history can lead your children directly to consider how various artists planned their paintings using drawings. Leonardo's cartoons are an obvious example of careful planning. On the other hand you could point out that Caravaggio painted directly on to his canvas without any reliance on sketches at all. Try the two approaches. Your children should also know the names of schools and individual artists and be able to explain why they like or dislike various paintings. You will find that **Copymaster 104** will be very helpful in placing individual artists in the correct periods and schools. Your children's use of specific technical terms will be improved.

PAINTING OBJECTIVES

Besides those objectives which concern knowledge and understanding, the National Curriculum PoS includes a number of specific painting goals. Your children should:

- use a sketchbook to record observations and ideas
- apply principles of colour mixing and
- modify their work in the light of its developments and their original intentions.

Before you start
Make sure that your children are well protected by overalls and that you allow time at the beginning and end of sessions to prepare and clear up. Let your children take their time over their work. Try to allow extended periods for planning and execution. It is worth demonstrating how to use paint pots and brushes effectively. Painting should not be limited to work on paper or small scale. Textiles and pottery can be painted and group murals can give children an exciting experience of changes to scale.

Materials and equipment
Key Stage 2 pupils need a variety of brushes: ranging from small, fine ones for detailed work to house-painting brushes for murals. A medium size bristle brush is too big for fine work and too small for mural work. It may be a false economy to buy particularly cheap synthetic brushes. Good quality brushes last longer and are much better for developing manual skills. Your children will need sizes 3, 5 8 and small decorating brushes. Get your children to practise using brushes. Exercises such as washes and careful application of paint (see Activities 291, 299 and 302) are good. Your children can also extend the drawing exercise of handwriting patterns by using flowing painted lines. Get them to paint a series of flowing

continuous lines. They will need to experiment to find the right consistency of paint.

Set them the task of painting a line in black, over the surface of a piece of paper. When complete, ask them to colour the open shapes in a way that is attractive to them. Ask them to make examples of straight, curved, swirling, bent and zig-zag lines. When working on a larger scale children will need to experiment to find the right consistency of paint for the brushes they are using. Provide a limited palette of water-based acrylic colours at first: brilliant red, crimson, brilliant blue, cobalt blue, brilliant yellow, lemon yellow, black and white. This limited palette can then be supplemented with the following colours: orange, purple, leaf green, burnt Sienna and Van Dyke brown. Your children will also need other materials such as card and papers, drinking straws, lino printing rollers, marbling colours, mixing trays, other paints such as true watercolours, powder finger paints, tempera blocks and cold-water dyes such as Brusho®; paper clips, pencils and crayons, scrap materials, sponges for pads plus a sketchbook.

Activity 286: Using a sketch book
Sketchbooks should be the usual way to record information, try out drawing techniques and media, and rough out imaginative compositions and designs. Set your children tasks regularly related to the use of sketchbooks. Get them to record the shapes, colours and textures of natural and made objects, paying particular attention to getting colours right. You can set tasks that link to the use of **Copymaster 39** (colour palette) to help colour mixing exercises. Use **Copymaster 50** (cropping aid) to select elements from photographs from which to make studies.

Activity 287: Planning
Children are happy when drawing or painting directly. As they develop they will need opportunities to plan paintings. Such planning will involve discussion and the collection and use of all kinds of source materials. Collect all kinds of visual resources such as: illustrations from magazines, photographs, shells, seeds, rocks and minerals, mechanisms and machine

parts, prints, sketches, notes and books of all kinds. Try to prevent painting being seen as 'colouring-in' drawings. Painting as a process probably has more to do with sculpture than it does with drawing. It can be useful, nevertheless, to plan paintings by drawing. Use **Copymaster 8** to help enlarge sketches on to larger pieces of paper for painting.

SKILFUL USE OF MATERIALS AND TOOLS

C39, 40, 41, 94–5

Activity 288: Colour palette and the blues
Use **Copymaster 39** and the limited palette of colours. Ask your pupils to mix the colours specified. Then, using the additional colours, set the following exercise. Using **Copymaster 94** mix 100 different blues (browns, whites, greys, reds, etc).

You need
Paint, palettes, brushes and **Copymasters 39** and **94**.

Activity 289: Complementary colours
Use **Copymasters 41** and **95**. Explain that complementary colours are those colours, which when mixed, produce a neutral grey. To start with you have to establish some norms. For example start with red and green. In the first instance get your children to mix up a red that is a 'mid' red. Looking at the colour circle on Copymaster 41, your children can see that this is a red

that is neither orange nor purple. In a similar way the green will have to be neither blue nor yellow but exactly half way, a pure mid-green. Also, both the mid-red and mid-green will have to be a mid tone. This means that if you took a black and white photograph of the colours they would appear to be exactly the tonal value of a mid-grey, neither black nor white but exactly in the middle. If the red is a little dark then your children will have to mix a little white to adjust its tonal value. Do the same for orange and blue and then for purple and yellow. For purple especially your children will have to adjust the tonal quality by adding a little white. They will also need to add a little purple to the yellow to make it darker. When the six colours are ready choose a pair of these 'mid' colours (red and green for example) and paint one pure colour in the right place on the colour wheel. Add a little of the complementary colour to it progressively and continue until the first two segments of the colour circle are finished. Then complete the circle by following the same procedure with the other pairs of colours. Follow this up by using **Copymaster 95**. Paint small squares and bands as described. Get your children to paint carefully around these with the appropriate pairs of complementary colours. Make each colour butt up against the other. Discuss with your children the visual effect of close proximity of complementary colours. Now repeat the exercise but paint a thin black line between the different colours. Make sure that the lines are precise and well finished. Now look at the second set. What difference is there?

Activity 290: After images
Use **Copymaster 40**. Get your children to complete the exercise carefully. After staring at the painted rectangles for about 30 seconds your children should see the complement of the colour that they were staring at. Where they saw mid-purple they should see a luminous yellow. Complete the designs. Discuss what they have seen. Can they make designs using bright pairs of colours? Consider the work of Vasarely and Seurat and their use of complementary colours.

Mid colours diagram

117

APPLYING COLOURS

Small flat areas

Being able to apply colour in the right density, chroma and tone is fundamental to painting whether using the cheapest water-based paint or the finest artist's oil colour. You can help your children to improve their control over paint in many ways. Perhaps the simplest yet most demanding exercise is as follows. Give each child a piece of A4 cartridge paper, get them to square it up with 64 squares like the chessboard (so that the overall square fills up the width of the paper). Use fine pencil lines and try to make sure that it is drawn accurately. Erase any excess or untidy lines. Let each child choose one good quality colour with which to work (a dark colour is easier to use). They will also need a good size 3 or 4 brush, some blotting paper and a mixing palette.

The object of the exercise is to complete the grid exactly in the manner of a chess board. Each alternate square is to be painted with an even, flat layer of paint. If your children work from top to bottom their work will dry and allow them to progress. When the entire sheet is dry get them to turn it around so that they can go over all the painted squares again with a flat coat of colour. The edges of the squares should be clean and straight. Remove any excess paint with blotting paper.

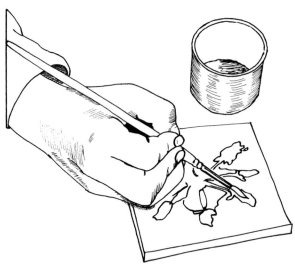

Painting with care

Activity 291: Washes and overlaying transparent colours

It is sometimes necessary to apply a thin wash of colour over the whole of a piece of paper as a background. These washes and transparent thin layers of colour, (either acrylic or watercolour) are applied as follows: With a clean, large brush (or piece of wet sponge) apply clean water in consecutive bands across a sheet of clean paper until it is wet all over. While the paper is still wet, apply the chosen background colour from top to bottom, the paint will blend together and produce a soft impression. Different colours can be applied to the wash

before it dries or your children can wait until the wash has dried before working into it or over it. When using acrylic colours a glazing approach can be followed if each layer of colour is allowed to dry thoroughly before continuing with additional layers.

Activity 292: Masking

Your children can use a variety of masks to make clean crisp motifs in their paintings. There a number of 'low-tack' masking sheets that can be cut, placed on to the paper and spattered or painted over. Once the mask is removed the outlined shape can be worked on or left as required. Try the following to produce equally spaced lines or different colours. Cut enough strips of Sellotape® for the job in hand. Stick each piece carefully on to clean Formica®, peel them off and re-stick a few times to remove a large proportion of the stickiness from the tape. These strips can now be applied to the surface of paper that is to be painted. Press them down quite firmly in place. Either spatter or use creamy paint to make the design. Let the paint dry and then carefully, as shown in the diagram, peel off the Sellotape®. Your children can get better, sharper lines using Sellotape® than by using the more expensive masking tapes.

For information about other resist methods refer to the Drawing, Ceramics and Textiles skills sections.

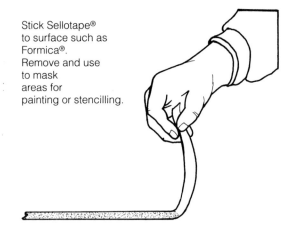

Stick Sellotape® to surface such as Formica®. Remove and use to mask areas for painting or stencilling.

Remove Sellotape® carefully by pulling at angle from the paint.

'De-sticking' Sellotape® and masking methods

Activity 293: Impasto

Paint can be given different kinds of textures by the addition of quantities of sand, semolina, Polycell®, sawdust and liquid detergent. PVA paints are most suitable as they already include a glue base that can fix any added materials. Thickened paint can be applied with brushes and palette knives and is very useful as a medium for fixing collage materials, such as buttons, sequins or papers and fabrics.

Activity 294: Monotypes from oil paints

This is really an extension of work that your children do with finger paints. Use a piece of plate glass (stick some masking tape around and over the edges to make it easy to see and hold). Mix a little oil paint and a small quantity of white spirit with a metal palette knife. Spread this around and use brushes to make a design. Place a clean piece of newsprint on to the wet surface and rub down well. Remove and hang to dry.

Vary this by including more than one colour. Put one colour in one area and another in a different corner so that pure and mixed colours can co-exist. Take a piece of card smaller than the glass and cut it to produce notches of different thicknesses. Draw this comb through the paint to produce a pattern and then place a piece of clean paper on the surface. Take a print as described above.

Activity 295: Brushes, sponges and rollers

Using different kinds of tools and materials to apply paint can produce different kinds of marks. You need to provide a variety of tools to use. They may include sponges, brushes of different sizes, found objects, card and, of course, fingers and hands. Make an organised collection of scrap materials (soft, hard, textured, smooth), various brushes, soft and hard rollers, and fabrics. Give the children scrap paper and some good paper to work on after they have experimented. They will also need sponge pads and plastic trays into which the colour can be worked. Ask your children to produce as many kinds of marks as the can, applying paint to make up images and pictures. At first it is important that your children try out their experiments on scrap paper, otherwise they will waste a lot of materials. Pressing scraps into a pad of paint or dye and being applied to paper may result in pictures that have been made from marks using only soft or hard materials. Children may use rollers by charging them with colour and rolling across paper as a background for further painting, or they may pick up an image from an already painted object and transfer it to the paper on the surface of the roller.

Activity 296: Dry and wet, paper and paint

Provide pieces of two or three types of paper; such as sugar, cartridge and newsprint, also make available powder paint, PVA paint and Brusho®. Cut the pieces of paper into two, then get your children to soak one piece of each type of paper in turn with a wet sponge and ask them to drop powder paint, drip PVA and float Brusho® on to the surfaces of the papers. Now ask them to see what happens when the same is done on dry paper and what happens if you wash dry powder paint over a piece of dry paper. Discuss with your children whether certain techniques they have used might be good for painting skies, seascapes or faces. Can they apply colours in different ways, using scrap materials for example? Mount and display good examples of wet and dry work.

Activity 297: Optical mixing

Use **Copymaster 97** as a way to teach optical mixing of colours. Give each child a copy and ask them to start at one edge with alternate colours of green and blue. As they progress across the sheet introduce occasional reds, and yellows, further across add oranges, purples and light tints of all the colours used. Stand back and see what kinds of colours are produced.

Your children can also use straws to paint pictures in the style of Seurat. Place dots of pure colour alongside each other so that from a distance they appear to mix. As you stand further away the colours mix together.

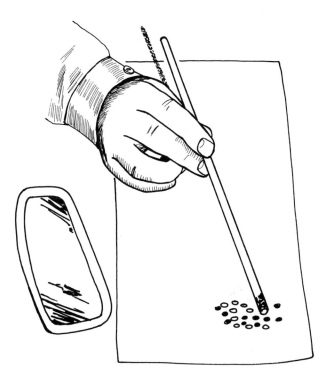

Using straws to paint

Activity 298: Camouflage

Cut a small interesting piece (approximately 5 cms square) from a magazine. Paste this section to the centre of a piece of cartridge paper. Using water-based paints, get your pupils to mix and match the various elements of the picture section. Try to match the colour and tonal values accurately, making a pattern radiating from and camouflaging the picture section.

REPRESENTING COLOURS

Activity 299: Small sky study
Look through a window or space between school buildings and, with a fine brush, study and graduate a small piece of white paper to match a small patch of sky. This exercise can also be undertaken with pen and ink using fine lines.

Activity 300: Still life
Using a limited palette you can set a variety of still life subjects. Include leaves, shells, minerals, bottles, found objects and mechanisms. Set the task of making as accurate representational pictures as possible. Ask your children to apply the paint so as to give a three-dimensional impression and to use varied shades of colours to give the impression of distance. Discuss again ideas about colour mixing theory.

Activity 301: Colour and shapes
Some shapes seem to suggest colours to be used. **Copymasters 42–3** and **96** contain a number of interwoven flat shapes. Your pupils should think about the colours which would most suit the shapes, then mix the colours and complete their design.

Activity 302: Copy the work of other artists
Collect a good range of art books with illustrations of Van Gogh, Klee, Leonardo, Modigliani, Rubens, Gainsborough, Constable, Rembrandt, and contemporary artists. Depending on your local circumstances try to arrange a visit to an Art Gallery. Such visits are an enormous advantage to young children, especially so if they are well prepared. Preparation is, in the main, simply to ensure that the practical activities linked to visits are relevant and properly resourced. If you are working on aspects of landscape then it is a simple matter to collect a rich and stimulating bank of resources to feed the pupils' own

Child's version of the Mona Lisa

work. Discussion, copying and emulating the work of other artists are all valuable activities.

Activity 303: Imaginative work
Poetry, stories and personal experiences can all stimulate imaginative work. Trips, videos and looking at the work of other artists can all be inspirational. The weather and environment can be harnessed to bring meaning and excitement to your children's work. You can establish a whole range of ideas and themes and suggest and direct ways of working. For most children the time spent in discussing subjects for work is well spent, remember that the quality of work is related to the stimulus provided.

Activity 304: Group work
Discuss a theme (try the National Curriculum suggestions of a windy or snowy day) and introduce it through stories or poems. Consider the size of the finished work and whether or not it will be painted on the wall or on pieces of paper which will then be fixed to the wall. Using the grid on **Copymasters 6** and **8** to make rough and finished designs of the whole mural incorporating everyone's ideas. Once the design is complete divide the class into pairs who will work together on specific elements of the mural. Each pair can use any of the following techniques: applying paint with rollers, feathers, fingers and large brushes; splatter and wet and dry methods; using dots; bubble patterns; impasto and marbling.

Once each pair has finished their section on a large piece of paper bring all the elements together and assemble them on the wall to complete the mural. Your pupils may experiment with different techniques before starting on their work proper. Cut samples from these experiments and mount them on a small piece of paper as a record of their achievements.

Activity 305: Collage
Collage is a bridge between two- and three-dimensional work and can combine all kinds of materials. These include tissues, newspaper, marbled paper, stamps, alphabets, fabrics, wool and string, plaster and sand, buttons, corks, found objects and a range of colours and glues. The various approaches to collage can include the skills of drawing, painting, modelling, cutting, folding, fixing and finishing. Collage involves the need to plan well and to make decisions before acting. You should aim to provide a good range of materials and to set appropriate tasks related to the PoS.

Activity 306: Line drawings and collage
One of the simplest forms of collage is to make an outline drawing and then fill the shapes in with other materials. Simple mosaics can also be made in this way.

For example you could get your pupils to make line drawings of a transformer or their pet. Use white chalk on coloured sugar paper to draw the different elements of their chosen subjects. Then get your children to use

Child doing line drawing collage

different coloured shiny paper or foil, torn into small pieces, fixed into place to make up the mosaic image. Alternatively, use shiny paper but instead of tearing it into small pieces, crumple up pieces and glue it into position.

Activity 307: Colour mixing through collage
A theme such as 'underwater' can provide new challenges to mixing colour by overlaying tissue papers. Use PVA mixed with water to make the tissue paper even more transparent. First you will need to provide the right stimulus for the work: a display, a visit to an aquarium, a range of books and pictures. Talk about colour mixing, transparency and changes to the quality of materials. Ask your pupils to make sketches and designs, to select their materials and test them out

before using them on the collage. They may need to scale up their work.

Activity 308: Multi-media assemblage
The task here is to use an extended range of materials including: sand, stones, rope, fabrics, found objects, metallic papers; to make an image of a subject such as 'mysterious landscape'. Before starting work discuss what kinds of unfriendly environments exist. What must it be like to be on Mars, or at the centre of the Earth? Talk about colour and texture combinations, materials and structures. A written description could be an important starting activity for the collage. Pupils can work individually or in groups creating images of their imaginary worlds. They may use prepared paper, either painted or marbled as a starting point or background, or work directly on to a stout piece of board. To produce a range of marks for a varied and unusual landscape will utilise many more techniques than those used in the activities above. The fixing of solid and 3D materials to a surface may involve the use of pins, nails, staples as well as glues and paints. Textures can be added by fixing layers of sands with PVA glue, a technique which can be used on flat and shaped surfaces. Papier mâché can be built up away from the surface of the board to give a relief effect.

Activity 309: Water-soluble pencils or pastels
Get our children to try out water-soluble pencils before tackling a finished piece of work. Apply strokes of pencils close together and blend them with a wet brush. Provide your children with a limited palette of pencils or pastels. You can set a variety of still life subjects. Include leaves, shells, minerals, bottles, found objects and mechanisms. Set the task of making as accurate representational pictures as possible by carefully blending and merging the colours.

▶ GLOSSARY OF TERMS

Acrylic colours Most useful liquid colours that include a fine adhesive that enables the paints to be used in thin transparent overlaid washes, impasto techniques (when used with thickeners), and collage.
Advancing and retreating colours Generally reds advance and blues retreat into a picture.

Background In a picture the parts that appear to be furthest away from the viewer
Binder Material used to hold pigments in suspension, such as PVA, oils or wax.
Bird's eye view A view from above a subject that includes the whole of the subject.
Blending Merging together two or more colours, tints or tones.

Broken colour A colour produced by adding pure colours together, such as when blue and orange are mixed.

Chiaroscuro Use of light and shade to produce dramatic moods in paintings, refer to Rembrandt and Caravaggio.
Chroma The quality of colour in pigments, i.e. not a tonal value but a description of the hue itself.
Collage Pictures made by fixing fabrics, papers and all kinds of found objects to a background support.
Colour circle A simplified way to show how colours mix and are complementary to each other.
Complementary colours Pure colours which, when mixed, produce a neutral grey (black in theory); such as blue and orange; red and green; yellow and purple.

Cool colours Those that seem to suggest a feeling of coolness, often thought to be the blue and green range of colours.

Dominant colour The main colour in a painting or colour scheme.

Encaustic Ancient painting system that uses hot wax as a binder for pigments.

Finger painting A method often associated only with infants. Making direct marks with fingers in paint is, however, very similar to methods used by professional artists and should be used progressively throughout Key Stage 1 and Key Stage 2.

Foreground The part of a picture that appears to be closest to the viewer.

Foreshortening A technique used to give an impression of depth to pictures, particularly figures.

Impasto Method of building up a thick, textured surface to paintings.

Landscape A picture whose subject is that of landscape or scenery.

Local colour The colour of an object itself in normal white light.

Medium The binder in which pigments are ground or suspended, PVA, oil or egg for example.

Miniatures Small paintings (such as those from Persia) and round or oval portraits painted in watercolour. Photography later took over this kind of artistic function.

Mosaic Small pieces of coloured tiles (tesserae) arranged so as to form pictures. Originally the images were set in plaster and were often made up from small pieces of coloured glass. For infants cut sticky paper is a simple introduction to this craft.

Mural Paintings done either directly or on a frame in a wall. Modern murals are often used to decorate the ends of houses, tube trains or panels around building sites.

Paint A material made by suspending pigments in a binding medium.

Pointillist Technical name given to painters such as Seurat who used small points of pure colour, juxtaposed to produce other colours by optical mixing (the colours appear to mix when viewed from a distance).

Restricted palette For some exercises it is sensible to restrict children's palettes to the primary colours and black and white. This will encourage experimentation with colour mixing.

Still life A subject that often includes fruit, bowls, fabrics, shells and other found objects arranged on a table.

Wash Paper is first wetted thoroughly and the washes of water colours are brushed over the surface in such a way that there are no hard edges, everything is smooth and soft. Often useful as a background to landscapes.

PRINT-MAKING

INTRODUCTION ▶

Printing has been used for many years as a way to communicate with a wider audience than is possible through hand drafted images and text. The main difference between painting and printing is that in print-making a mark or a picture is transferred from one surface or material to another. Also, overprinted colours and textures give a variety of results and marks and pictures can be repeated so that patterns are formed. The activities of stencilling, cutting and pressing produce images that have different qualities to those of painting and drawing. The ability to produce repeated images gives print-making an important position in art and design, and design and technology activities.

At Key Stage 1 children will probably have used simple relief printing methods such as rubbing and press-printing. They may also have used simple wax and stencil resists. At Key Stage 2 children will find the technical demands of more sophisticated printing techniques can be tackled more easily. While it may be sensible to start with black and white images, colour can be widely used and cutting tools can be introduced to small groups of well supervised children. The National Curriculum has only two examples of print-making at Key Stage 2. These are:

- Experiment with different ways of printing the same image, for example, sponge and hard rollers, etc.
- Take a number of different photographs from the

same position and make a montage to create a sense of space.

When planning your activities there are three types of printing to consider. Relief, resist printing and photography.

Relief printing
This includes hand and finger prints, monotypes, prints from found objects such as feathers, leaves and other textured and patterned surfaces. Card and other block prints (built up from string, PVA and bits and pieces) or lino and wood blocks also fall into the category of relief methods.

Resist printing
From simple to complex stencils (those used with stencil brushes or spattered paint to the more complex cut, painted and photo-sensitive stencils for screen printing). Latex (Copydex®) is often used for masking out on ceramics to which slips or glazes are then applied. Others include starch resists on fabrics, tie and dye, batik and other wax resist methods.

Photography
At Key Stage 2 black and white photography is most suitable as processing can be undertaken by your children.

RESOURCES FOR PRINT-MAKING C20–23, 70–73 ▶

A good way to introduce the range of printing that exists today is to make a display of different printed items. Collect as many kinds of prints as you can. Try to include: printed bags and packages (these are in the main produced by screen process methods); images from magazines. you will be able to get a range of qualities, some will be coarse (pictures made with big dots) or high quality fashion images, get your children to look at illustrations through magnifying glasses; photographs; limited edition prints from your local authority. These may include etchings, lithographs, lino prints, wood blocks, screen prints and engravings.

Try to get reproductions of Rembrandt's etchings, Bewick's wood blocks. Japanese wood blocks and lithographs by Lautrec, Matisse and Picasso. Look at contemporary wallpapers and compare these with those of William Morris. Use **Copymasters 70–73** for this. Try

to find out all you can about his work. Use it as a stimulus for your children in the production of their own block printed fabrics and illustrated books. This work can be linked to a general consideration of repeat patterns that are used in fabric, wallpaper and wrapping paper production. Look at the geometry of patterns. Include the complex forms of Islamic patterns (**Copymasters 20–23**), the use of half drop and rotated methods. Patterns can also be produced by overprinting with transparent colours using positive and negative shapes.

Pattern work has cross-curricular links. The science of growth, constructions of mathematics and the sourcing of patterns in the environment (buildings, pebbles, shells, animals and birds) are all relevant.

Besides this you should examine the picture making function of print-making, the everyday work of newspaper and book illustration and the fine art business of limited edition graphics.

Your children can also produce cards, posters and T-shirts. Let them choose the methods, colours and materials.

Many of the activities given below can be used to print on to paper, fabrics and other materials. You will find that throughout the topics section of this book a number of printing techniques are described in some detail.

Before you start
Your children should take an active part in managing print-making. They should learn to organise the printing area, become familiar with the safe and efficient use of tools and equipment. Get them to study comics, posters and illustrations of all kinds so that they may discover and then use the techniques in their own work. Doing this they will discuss and develop their own specific vocabulary.

Your children will need to plan, anticipate and experiment in order to obtain a variety of effects. They need to realise the need to organise the right sequence of using colours to achieve the desired effect in the finished work. Even though children will become more confident and capable you must reinforce the basic safety rules constantly. Tools must be sharp to work properly and are, in fact, less dangerous than blunt ones. Use safety rules and a cutting mat. Make sure that working surfaces are well protected as some of the colours used can stain permanently. If your children are going to use oil-based inks it is a wise precaution to use a barrier cream on their hands. Take care using solvents.

RELIEF PRINTING

Activity 310: Rubbings
Get your children to collect a good variety of manageable natural and made materials. Suitable items will include well grained pieces of wood, embossed wallpaper, stones, coins, string, bags, paper doilies, leaves, shells and bricks.

Crayons are particularly useful for taking rubbings, simply place a sheet of paper over the surface to be rubbed and while holding everything steady, apply the side of a crayon evenly across the image area. Children can build up a collection of rubbings which can be categorised and used in displays. This activity can be extended by first preparing a card or mixed material picture that can then be rubbed to produce a flat image. This is most easily done, working from simple designs of animals or scenes that are then built up by gluing cut sections of card, string or other scrap materials to a base board.

You need
Chunky wax crayons, lining paper or newsprint, materials from which to take rubbings.

Activity 311: Using found objects for printing
The same kind of objects as used in the above activity can be used to produce printed images. The simplest approach is to pour some liquid paint on to a pad of sponge that is contained in an old ice-cream box. Objects are pressed on to the pad and the paint-covered surface is then pressed on to a sheet of sugar paper.

Printing on to fabric can easily be done if you use dried leaves and dyes. Place the leaves on a sheet of newsprint and carefully, one at a time, apply dye to the leaf. Place the leaf face down on to the fabric and cover it with another piece of paper which is then rubbed gently to print the leaf on to the fabric. Remove the paper and the leaf carefully and repeat the operation with different colours and using a clean piece of paper for each printing.

You need
Paints or inks, pads of sponge or fabric, articles from which to print, natural fabrics such as cotton, backing papers, paper.

Activity 312: Creating simple patterns
Potatoes, carrots and cabbages can all be used to produce simple patterns on paper or fabric. Half a potato can be shaped so that a simple design can be repeated over a large surface. The design is pressed into the pad of paint or dye and applied to the paper or fabric. If you are using fabric, then it is a good idea to Sellotape® the surface on to the table, so that a regular and even impression is made. Before printing on fabric,

A rubbing

Simple patterns

it is good practice to try out the pattern on scraps of paper first, also it is best not to put too much dye or ink on the pad in one go.

You need
Paints or inks, pads of sponge or fabric, articles from which to print, natural fabrics such as cotton, vegetables, backing papers, paper.

Activity 313: Making a simple lino block print
The following description can be equally useful when working with 'Easiprint' polystyrene sheets (used with water-based inks only) from NES Arnold or wood or lino blocks.

Lino printing is such a good and often underused

activity that is focused upon here. Get your children to do quick sketches in pen and ink so that the results are bold and well-defined. Transfer the drawings (by tracing) to the block of linoleum. Emphasise that the areas which are cut away will be white in the final print. Get your children to cut the design out carefully and then take a print using black ink.

When your children are cutting the lino it is essential that they keep their hands out of harm's way as shown in the illustration. Reinforce this often. Try to encourage your children to cut even lines not wobbly lines of changeable width and depth (unless, of course, this is required by the design). Use the right size cutter. Do not use two or three cuts where one will do. Cut open areas almost down to the canvas support. Also mention to your children that 'you can't put it back', so make the cut on the safe side of the line being cut. (That is, cut on the side which is going to be white anyway so that a slight slip will not be a disaster).

When inking up the black, roll out an oil-based ink on a slab of plate glass or white glazed tile. If possible use a gelatin roller otherwise use a hard rubber roller. Do make sure that the ink is evenly spread but do not over roll it or it will dry out rapidly. Ink up the lino block. When your children ink the corners get them to work diagonally so that it is well covered. (Always ink up on a clean bed of newspaper or you will get into a mess.)

Place the printing paper on the inked up block, rub it down firmly in place. The results of the printing are going to depend almost entirely on how well your children burnish the back of the printing paper. Use the back of a desert spoon for burnishing. Rub and rub all over while holding the print in place. To check how things are going, gently raise one corner and replace if the ink covering is not dense or even enough. When happy with the ink density, remove the print and hang from a 'washing line' as shown in the illustration.

If your children wish to use more colours then they will need to register subsequent prints carefully. To do multi-colour prints with Key Stage 2 children stick to using one block which is cut away progressively for

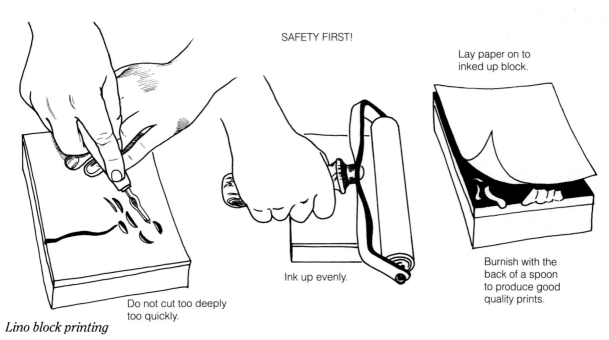

SAFETY FIRST!

Lay paper on to inked up block.

Ink up evenly.

Do not cut too deeply too quickly.

Burnish with the back of a spoon to produce good quality prints.

Lino block printing

different colours. Use a light colour for the first print and end up with a dark colour for the final cut. This rough and ready approach can be modified as children become more familiar with the ideas involved. Your children may well benefit most from working solely with black ink.

Activity 314: Monotype printing
Details of this technique can be found on page 119.

Activity 315: Marbling
Prepare your work area and materials well. Use a large photographic dish. Half fill it with clean water. Cut paper so that it is a little smaller than the size of the dish. To produce really effective marbled paper you need to prepare the bath of water using a derivative of seaweed. Follow the manufacturer's instructions and mix with water in the photographic dish. The water will thicken slightly. Drop oil-based inks on to the surface and use a feather or comb to make complex swirling multi-coloured patterns. (You can use more than one colour at a time). Stir the surface of the water so that the colour is dispersed over the whole surface. (Be gentle otherwise you may cause the colour to settle in blobs on the bottom of the tray.) Drop a sheet of paper on to the surface, remove and lay out face up on a piece of newsprint to dry. You can repeat this process on the same piece of paper with different colours.

Marbled papers can be used for many other craft activities including covering books, as backgrounds to collages or for finishing the interiors of model houses.

You need
Dishes, marbling colours, paper, a stick for stirring, combs or feathers, newsprint.

Activity 316: Printing with clay
This is similar to potato printing. Thump a small ball of clay on to a table. Press objects into the flat, printing surface. Tap the block once more on to the table to ensure its evenness. It can then be used for printing. Press the clay against a pad of ink or paint and take a print. Make sure that the children work in a clean way and wipe the blocks clean after each colour. Favourite clay printing blocks can be allowed to harden and can be reused over a long period of time. The clay printing blocks can be pulled to produce abstract forms.

You need
Clay, clay boards, texture making surfaces or tools, paints, paper.

Clay block printing

RESIST PRINTING

C70–73, 99

Stencils, in one form or another, are the basis of most resist methods. The following few activities are based on traditional stencil making techniques. They can be used or modified and used with screen printing. Stencilling involves dabbing, squeezing or squeegeeing ink or paint through openings in a sheet of stout paper or thin card so that an impression or print is left on the surface underneath. For stencilling on white or tinted paper use water-based poster paints, acrylic paints or inks. For stencilling on fabrics use dyes and special fabric printing colours and crayons.

Activity 317: A simple stencil
Give your children a piece of thin card. Get them to draw a square in the centre (make the square about 3 cms × 3 cms). Use a safety rule, cutting mat and craft knife and get your children to cut out the square. (See the illustration on the page facing.) Note that your children should cut from the corners of the square and move their work around to complete the task. Keep the cut out square and the sheet with the square opening. Both will be used as stencils. Give your children a choice of tinted A4 card and two or three stencilling colours. Now your children should produce a regularly spaced border around the edge of the card by stencilling through the square using either a stencil brush or small piece of sponge. When complete get them to use the cut out square piece of card for edge stencilling a pattern in the centre of the card to make up an interesting abstract composition. When edge stencilling, your children need not go all the way around the square, just one, two or three edges can be used if wished. When using a stencil brush make sure that paint is only picked up on the end of the brush. Make sure that the work is kept still while stencilling otherwise smudging will result.

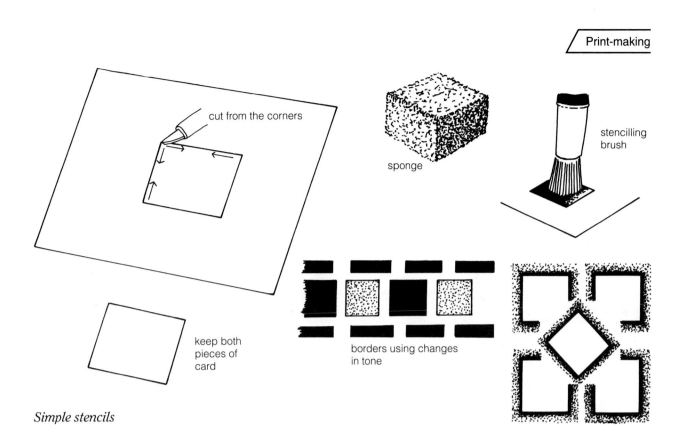

Simple stencils

edge stencil pattern

Activity 318: Using complementary stencil plates

If you look at the illustration you will see how a single sheet can be cut and used to stencil the inside and outside edges as part of a pattern. Get your children to make up pairs of stencils for more complicated edge stencilling.

You need
A4 paper/thin card, tinted card to stencil on to, paint, sponge or stencilling brushes, trays for paint.

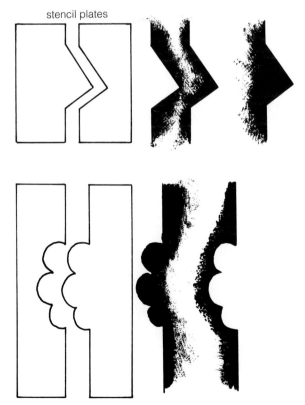

Complementary stencil plates

Activity 319: Stencils with ties

Complex stencils need supports, these are called ties. The illustration below shows ties used in a leaf stencil. The black areas are the open parts of the stencil, the white strips are the ties. Ties can be an important decorative element in stencils. Get your children to design and make up snowflake designs based on a simple square and utilising ties as part of the pattern. The square can be folded and then cut to assist symmetry.

You need
A4 paper/thin card, tinted card to stencil on to, paint, sponge or stencilling brushes, trays for paint.

Stencil with ties

127

Activity 320: Floral stencils

Discuss the William Morris designs as shown in **Copymasters 70–73**. Use your children's observational drawings of flowers as a starting point for making stencils. Use both parts of the cut stencils, the inside and outside. Try overlapping stencilled images.

You need
Copymasters 70–73, flowers, drawings, A4 paper/thin card, tinted card to stencil on to, paint, sponge or stencilling brushes, trays for paint.

Activity 321: Patterns from stencils

If your children use regular shapes such as squares, triangles, rectangles or even circles they can produce patterns on paper or fabrics. **Copymaster 99** shows simple networks based on shaped stencils. These outlines are drawn on fabric or paper so that stencils can be repeated and positioned accurately.

SCREEN PROCESS PRINTING

There a number of factors common to all screen printing, these are described below.

Supplies

Use a strong wooden frame as shown in the diagram. Use brown, water-based tape to secure the internal edges of the stretched fabric (organdy, a fine nylon or voile). Make sure you seal both surfaces of the fabric in the way shown. You will then need to coat the brown tape with button polish to make it tough and waterproof. Give it two good coats. You now have a tough screen, suitable to print high quality images.

Do not waste money on cheap frames. They do not last and will be expensive in the long run. A couple of solid frames from Sericol will last you for a long time. Also buy good (soft quality) squeegees from Sericol. Don't waste money on cheap ones. Even young children can also hold these chunky squeegees with surprising ease. Take care as there are some particularly bad screen inks available from a few suppliers. As screen printing can be done on fabrics and paper I suggest that you buy one ink type that will work well on both surfaces. Buy a few 1 litre tubs of Texiscreen inks from Sericol. These are self-curing, water-soluble inks which are safe to use.

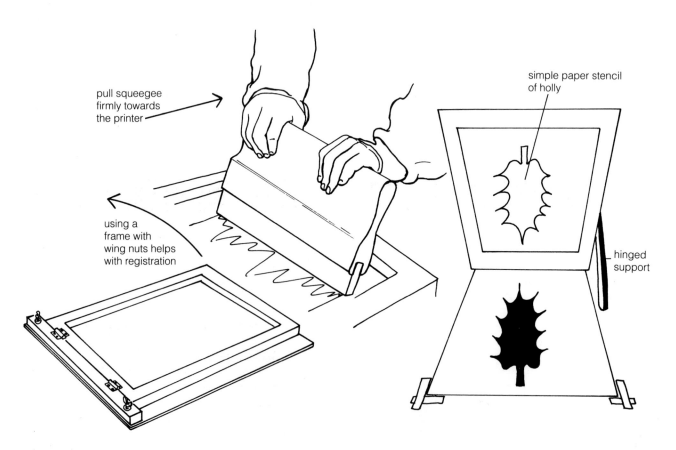

pull squeegee firmly towards the printer

using a frame with wing nuts helps with registration

simple paper stencil of holly

hinged support

Screen printing

You will get excellent results if you wish to produce T-shirts or posters. The cost of these inks is lower than those sold in small quantities, and they are far better and easier to use. It is a good idea to buy mono-filament nylon from a similar supplier. This is tough and cleans reasonably easily and does not sag like organdy.

The diagrams illustrate a simple but effective way to manage printing. Using a hinged device like the one shown will enable your children to register subsequent colours quite easily. Keep solvents and oil-based inks under close supervision.

Activity 322: Screen printing with paper stencils

Make up paper stencils large enough to cover the open area of the screen. You do not need any ties even for very complicated designs. Place the stencil on a clean piece of newsprint. Place the screen on top so that the paper stencil is nicely positioned to cover the whole open area of the screen. Pour a little paint or ink along one edge of the screen, taking care not to let it go into the area where the stencil openings are (see the diagram). Now using a squeegee held at the angle shown draw the ink across the screen. This action accomplishes two things. First it sticks the stencil to the underside of the screen, second it makes your first print as ink is forced through the open areas of the paper stencil. There are a number of stencil sheet materials (water and spirit based). These are cut in a similar way to paper but fixed either by application of heat, water or solvent. (Obviously water-based ones are not really suited to water-based inks.)

Activity 323: Painted screen stencils

There are a number of excellent cheap stopping mediums available. These are generally better than water-soluble PVA as they are much easier to use and clean out after printing is completed. The process is incredibly simple. Give your children a clean, prepared screen. Turn it over so that the wooden frame is underneath and the whole fabric surface facing up. A design is painted using the water-based stopping medium. The painted areas will not print while the open areas will. Dry the screen very thoroughly using a blow drier or hair drier. (Remember to dry hands before using electrical equipment!) Set up the screen as normal and print. Using oil-based inks is most satisfactory as water-based inks will tend to dissolve the stopping medium after a short time. This approach can be extended by getting your children to draw directly on the underneath of the screen with waxy chalk such as lithographic crayons. Use these firmly and when the drawing is complete squeegee over with water-soluble stopping agent. When this is dry remove the wax with white spirit. This will produce a stencil of the original drawing. Molten wax can be also used to produce direct stencils.

If you are going to use Texiscreen inks which are water-soluble then use a blocking medium that is not soluble in water. Buy a ready-made, safe type and remove the stencils carefully after use to make sure that the screen is ready for further use.

Activity 324: Photo-stencils

If your children do drawings on tracing paper using opaque black or dark medium then they can transfer the images very accurately to screens without overly complicated equipment. Buy a small quantity of light sensitive emulsion and the separate sensitiser. (These can be mixed up and kept in a light-proof bottle for up to about three months or so.) In subdued light apply an even coat to the clean screen (follow manufacturer's instructions). Dry thoroughly using a hair drier. Place the silhouette drawing in close contact with the underneath surface of the screen. Either expose this to an ultraviolet source (take care of eyes!) for a few minutes or place in strong sunlight. (Take care not to let light hit the upper surface of the screen or it will cure it where it strikes and ruin your stencil). Wash out the screen with water. Dry thoroughly. You will see that a perfect image of the drawing has been transferred to the screen as a stencil enmeshed in the screen itself. Print in the normal way.

PHOTOGRAPHY

Fox Talbot thought of photography as 'the pencil of nature'. This rather beautiful description explains how the light that is reflected from a scene strikes a photo-sensitive material and produces a latent invisible image. The problem that faced early photographic experimenters was trying to convert this latent invisible image into a permanent visible picture. You can trace this exciting episode again with your children and you do not need a darkroom for the first of the activities.

Activity 325: Fading and shadows

Place a few pieces of different coloured papers on the windowsill and place on top a few objects that you're not going to need for a few weeks. Try things like a pair of scissors, comb, magnifying glass and anything with an interesting shape. The colours will fade rapidly in bright sunlight. Check them occasionally and when ready remove all the objects. Discuss the results. Which colours faded the most? Repeat this with dyeline and other architect's copy paper.

You need
A variety of coloured papers and interesting objects.

Activity 326: Camera obscura

Get your children to use **Copymaster 100** to make up their own simple *camera obscura*. Discuss why the images are inverted.

You need
Copymaster 100, small cardboard boxes, tracing paper, Sellotape®.

Activity 327: Photograms

Making photograms is a simple and effective way to introduce processing photographic materials to your children. Photograms are images on photographic paper made without negatives. They are high contrast and very dramatic. For black and white processing you need three chemical solutions and a final washing in running water. The solutions (for paper and all black and white films) are used in the following order: developer, stop bath, fixer. Make up the solutions according to the manufacturer's instructions. Try to keep to the right temperatures and do not contaminate solutions by using unwashed mixing jugs. In a darkroom, under safelight conditions arrange some transparent or semi-transparent and interestingly shaped objects on to a piece of photographic paper. Letters, leaves, plastic rules, feathers and scissors are good. Turn on the exposing light (either the enlarger or a low wattage white bulb) for a few seconds. You will need to experiment with the exposures. Now process the paper, develop for two minutes (or the time specified by the manufacturer), rinse the paper in the stop bath, then fix and wash the finished print. This is the same procedure as printing an ordinary black and white photograph. The only difference is that in that case you place a negative film in the enlarger and project the image on to a piece of photographic paper on the baseboard of the enlarger.

You need

Objects, chemical solutions, photographic paper, tongs for handling the paper while in solutions, rubber gloves, thermometer, safelight, enlarger or desk lamp with low wattage bulb.

Activity 328: Processing a black and white film

After having taken the photographs you can process the film quite easily. Check the darkroom first as the film is extremely sensitive to light. (Sit inside the room for five or six minutes, if you can see a piece of white paper after that time then it is not light proof enough so cover any cracks with loose fitting black polythene). Also your children will need to be able to breathe so make sure that it is ventilated. The first and most important thing to do is to check exactly where the things that you will need are located. Place in known positions (and in such a way that they will not roll on the floor!) scissors, unopened film cassette, developing tank, lid, spiral and collar. They must all be clean and dry – a damp spiral is a disaster when trying to load the film. When you are sure where everything is you are ready. Switch off all the lights (including safelights). Take the cassette in one hand and, with the protruding shaft underneath, press it firmly down on to the dry work surface. This will pop off the retaining end cover from the top. Carefully withdraw the film holding it so that it does not unroll. Pick up the scissors and carefully cut the leader strip as shown in the diagram. Do not worry about the leader strip – let it fall on the floor. Put the scissors down away from you. Still holding the film, pick up the spiral with your other hand. The spiral should be positioned so that the open end faces you. Thread the shaped end of film on to the spiral until it is secured by the small ball bearings or other device. Let the roll of film rest on the work surface in front of you while you now hold the spiral in both hands. Hold the left side stationary while with forward and backward motions you move the other side of the spiral. This will drive the film on to the spiral until it is completely loaded. Cut off the central plastic core to the cassette. Place the spiral in the tank, put on the collar, lid and any plastic cover. Check that you have not cross threaded the lid. Switch on the main light. Follow the manufacturer's instructions to process the film with developer, stop, fix and wash. Try to keep to the right temperatures. After washing remove the lid. Use a final rinse aid such as Kodak's Photo-Flo and hang up to dry. Cut into sections, file, date and name the negatives. Use **Copymaster 49** for photo planning.

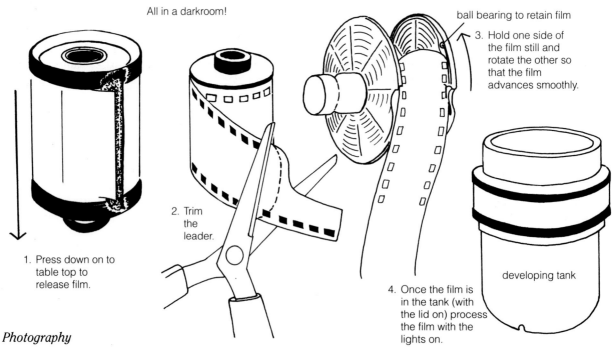

All in a darkroom!

1. Press down on to table top to release film.

2. Trim the leader.

ball bearing to retain film

3. Hold one side of the film still and rotate the other so that the film advances smoothly.

4. Once the film is in the tank (with the lid on) process the film with the lights on.

developing tank

Photography

Activity 329: Making a print
Place a negative in the negative holder of the enlarger. Project this at the chosen size on to a piece of white paper under safe-light conditions. Focus the image and then stop down the lens to f11. Switch off the enlarger. Now you will make a test strip. Place a piece of photographic paper in position under the enlarger lens on the baseboard. Cover all but one fifth of the paper with a box lid or piece of card, so that a strip is showing. Switch the enlarger on for five seconds. Repeat this process moving the box lid a fifth over each time so that eventually the paper will be crossed with the bands of five, ten, fifteen, twenty and twenty-five seconds' exposures. Develop and fix the strip. Now with the main light on check to see which exposure is the best. Find a strip that includes good pure whites and also solid blacks. Then use the chosen exposure to make the finished print. The f numbers on the enlarger lens and on cameras indicate the amount of light passing through the lens. For example f11 allows twice the light to pass as does f16 or four times that of f22, your children can think of it as being similar to the volume control on a hi-fi or a tap for water.

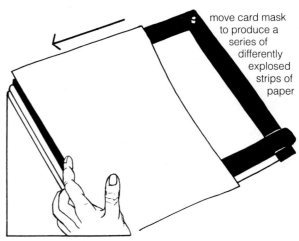

move card mask to produce a series of differently explosed strips of paper

Making a test strip

GLOSSARY OF TERMS ▶

Block print A relief print taken from a block that has been incised or built up to provide a printing surface.

Card prints Prints taken from cut out shapes of card, sometimes individual elements can be printed separately to make up a composition such as a face.

Decal Prints on to transfer material which can then be fixed on to fabrics, especially T-shirts.

F. Number The aperture of a lens: f22 is small, f5.6 is large.

Linocut Block printing method described above in Activity 253.

Marbling Resist method of producing monotype images from the surface of water.

Monotype One-off prints from fingerpaints or other kinds of paint. Designs are made by using the media on a smooth surface such as perspex or formica and picking up the image on a piece of paper by smoothing over it when placed on top of the wet surface.

Newsprint Plain white paper used in production of newspaper, cheap and tough.

Pad and block printing Using a block (potato, impressed clay, lino or polystyrene block) inked up with a loaded pad of paint/dye. Paper placed over the inked-up block is burnished with the back of a spoon and picks up an impression.

Paper-stencil screen process method Described in detail above in Activity 322.

Press printing Inked-up blocks pressed against paper of fabric.

Relief prints – assemblages A backing board is used to affix found objects or lines of PVA glue or string. The finished assemblage is then inked up and a print is taken in the normal way.

Resist Method of printing when the passage of ink on to the receiving surface is halted, for infants the most common method of resist printing is simple stencil work, where ink only passes through the open areas of the stencil

Rollers Soft (sponge) and hard rubber rollers are used to roll out ink on to plates or to ink up blocks directly. Soft rollers can be used for stencil work. Gelatin rollers are excellent for off-set printing. They can pick up the finest details but need to be cared for and cannot be used with water-based paints or inks.

Rubbings Basic method for introducing printing to young children. Paper placed over the surface from which an impression is required is rubbed firmly with chunky wax crayons.

Serigraphy silk screen or more correctly screen process printing All refer to the process outlined in its simplest form in Activities 322–4.

Stencilling Holes and shapes cut into paper or manila are used to produce simple or complex prints on a variety of surfaces.

TEXTILES

INTRODUCTION

General points
As with other skill areas there are a number of activities involving textiles and jewellery to be found in the topics section. Those activities are cross referenced below, avoiding duplication. This skill area, more than any other, will depend very much on you collecting a range of scraps.

Make a collection of all kinds of scraps including wool, cotton and synthetic fabrics, cottons, silks, needles, dyes, dye baths, plastic buckets, polythene sheets for protecting tables, batik equipment, dry sticks, raw wool for spinning and dyeing, embroidery frames, string, twine and cords, tracing paper, pencils and scissors, stuffing materials, sequins and buttons, an iron, newsprint and wax. Organise your junk boxes well, according to colour, texture and types of materials.

Activity 330: Appliqué
See Activities 109, 143, 205 and 227. Get your children to make a drawing of a chosen subject or favourite scene. (They may use images from magazines.) Trace the drawing as a simple outline pattern. Square up the drawing as in the illustration and transfer the outline to a piece of backing fabric of the chosen size. Cut pieces of fabric for each area in suitable colours and apply these to the backing either by gluing or by sewing. This kind of picture can be enhanced considerably by using felt tip

pens to add detail to the flat areas of colour. Felt is particularly useful as a material for making the main areas. Felt can be used for making simple bags, glove puppets and stuffed soft toys.

Activity 331: Mirror craft from India
This is an extension of appliqué. Collect scraps of safe reflective materials such as variously coloured flexi-mirrors. Cut these into small pieces. Use two pieces of felt in contrasting colours. Using a stencil or other silhouetted design draw the sections of the design on to one piece of felt. Cut holes carefully to produce the desired pattern or picture. Find pieces of coloured flexi-mirror to fill some of the holes completely. Glue these in place behind the openings, completely filling the holes. This piece of felt can now be placed on the backing piece and stuck down. If not all the holes have been backed with flexi-mirror then the contrasting colour of the felt backing will add to the variety of the design.

You need
Scraps of flexi-mirror, scissors, glue, felt.

Activity 332: Dyeing
A selection of cochineal, henna, indigo, madder and yew chips can all be used to produce natural dyes. Most natural dyes require mordants to make the colours fast. Check with your supplier for specific information about the right mordants.

Natural fabrics and raw wool are suitable for dyeing with natural dyes. If you are using wool you will first need to scour (clean) it. To do this first open out the fleece in hot water (50 degrees). Leave it in the bowl until the water is cold. Prepare another bowl of soapy water of hand temperature. Place the fleece in the soapy water and squeeze it to flush out the dirt and natural grease (lanolin). You will need to repeat this and then rinse it in tepid water. If you are going to dye yarn prepare it in the form of tied skeins.

If you use lichen first then you will not need to use a mordant as it is naturally fast. Collect lichen in damp weather. In a large bowl layer lichen, fabric, lichen and so on. Cover with soft water and heat gently for two or three hours. Remove, rinse and dry.

The most common mordants are tin, alum, iron and chrome, Test these carefully with some of the range of natural dye sources given above. Natural dyestuffs have to be boiled with mordants so, for safety reasons, you will have to do this yourself. When prepared your children can test and record results.

copy on to squared up backing fabric

stitch fabric pieces into place

Appliqué

You need
Large and small containers, dyebaths (a big stainless
steel bowl to hold hot liquids), saucepans, smooth sticks
for stirring, muslin bags for holding dyestuffs, sieve,
scales, hot ring, soft water (if possible).

Activity 333: Embroidery

Please refer to Activities 204 and 205 **Copymasters
101–102** contain designs that your children can use
either as the basis for pictures or as decorative motifs. In
all there are over 50 different embroidery stitches. Your
children need to learn just one, cross stitch, to make
really lovely things. Cross stitch is easily done on canvas
by counting the threads – pattern and background are
all worked in the same stitch. You can do cross stitch in
two ways. One is to sew one diagonal of each stitch all
the way along one row, and coming back to complete it
by putting in the second stitch. The other way, more
satisfactory, is to complete each cross as one goes along.
In either case, each cross must be identical, the first
stitch always in the same direction and the second in
the opposite. Your children can make up their own
simple designs using **Copymaster 103** and coloured felt
tip pens. Simply mark crosses as part of the design and
transfer to canvas or Binca®.

You need
Plastic or, real canvas or Binca®, needles, embroidery
cottons, **Copymasters 101**, **102**, scissors, felt tip pens,
pencils.

Activity 334: Spinning

You may be lucky enough to have someone in your
school who can spin. Even if you don't, your children
can have a lot of fun just using finger spindles. To
extend this simple activity, try to arrange to borrow a
simple spinning wheel such as the Louet type and a
number of finger spindles. Before spinning with either
the wheel or spindles you will need to prepare the fleece.
(If you have difficulty getting hold of fleece contact the
Wool Board.) Use clean fleece. First take a little fleece
and place on one of the pair of carders, comb the fleece
for a few minutes with the other carder to align the
fibres. This produces a 'rollag' which is essential for
spinning. Attach a strand of ready spun wool from the
end of the rollag to the spinning wheel or spindle and
then start spinning. Try to tease a little of the rollag
gently on to the spindle in a spun form. This will take
practice but is a lot of fun.

You need
Finger spindles, spinning wheel, clean fleece, carders,
knitting wool.

Activity 335: Batik

Please refer to Activities 108 and 144 in the topics
section. Batik extends the simple wax resist drawing and
painting methods that your children are probably
already familiar with. Your children can use cotton or
silk for batik. The fabrics can either be stretched on a
frame or simply laid on to sheets of clean newsprint on
a table. Designs can either be made directly on the fabric
(outlined in chalk first) or transferred from sketches.

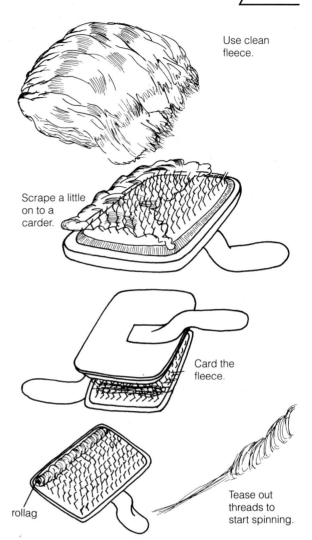

Use clean fleece.

Scrape a little on to a carder.

Card the fleece.

rollag

Tease out threads to start spinning.

Making a rollag

Restrict the size of the work, in the first instance, to
30 cms square. (Batik on silk can be extended by using
silk paints.) Hot wax can be applied to the fabrics by
brush or tjantings (wax pens). When the first part has
been done, crumple up the fabric to crack the wax
drawing. Place the fabric in a bath of cold water dye
(Dylon®) with a fixative (salt). The material will absorb
the dye except where the wax has been applied. Remove,
rinse, dry and then iron between sheets of newsprint
(not newspaper!) to remove the wax. Repeat with
different colours until the desired effect is achieved. Try
to remove all the wax at the end of the process otherwise
the fabrics will feel heavy and horrid, not the beautiful,
delicate and softly decorated pieces of cloth that they
can be.

Jackson Contra-Banned of Huddersfield sell an
excellent set of batik samples from Bali that clearly
show sequences of the processes of waxing and dyeing
involved in batik work. You may find that a set for
display and reference will be a useful addition to your
resource collection.

You need
Tjantings, brushes, wax and suitable heater (double
boiler) or a specially made batik wax pot (NES Arnold),
cotton or silk, pencils, paper, newsprint, dyebath
(plastic bowl), cold water dyes and an iron.

Activity 336: Tie dye

This is another resist method. Take a length of cotton and tie it at selected points, tightly and in some cases more loosely. Soak the fabric with water then immerse in a bath of chosen and prepared cold-water dye. Leave for a while (an hour or so), remove, rinse until the water runs clear. Open, retie and repeat the process until the results are pleasing. Finally dry and iron.

You need
Cold water dyes, dyebath, cotton, string and an iron.

Activity 337: Weaving

Weaving can be introduced by making simple 'shoebox' looms or by using some of the commercially available looms. To add variety to your children's weaving collect all manner of threads and tie them together at random. Use this assemblage of threads to make unusual woven fabrics.

Printing on fabrics

Pad and dye, screen process, stencilling, tie and dye and batik are all methods of colouring fabrics with random or repeating motifs. Please refer to Activities: 43, 71–3, 108 and 144, in the topics section.

GLOSSARY OF TERMS ▶

Appliqué Decorative art in which pieces of material are fastened to a surface to form a design. Cloth is often sawn or glued in place.

Basketwork It involves weaving strong fibres to produce baskets, or materials are first coiled together and then stitched coil by coil to form containers. Many people agree that this kind of fabric work is the earliest of all.

Beadwork It involves threading different kinds of beads on a cord. They are also used in other craftworks such as macrame, knitting, crochet, embroidery and metal jewellery.

Dyes Materials used to colour fabrics.

Embroidery Pictures and patterns made usually on canvas or linen by combining a variety of stitches and coloured threads.

Findings Small fittings for jewellery, connectors and clasps.

Knitting Interlocking loops of yarn which form a fabric, often produced on knitting needles.

Macramé Heavy, coarse lacework that can be used in abstract designs and a form of sculpture.

Resist The use of a resisting material, such as wax, to form patterns and images on fabrics when dyed.

Rollag Clean fleece that has been carded so that all the fibres are roughly parallel and ready to be fed on to the spinning bobbin.

Sewing Fastening of fabrics by using thread stitches. Simple stitches such as blanket stitch are suitable for infants.

Spinning Method of producing yarn by twisting raw material (often wool) into a fine thread.

Tassels Decorative finish to cords and ropes.